SECOND EDITION

GRAMMAR BOOK

Australia • Brazil • Mexico • Singapore • United Kingdom • United States

Contents

			Page
Unit 1			
Lesson 1	*Have/has got* (affirmative)		4
Lesson 2	*Have/has got* (negative)		6
Lesson 3	*Have/has got* (questions and short answers)		8
Unit 2			
Lesson 1	Present simple: *be* (affirmative)		10
Lesson 2	Present simple: *be* (negative)		12
Lesson 3	Present simple: *be* (questions and short answers)		14
Review: Units 1–2			16
Unit 3			
Lesson 1	*There is / There are* (affirmative, negative, questions and short answers)		18
Lesson 2	Possessive adjectives		20
Lesson 3	*A, an, the*		22
Unit 4			
Lesson 1	Countable and uncountable nouns: *some/any*		24
Lesson 2	*How much …? / How many …?*		26
Lesson 3	Object pronouns		28
Review: Units 3–4			30
Unit 5			
Lesson 1	Present continuous (affirmative)		32
Lesson 2	Present continuous (negative)		34
Lesson 3	Present continuous (questions and short answers)		36
Unit 6			
Lesson 1	*Can/can't* (affirmative, negative, questions and short answers)		38
Lesson 2	*Must/mustn't* (affirmative and negative)		40
Lesson 3	Imperatives (affirmative and negative); *Let's*		42
Review: Units 5–6			44

Contents

		Page
Unit 7		
Lesson 1	Present simple (affirmative)	46
Lesson 2	Present simple (negative)	48
Lesson 3	Present simple (questions and short answers)	50
Unit 8		
Lesson 1	Adverbs of frequency	52
Lesson 2	Comparatives	54
Lesson 3	Superlatives	56
Review: Units 7 – 8		58
Unit 9		
Lesson 1	Past simple: *be* (affirmative)	60
Lesson 2	Past simple: *be* (negative)	62
Lesson 3	Past simple: *be* (questions and short answers)	64
Unit 10		
Lesson 1	Past simple (regular verbs, affirmative)	66
Lesson 2	Past simple (irregular verbs, affirmative)	68
Lesson 3	Past simple (negative)	70
Review: Units 9 – 10		72
Unit 11		
Lesson 1	Past simple (questions and short answers)	74
Lesson 2	*Be going to* (affirmative)	76
Lesson 3	*Be going to* (negative)	78
Unit 12		
Lesson 1	*Be going to* (questions and short answers)	80
Lesson 2	Future simple (affirmative)	82
Lesson 3	Future simple (negative)	84
Review: Units 11 – 12		86

Lesson 1

1 Read.

I've got a cool T-shirt!

Have/has got (affirmative)

We use **have got** to say that a thing belongs to a person, or to describe a person or a thing. When we speak, we usually use the short form.

I **have got**	I**'ve got**
you **have got**	you**'ve got**
he **has got**	he**'s got**
she **has got**	she**'s got**
it **has got**	it**'s got**
we **have got**	we**'ve got**
you **have got**	you**'ve got**
they **have got**	they**'ve got**

I**'ve got** two cats.
Mary**'s got** a computer.
The cat**'s got** green eyes.

2 Write *'ve got* or *'s got*.

1 I <u>'ve got</u> two ducks.

2 The goat _____ a black tail.

3 She _____ three cows.

4 You _____ a chicken.

5 We _____ two black horses.

6 They _____ a small farm.

4 UNIT 1

3 Write 've got or 's got. Then match.

1 The sheep __'s got__ two baby sheep.

 a

2 He _____ a farm.

 b

3 They _____ big ears.

 c

4 We _____ a horse on the farm.

 d

5 It _____ long hair.

 e

4 Say it! Tick and say.

	Me	My friend
🛋️ (lamp)		
🖥️ (desk)	✔	
💻 (computer)		✔
🛏️ (bed)		
🪑 (chair)		
📚 (books)		
🖍️ (crayons)		
✏️ (pencils)		

I've got a desk in my bedroom.

I've got a computer.

Lesson 2

1 Read.

I haven't got a white T-shirt.

Have/has got (negative)

We put the word **not** after **have/has** to say that a person or a thing hasn't got something. When we speak, we usually use the short form.

I **have not got**	I **haven't got**
you **have not got**	you **haven't got**
he **has not got**	he **hasn't got**
she **has not got**	she **hasn't got**
it **has not got**	it **hasn't got**
we **have not got**	we **haven't got**
you **have not got**	you **haven't got**
they **have not got**	they **haven't got**

I **haven't got** a pet.
She **hasn't got** a big bedroom.

2 Circle.

1 We **haven't got** / **hasn't got** cows on the farm.
2 They **haven't got** / **hasn't got** a tractor.
3 She **haven't got** / **hasn't got** sheep.
4 The cow **haven't got** / **hasn't got** long hair.
5 I **haven't got** / **hasn't got** a goat.
6 Mara and Lara **haven't got** / **hasn't got** a cat.
7 The field **haven't got** / **hasn't got** trees.
8 You **haven't got** / **hasn't got** a horse.

3 Write *have got*, *haven't got*, *has got* or *hasn't got*.

1 Sonia __has got__ a cat.
   She __hasn't got__ a dog.

4 He _____ a sister.
   He _____ a brother.

2 Marta _____ a cat.
   She _____ a dog.

5 It _____ wings.
   It _____ a tail.

3 We _____ a bird.
   We _____ a fish.

6 The tree _____ mangoes.
   It _____ apples.

4 Write.

This is Sammy. Sammy and his family (1) __have got__ (✔) a shop. The shop (2) _____ (✘) teapots. It (3) _____ (✔) beautiful rugs. Sammy (4) _____ (✔) lots of brothers and sisters. He (5) _____ (✘) a cat. He (6) _____ (✔) a good friend called Hassan.

LESSON 2

Lesson 3

1 Read.

Have you got horses and cows on the farm?

No, I haven't.

Have/has got (questions and short answers)

We put **have** or **has** at the beginning of a question to ask if a person has got something. We can give short answers with **Yes** or **No**, the person, and **have/has** or **haven't/hasn't** without the word **got**.

Have I **got** ...?	Yes, I **have**. / No, I **haven't**.
Have you **got** ...?	Yes, you **have**. / No, you **haven't**.
Has he **got** ...?	Yes, he **has**. / No, he **hasn't**.
Has she **got** ...?	Yes, she **has**. / No, she **hasn't**.
Has it **got** ...?	Yes, it **has**. / No, it **hasn't**.
Have we **got** ...?	Yes, we **have**. / No, we **haven't**.
Have you **got** ...?	Yes, you **have**. / No, you **haven't**.
Have they **got** ...?	Yes, they **have**. / No, they **haven't**.

Has Nancy **got** a bird?
Yes, she **has**. / **No**, she **hasn't**.
Have you **got** a fish?
Yes, we **have**. / **No**, we **haven't**.

2 Write and match.

1 <u>Have</u> you <u>got</u> a toy tractor?
2 _____ your friend _____ a horse?
3 _____ worms _____ legs?
4 _____ you _____ a cat?
5 _____ we _____ water?
6 _____ your classroom _____ a window?

a No, she hasn't.
b No, I haven't.
c No, they haven't.
d Yes, I have.
e Yes, it has.
f Yes, we have.

3 Write.

1 Sue / a fish
   Has Sue got a fish?   Yes, she has.

2 Tim and Sue / bird
   _____   _____

3 Tim / a cat
   _____   _____

4 Tim and Sue / a dog
   _____   _____

4 Say it!

barn   chicken   cow   dog   duck   goat   horse   sheep   tractor

Has the farmer got a dog?

No, she hasn't.

Has she got sheep?

Yes, she has.

2 Lesson 1

1 Read.

Hi. My name is Ana. I'm eight.

Present simple: be (affirmative)

To say who a person is, or what a thing is, and to introduce ourselves, we use the verb **be**. When we speak, we usually use the short form.

I **am**	I**'m**
you **are**	you**'re**
he **is**	he**'s**
she **is**	she**'s**
it **is**	it**'s**
we **are**	we**'re**
you **are**	you**'re**
they **are**	they**'re**

I **am** Alison.
A potato **is** brown.
Computer games **are** fantastic!

Note: In English we always use a personal pronoun with a verb, for example, **we are**. The words **am, are, is** go after the personal pronouns (**I am, you are, he is, she is, we are, they are**), or after the name of a person, animal or thing.

2 Circle.

1. We **'m** / **('re)** happy children.
2. It **'re** / **'s** a big cat.
3. They **'s** / **'re** best friends.
4. You **'m** / **'re** a good boy!
5. It **'m** / **'s** my book.
6. She **'s** / **'re** very tall.
7. We **'m** / **'re** cool!
8. He **'s** / **'re** my friend George.

3 Match.

1 Ana and Sofia
2 Alex
3 Cats
4 The stars
5 I

a is eight years old.
b am seven years old.
c are animals.
d are friends.
e are in the sky.

4 Write *am*, *are* or *is*.

My name (1) ___is___ Lucas.
I (2) _____ in the photo. That man (3) _____ Grandpa, and the little boy (4) _____ my brother, John. We (5) _____ by a lake. Fishing is fun! Mum and Dad (6) _____ at home. They (7) _____ with my sister. She (8) _____ only two!

5 Say it! Write and say.

What's your name?

My name is Lucy.

My name is Maria. What's your name?

	You	Your friend
What's your name?		
How old are you?		
What's your favourite colour?		
What's your friend's name?		
What's your mum's name?		

Lesson 2

1 Read.

My cat isn't very cute in this photo!

Present simple: be (negative)

We put the word **not** after **am**, **are** and **is** to say who a person isn't or what a thing isn't. When we speak, we usually use the short form.

I **am not**	I**'m not**
you **are not**	you **aren't**
he **is not**	he **isn't**
she **is not**	she **isn't**
it **is not**	it **isn't**
we **are not**	we **aren't**
you **are not**	you **aren't**
they **are not**	they **aren't**

He **isn't** five years old.
They **aren't** sad.

2 Write *are*, *aren't*, *is* or *isn't*.

1 The sky ___is___ blue. It ___isn't___ green.

2 Paul _____ a boy. He _____ a girl.

3 The sun _____ blue. It _____ yellow.

4 Elephants and giraffes _____ small. They _____ big.

5 It's the weekend. Students _____ at school. They _____ at home.

6 Aunts _____ women. They _____ men.

12 UNIT 2

3 Match.

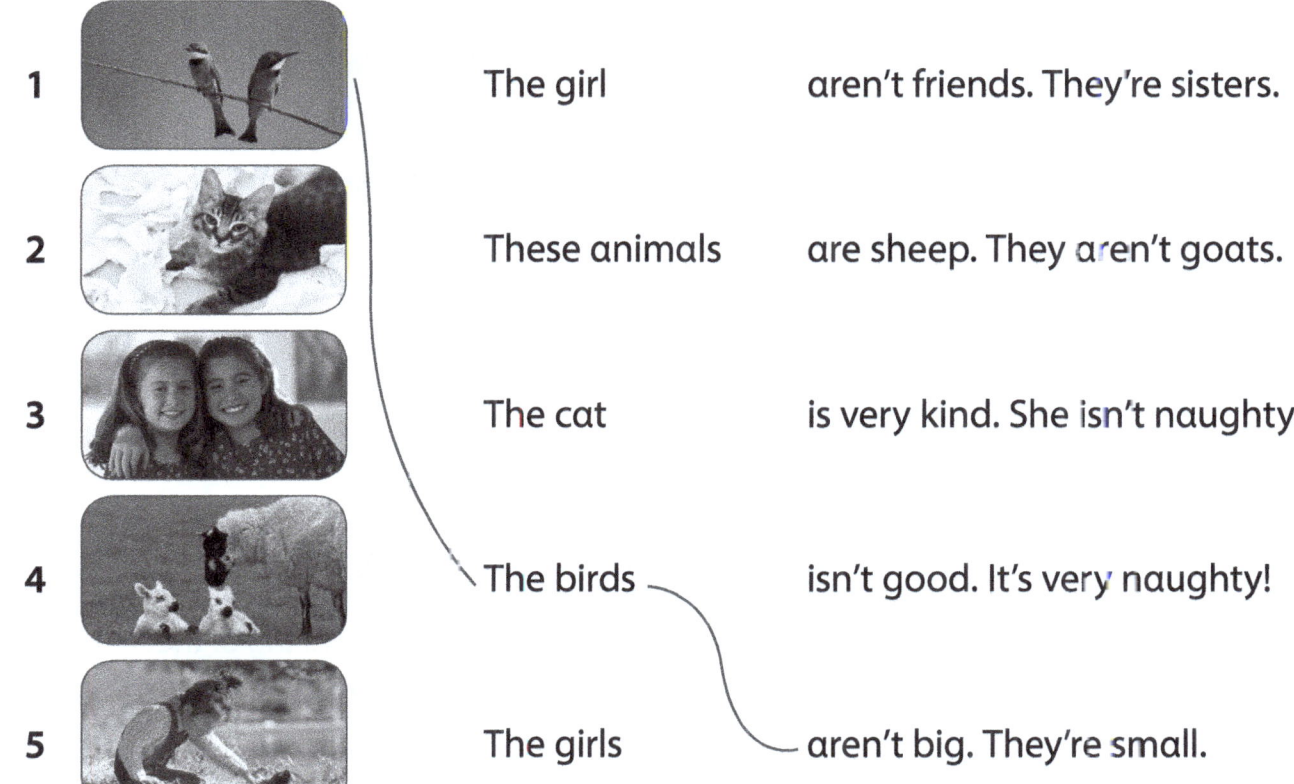

1 The girl — aren't friends. They're sisters.
2 These animals — are sheep. They aren't goats.
3 The cat — is very kind. She isn't naughty.
4 The birds — isn't good. It's very naughty!
5 The girls — aren't big. They're small.

4 Write *am, am not, is, isn't, are* or *aren't*.

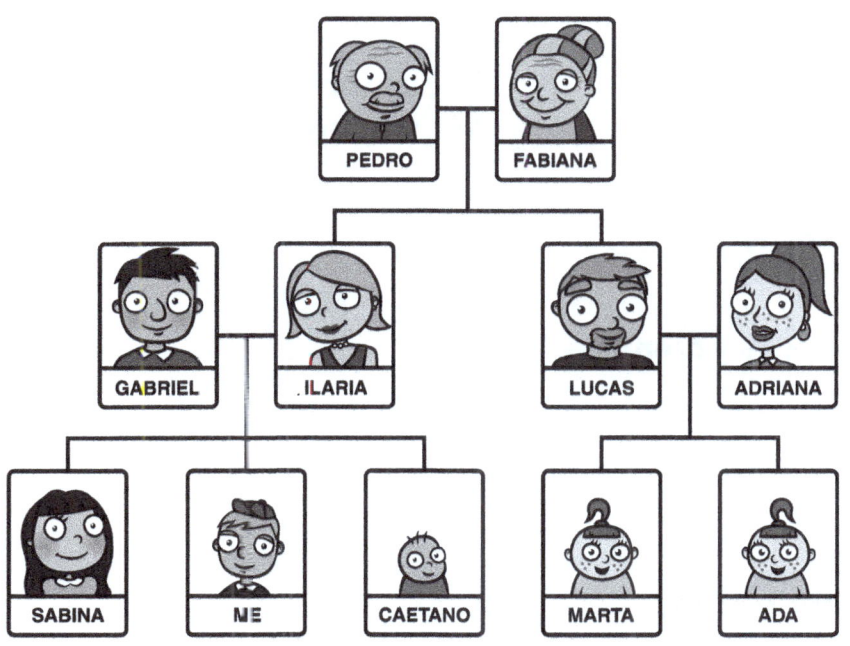

1 Gabriel and Lucas <u>aren't</u> brothers.
2 Marta and Ada _____ twins.
3 Caetano and I _____ twins.
4 Lucas _____ Ilaria's husband.
5 Pedro and Fabiana _____ husband and wife.
6 I _____ a baby.
7 I _____ Gabriel and Ilaria's son.
8 Ilaria and Lucas _____ brother and sister.

Lesson 3

1 Read.

Are you hungry? — Yes, I am.

Present simple: be (questions and short answers)

To ask questions with the verb **be,** we put **Am**, **Are** or **Is** at the beginning of the question. We give short answers with **Yes** or **No**, the correct person, and **am**, **are** or **is**.

Am I ...?	Yes, I **am**. / No, I**'m not**.
Are you ...?	Yes, you **are**. / No, you **aren't**.
Is he ...?	Yes, he **is**. / No, he **isn't**.
Is she ...?	Yes, she **is**. / No, she **isn't**.
Is it ...?	Yes, it **is**. / No, it **isn't**.
Are we ...?	Yes, we **are**. / No, we **aren't**.
Are you ...?	Yes, you **are**. / No, you **aren't**.
Are they ...?	Yes, they **are**. / No, they **aren't**.

Are you happy?
Yes, I **am**. / **No**, I**'m not**.

Are they tired?
Yes, they **are**. / **No**, they **aren't**.

2 Write.

1 Is tea hot? <u>Yes, it is.</u>
2 Is your grandpa old? _____
3 Are your friends young? _____
4 Are sharks cute? _____
5 Is your teacher tall? _____
6 Are you and your friends fun? _____
7 Are you from Greece? _____
8 Is cake yummy? _____

3 Write and match.

1 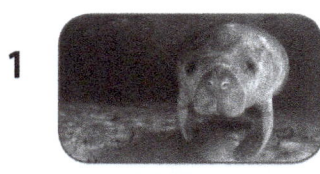 ? / a / fish / it / is
    Is it a fish?   **a** Yes, they are.

2  ? / they / are / flowers   **b** No, it isn't.

3  ? / young / they / are   **c** No, he isn't.

4  ? / baby / is / he / a   **d** No, they aren't.

5  ? / at / school / you / are   **e** Yes, it is.

6  ? / is / winter / it   **f** No, I'm not.

4 Say it!

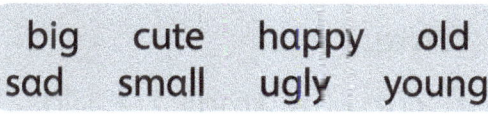
big   cute   happy   old
sad   small   ugly   young

Is it an animal?
Is it cute?
Is it small?
Is it a horse?

Yes, it is.
Yes, it is.
No, it isn't.
Yes, it is.

LESSON 3   **15**

Review

1 Write *have got, haven't got, has got* or *hasn't got*.

Butterflies (1) __have got__ wings and they (2) _____ tiny legs. They (3) _____ arms.

A tiger (4) _____ big legs and big paws. It (5) _____ big teeth, too! It (6) _____ big ears.

2 Write *Have* or *Has*. Answer about you.

1 __Have__ you got a computer?   __Yes, I have. / No, I haven't.__

2 _____ your dad got a big car?   _____

3 _____ you got a fish in your classroom?   _____

4 _____ your mum got a sister?   _____

5 _____ your friends got bicycles?   _____

3 Write.

1 cats / ✔ small / ✘ big
   __Cats are small. They aren't big.__

2 sun / ✔ yellow / ✘ red
   _____

3 I / ✔ eight / ✘ nine
   _____

4 He / ✔ hungry / ✘ thirsty
   _____

5 You / ✔ tired / ✘ angry
   _____

4 Write and match.

1. __Is__ your mum young? — c Yes, she is.
2. _____ you and your friends hungry?
3. _____ they happy?
4. _____ your cat hungry?
5. _____ he your brother?
6. _____ you thirsty?

a Yes, it is.
b Yes, he is.
c Yes, she is.
d Yes, they are.
e No, we're not.
f Yes, I am.

5 Write.

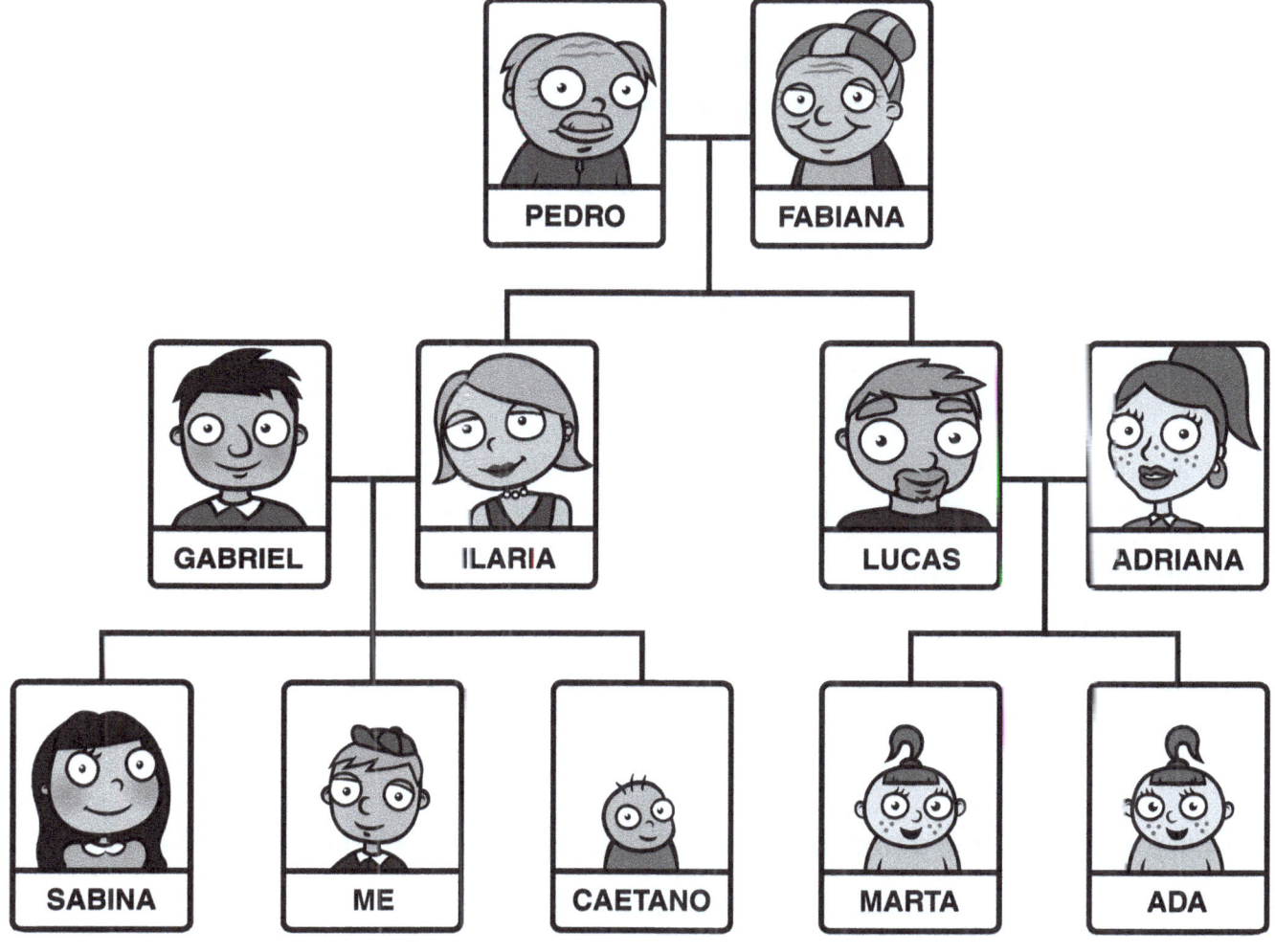

1. Has Sabina got a husband? — No, she hasn't.
2. Are Lucas and Ilaria brother and sister? _____
3. Are Marta and Sabina twins? _____
4. Is Caetano a baby? _____
5. Is Adriana Gabriel's wife? _____
6. Have Fabiana and Pedro got two sons? _____

3 Lesson 1

1 Read.

Are there stairs in your house?

No, there aren't.

There is / There are (affirmative, negative, questions and short answers)

To say what exists in a place, we use **there is** for one thing, and **there are** for more than one thing. The short form of **there is** is **there's**.

There is a bird in the tree.
There's a spider in your bag.
There are two computers in my room.

We put the word **not** after **there is** and **there are** to say that there isn't a thing.

There isn't a photo in my notebook.
There aren't any skateboards in this shop.

To ask if there is a thing, we put **Is/Are there** at the beginning of the question. We can give short answers with **Yes** or **No**, and **there is/are** or **there isn't/aren't**.

Is there a pen on the book?
Yes, there is. / No, there isn't.

Are there five oranges on the table?
Yes, there are. / No, there aren't.

2 Write *there is, there are, there isn't, there aren't, is there* or *are there*.

1 ___Is there___ a table in the living room?
No, ___there isn't___ .

2 _____ stairs in your grandma's house?
Yes, _____ .

3 _____ five bedrooms in our house. It's a big house!

4 _____ windows in your living room?
No, _____ .

5 _____ toys in your living room?
No, _____ . But _____ a lot of toys in my bedroom!

3 Write.

1. __There is__ (✔) a computer in my room. __There isn't__ (✘) a TV.
2. _____ (✔) drawings on my walls. _____ (✘) photos.
3. _____ (✔) a door in our kitchen. _____ (✘) windows.
4. _____ (✘) a computer in the living room. _____ (✔) a lamp.
5. _____ (✘) books on my desk. _____ (✔) toys!
6. _____ (✔) two computers in our bedroom. _____ (✔) toys, too.

4 Write.

1. __Are there__ photos on the wall?
   __Yes, there are.__

2.  _____ a rabbit in the box?
   _____

3.  _____ chairs behind the desk?
   _____

4. _____ a cat in the bag?
   _____

5.  _____ apples in the basket?
   _____

5 Say it! Colour and say.

Is there a green bed?

No, there isn't. There is a grey bed.

LESSON 1

Lesson 2

1 Read.

"Whose ball is that?"

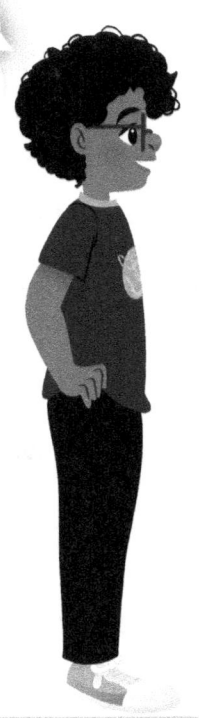

"It's my brother's."

Possessive adjectives

We can use **possessive adjectives** to show whose a thing is.

my	**its**
your	**our**
his	**your**
her	**their**

It's **my** ball.
It's **her** book.

We put **'s** after the name of a person or animal to show whose thing it is.

It's Uma**'s** bike.
They're Lucca**'s** books.
It's the cat**'s** toy.

To ask who a thing belongs to, we use **Whose ...?** We answer with **It is ...** or **They are ...** and the **possessive adjective** (**my**, **your**, **his**, etc.), or **'s** after the name of a person or animal.

Whose pencil is this?
It's **my** pencil.

Whose bike is this?
It's Jerry**'s** bike.

Whose socks are these?
They're Mark**'s** socks.

2 Circle.

1 John has got a big toy box. **(His)** / **Its** toy box is very tidy.
2 Look at Mia. **His** / **Her** socks are red.
3 We are twins. **Our** / **Her** clothes are the same.
4 Hi, Anna! Is this **your** / **their** new doll?
5 We've got many toys and books! **Our** / **Their** bedroom is messy.
6 I've got a cat. **Its** / **Their** eyes are green.
7 I'm at school. **My** / **Your** English lesson is fun.
8 My parents have got lots of books. **Our** / **Their** books are on the bookshelf.

3 Write.

1 Whose toys are these? They're Helen's toys.

2

3

4

5

6

LESSON 2   21

Lesson 3

1 Read.

"Look! A cat in a box. The cat is cute!"

A, an, the

We use **a** and **an** to talk about one person, animal or thing. We use **the** instead of **a/an** to talk about a specific person, animal or thing, or to talk about it again. We use **a** before consonants and **an** when the word begins with a vowel (a, e, i, o, u).

There's **a** rug and **a** table. **The** rug is blue and **the** table is brown. There's **an** apple on **the** table.

We also use **the** to talk about something which is unique, for example, **the** sky, **the** moon, **the** sun.

The moon and **the** sun are very far away.
The sky is blue.

2 Write *a*, *an* or *the*. Then match.

1 __the__ moon   a

2 _____ elephant   b

3 _____ flower   c

4 _____ orange teddy bear   d

5 _____ sun   e

6 _____ pencil   f

22 UNIT 3

3 Circle.

1. This is **a** / **an** dog and that's **a** / **an** cat.
   The / **A** cat is white and **a** / **the** dog is brown.

2. This is **a** / **an** grey box and that is **a** / **an** spider.
   A / **The** spider is on **a** / **the** box.

3. This is **a** / **an** aeroplane in **a** / **the** sky.
   A / **The** aeroplane is red and **a** / **the** sky is blue.

4. Andrew is on **a** / **an** green boat. He is wearing **a** / **an** orange mask.
   A / **The** mask is big.

4 Write *a*, *an* or *the*. Then colour.

In Pedro's bedroom, there's (1) __a__ very cool bed. (2) _____ bed is (3) _____ car! It is red and black. There is (4) _____ shelf on the back of (5) _____ car. (6) _____ shelf is purple. There is (7) _____ ball on (8) _____ shelf. (9) _____ ball is green and blue. There's (10) _____ teddy bear in front of (11) _____ bed. (12) _____ teddy bear is brown. There are three crayons on (13) _____ floor: (14) _____ orange crayon, (15) _____ red crayon and (16) _____ blue crayon.

4 Lesson 1

1 Read.

I've got some fruit.

No, I haven't. But I've got some apples!

Have you got any bananas?

Countable and uncountable nouns: some/any

Nouns which we can count are called **countable nouns,** and they have singular and plural forms: orange, oranges.

Nouns which we can't count are called **uncountable nouns** and have only got a singular form: water.

To talk about a number of people, animals or things we can count, we use the words **some** or **any** with a plural countable noun. **Some** goes in affirmative sentences, and **any** goes in negative sentences and in questions.

I've got **some** oranges.
I haven't got **any** oranges.
Have you got **any** oranges?
There are **some** sandwiches.
There aren't **any** sandwiches.
Are there **any** sandwiches?

When we want to talk about the amount of a thing we can't count, we use the words **some** or **any** with an uncountable noun. **Some** goes in affirmative sentences, and **any** goes in negative sentences and in questions.

We've got **some** fruit.
We haven't got **any** fruit.
Have you got **any** fruit?
There's **some** bread.
There isn't **any** bread.
Is there **any** bread?

2 Find eleven words. Circle countable nouns. Underline uncountable nouns.

waterbtomatoesajuicecmangoeslapplespmilkulemonadekqricewbiscuitsrstrawberriesghmeat

3 Circle.

1 Chang hasn't got **some** / **any** water.
2 Has Chen got **some** / **any** oranges in his school bag?
3 There is **some** / **any** chocolate in the box.
4 Is there **some** / **any** lemonade in the fridge?
5 There are **some** / **any** sandwiches in my lunch box.
6 Have you got **some** / **any** apples in your bag?

4 Write *some* or *any*.

1 She hasn't got __any__ fruit.
2 There isn't _____ milk in the bottle.
3 He's got _____ oranges.
4 There's _____ bread on the table.
5 They've got _____ sweets.
6 There isn't _____ juice in the fridge.

5 Write *are, aren't, is* or *isn't* with *some* or *any*.

1 There __aren't any__ grandparents.
2 There _____ sandwiches.
3 There _____ cake.
4 There _____ drinks.
5 There _____ fruit.
6 There _____ trees.
7 There _____ animals.

LESSON 1 25

Lesson 2

1 Read.

How much …? / How many …?

To ask the number or amount of people, things or animals, we use **how much** or **how many**. If we can count them, we use **how many**. If we can't count them, we use **how much**.

How many …?
biscuits
sandwiches
oranges

How much …?
fruit
sugar
chocolate

How many apples are there? There are ten.
How much sugar has he got? A lot.
How much fruit is there?
How many pieces of fruit are there?

2 Circle.

1 How **much** / **many** fruit is there?
2 How **much** / **many** pieces of pizza have you got?
3 How **much** / **many** water is there?
4 How **much** / **many** sandwiches has she got?
5 How **much** / **many** lemonade is there in the fridge?
6 How **much** / **many** sugar is there?
7 How **much** / **many** pieces of chocolate has she got?
8 How **much** / **many** chocolate is there?

3 Write *How much* or *How many*.

1. <u>How much</u> milk is there?
2. _____ sandwiches are there?
3. _____ strawberries are there?
4. _____ water is there?
5. _____ orange juice has she got?
6. _____ pieces of chocolate have they got?
7. _____ mangoes are there on the table?
8. _____ biscuits are there?

4 Say it!

How much water is there?

There is a lot.

LESSON 2

Lesson 3

1 Read.

Object pronouns

A **pronoun** is a word that replaces the name of a person or thing. A **subject pronoun** replaces the name of the person or thing that does the action.
<u>Mary</u>'s got ten biscuits. **She**'s also got some chocolate.

Object pronouns replace the name of a person or thing after a verb or a preposition (words like *at*, *for*, *to*, etc.).

I've got a cake for <u>Andy</u>. The chocolate is for **him**, too.
Give **me** that toy!
Look at **them**! They've got a lot of toys.

Subject pronouns	Object pronouns
I	me
you	you
he	him
she	her
it	it
we	us
you	you
they	them

2 Match.

1 This is for your brother.   a Look at them.
2 This is for you and me.   b Look at her.
3 Give the chocolate to your sister.   c This is for him.
4 Look at Ana.   d Give it to her.
5 Look at Marco and Simon.   e This is for us.
6 Give the flowers to your brother.   f Give them to him.

3 Circle.

1 Yum! A chocolate biscuit! I want **them / (it)**
2 Ken's got a big cake. Look at **us / it**.
3 I'm thirsty. Mum, give **me / him** some lemonade, please.
4 That yoghurt is mine. Don't touch **her / it**.
5 Say that again, please. I can't hear **you / me**.
6 Dad is very tired. Don't wake **us / him** up.
7 Grandma, look at **us / them**. We've got a lot of snacks.
8 Look at those yummy nuts. Let's eat **them / it**.

4 Write.

1 Your ice cream is very big. Can I taste __it__ ?
2 I'm behind the sofa. My friends can't see _____ !
3 Mum is very tired. Let's help _____ .
4 We've got a lot of snacks. Come and eat with _____ .
5 Look at _____ ! They're winning!
6 The dog is hungry. Give _____ some food.
7 Look at _____ . He's on the tree.
8 Please give _____ some water. I'm very thirsty.

5 Say it!

Is there any yoghurt for Maria?

Yes, there's some yoghurt for her.

	Maria	I	Angelo	Maria and I	Maria and Angelo
(yoghurt)	✔				
(bowl)			✔		
(glasses)					✔
(chocolate)		✔			
(nuts)				✔	

Review

1 Write *There is, There isn't, There are* or *There aren't*.

1. __There are__ three pictures on the wall.
2. _____ a lamp near the window.
3. _____ a lamp near the TV.
4. _____ books on the bookshelf.
5. _____ a sofa in the living room.
6. _____ a small table near the sofa.
7. _____ a rug near the sofa.
8. _____ books on the table.

2 Write.

1. __Whose lunch box is this?__   It's Marta's lunch box.
2. _____   It's Ahmed's toy box.
3. _____   They're my books.
4. _____   They're my sister's teddy bears.
5. _____   It's my brother's snack.

3 Circle.

1. Look! There's **(a)**/ **an** red aeroplane in **a** /**(the)** sky.
2. What's that? It's **a** / **the** toy.
3. This is **a** / **the** photo of a cat.
4. I'm hungry. I want **a** / **the** snack.
5. **A** / **The** sun is in **a** / **the** sky.
6. **A** / **The** teddy bear in the photo is my brother's.
7. I've got **a** / **an** orange umbrella.
8. Is that **an** / **the** ant?

30 UNITS 3 – 4

4 Write *some* or *any*.

1 There isn't __any__ lemonade.
2 Is there _____ orange juice in the fridge?
3 There are _____ snacks on the table.
4 Is there _____ sugar in those biscuits?
5 Are there _____ sandwiches in your lunch box?
6 I've got _____ sweets.

5 Write.

> bread   cake   cheese   crisps
> pieces   pizza   sandwiches   water

1  __How much pizza__ is there?

2  _____ of pizza are there?

3  _____ are there?

4  _____ is there?

5  _____ have you got?

6 _____ are there?

7  _____ is there?

8  _____ have we got?

6 Match.

1 I'm thirsty!
2 They've got funny hats.
3 It's Mum's birthday.
4 We're thirsty!
5 That's the new toy box.
6 We've got funny hats.

a We want some lemonade, please.
b Put it in your room.
c Let's buy her some flowers.
d Look at them!
e Give me some water, please!
f Look at us!

5 Lesson 1

They're playing in the snow.

1 Read.

Present continuous (affirmative)

To talk about something which is happening now, at the moment of speaking, we use the **present continuous**. This tense is formed with **am/are/is + verb + –ing**.

When we speak, we usually use the short form.

I **am** play**ing**.	I**'m** play**ing**.
You **are** play**ing**.	You**'re** play**ing**.
He **is** play**ing**.	He**'s** play**ing**.
She **is** play**ing**.	She**'s** play**ing**.
It **is** play**ing**.	It**'s** play**ing**.
We **are** play**ing**.	We**'re** play**ing**.
You **are** play**ing**.	You**'re** play**ing**.
They **are** play**ing**.	They**'re** play**ing**.

Note: When the verb ends in **–e**, we drop the **–e** before adding **–ing**.

| take | → | She's tak**ing** a photo. |
| have | → | We're hav**ing** breakfast. |

When the verb has got only one syllable and ends in **consonant-vowel-consonant**, we double the consonant that is at the end of the verb.

| win | → | We're win**ning**. |

2 Find eight verbs. Then write them in the present continuous.

win̄ferunkoswimlewatchbkotakexiwritemnhelpoflhave

1 __winning__
2 _____
3 _____
4 _____
5 _____
6 _____
7 _____
8 _____

3 Write.

dance   drink   make   ~~wear~~   win   write

1 The hockey players ___are wearing___ red clothes.

2 Samantha _____ the race.

3 We _____ a snowman.

4 Lisa _____ in her diary.

5 Steve and Liz _____ hot chocolate.

6 They _____ .

4 Write.

1 Mark / have fun / in Canada
   ___Mark is having fun in Canada.___

2 Chrissy and Mary / sleep / in their bedrooms
   _____

3 we / play / a fun game
   _____

4 the children / take / photos
   _____

5 that boy / eat / our food
   _____

6 you / run / fast
   _____

LESSON 1   33

Lesson 2

1 Read.

I'm not watching TV. I'm reading a book.

Present continuous (negative)

We use the **present continuous** with the word **not** after **am, are, is** to say that a person is not doing an action now. When we speak, we usually use the short form.

I **am not** play**ing**.
You **are not** play**ing**.
He **is not** play**ing**.
She **is not** play**ing**.
It **is not** play**ing**.
We **are not** play**ing**.
You **are not** play**ing**.
They **are not** play**ing**.

I**'m not** play**ing**.
You **aren't** play**ing**.
He **isn't** play**ing**.
She **isn't** play**ing**.
It **isn't** play**ing**.
We **aren't** play**ing**.
You **aren't** play**ing**.
They **aren't** play**ing**.

2 Circle.
1 The children **aren't** / **isn't** doing their homework.
2 Mum **isn't** / **aren't** playing a game.
3 The cat **isn't** / **aren't** climbing a tree.
4 I **'m not** / **aren't** sleeping.
5 We **isn't** / **aren't** riding our bicycles.
6 It **aren't** / **isn't** snowing today.
7 He **'m not** / **isn't** listening to the lesson.
8 They **isn't** / **aren't** watching the film.

3 Write.

1 Megan / climb / a mountain — _Megan isn't climbing a mountain._
2 I / sit / at my desk
3 the boys / swim
4 it / snow / today
5 we / have / fun
6 you / listen / to me
7 Emily / play / football
8 they / ride / their bikes

4 Write.

The butterfly (1) _isn't flying_ (fly). It (2) _'s sitting_ (sit) on a flower.

The children (5) _____ (have) a picnic. They (6) _____ (run) and jumping.

The children (3) _____ (have) fun on the beach. They (4) _____ (sleep).

We (7) _____ (sit) at home. We (8) _____ (play) in the snow.

LESSON 2 35

Lesson 3

1 Read.

What are you doing?

I'm playing a video game.

Present continuous (questions and short answers)

To ask if someone is doing an action at the moment, we simply put **Am**, **Are**, **Is** at the beginning of the question. We give short answers with **Yes** or **No**, the correct person, and **am**, **are** or **is**.

Am I play**ing**?	Yes, I **am**. / No, I**'m not**.
Are you play**ing**?	Yes, you **are**. / No, you **aren't**.
Is he play**ing**?	Yes, he **is**. / No, he **isn't**.
Is she play**ing**?	Yes, she **is**. / No, she **isn't**.
Is it play**ing**?	Yes, it **is**. / No, it **isn't**.
Are we play**ing**?	Yes, we **are**. / No, we **aren't**.
Are you play**ing**?	Yes, you **are**. / No, you **aren't**.
Are they play**ing**?	Yes, they **are**. / No, they **aren't**.

To ask what a person is doing at the moment, we use **What** at the beginning of the question. We answer with the **present continuous**.

What are you doing?
I'm making a cake.
What is Peter eating?
He's eating popcorn.

2 Write and match.

1 __Is__ he __making__ (make) a fire?   a Yes, they are.
2 _____ we _____ (eat) burgers?   b No, it isn't.
3 _____ it _____ (sleep) in a bed?   c Yes, she is.
4 _____ Mum _____ (cook) dinner?   d Yes, I am.
5 _____ you _____ (have) fun?   e No, he isn't.
6 _____ Bob and Alice _____ (walk)?   f Yes, we are.

3 Write about you.

1 <u>Is</u> your dad watching TV?   <u>Yes, he is. / No, he isn't.</u>
2 _____ your friends listening?   _____
3 _____ your mum working?   _____
4 _____ you sleeping at your desk?   _____
5 _____ you and your friends studying?   _____
6 _____ your teacher sitting next to you?   _____

4 Write and match.

1 <u>What is</u> Dad <u>watching</u> (watch)?   a My favourite jeans.
2 _____ you _____ (wear)?   b A big sandwich.
3 _____ the children _____ (play)?   c TV.
4 _____ Alberto _____ (eat)?   d Her homework.
5 _____ Susan _____ (do)?   e A video game.

5 Say it!

What is he doing?   He's watching TV.

6 Lesson 1

1 Read.

Can you snowboard?

No, I can't. But I can ski!

Can/can't (affirmative, negative, questions and short answers)

We use the word **can** and a verb to say what we are able to do. We use **cannot** or **can't** to say what we are not able to do. When we speak, we usually use the short form, **can't**.

I/you/he/she/it/we/you/they **can** ski.
I/you/he/she/it/we/you/they **can't** ski.

We also use **can** to say that something is allowed and **can't** to say that something is not allowed.

You **can** watch TV.
You **can't** go to the park.

To ask if a person is able or allowed to do something, we put **Can** at the beginning of the sentence. We answer with **Yes** or **No**, the correct person, and **can** or **can't**.

Can I/you/he/she/it/we/you/they **ski**?

Can she **speak** English?
Yes, she **can**. / **No**, she **can't**.
Can I ride my bike?
Yes, you **can**. / **No**, you **can't**.

2 Circle.

1 Fish **can** / **can't** walk.
2 Dogs **can** / **can't** run.
3 Sharks **can** / **can't** play video games.
4 Teachers **can** / **can't** sleep in the classroom.
5 Children **can** / **can't** shout in the lesson.
6 Elephants **can** / **can't** eat leaves.
7 Dolphins **can** / **can't** swim.
8 Babies **can** / **can't** ride a bike.

3 Write and answer about you.

1 Can you watch TV all day? Yes, I can. / No, I can't.
2 Can your best friend ride a bike? _____
3 Can you ski? _____
4 Can your dad make yummy cakes? _____
5 Can your teacher play the piano? _____
6 Can you draw beautiful pictures? _____
7 Can you and your friends play football? _____
8 Can your mum and dad sing songs? _____

4 Write.

	ski	run	ride a bike	ice-skate
Mum	✔	✘	✔	✘
Dad	✔	✔	✔	✘
The twins	✘	✔	✔	✔

1 Mum / run
   Can Mum run?
   No, she can't.
2 Dad / ride a bike
   _____
   _____
3 the twins / ice-skate
   _____
   _____
4 Mum / ski
   _____
   _____

5 Dad / ice-skate
   _____
   _____
6 the twins / ski
   _____
   _____
7 Mum / ice-skate
   _____
   _____
8 Dad / run
   _____
   _____

Lesson 2

1 Read.

"You must listen to your teachers!"

Must/mustn't (affirmative and negative)

We use the word **must** with a verb to say what we have to do. We put the word **not** after **must** to say what we are not allowed to do. When we speak, we usually use the short form: **mustn't**.

I/you/he/she/it/we/you/they **must**
I/you/he/she/it/we/you/they **mustn't** or **must not**

Lee **must** listen to his mum.
We **mustn't** shout in class.

2 Write.

| catch | ~~eat~~ | go | listen | make | throw |

1 You __must eat__ your dinner.

4 They _____ to the teacher.

2 They _____ the bus.

5 He _____ the ball.

3 She _____ a cake.

6 They _____ to bed.

3 Circle.

1 Dogs **must** / **mustn't** eat chocolate.
2 Children **must** / **mustn't** go to bed at twelve o'clock.
3 Babies **must** / **mustn't** eat sweets.
4 Students **must** / **mustn't** go to school on Monday morning.
5 We **must** / **mustn't** listen to the teacher.
6 The teacher **must** / **mustn't** talk on her mobile phone.

4 Write *must* or *mustn't*.

1 You ___mustn't___ shout in the classroom.
2 In basketball, you _____ throw the ball.
3 You _____ jump in the classroom.
4 You _____ kick a football.
5 You _____ run on ice.
6 You _____ do your homework.

5 Say it!

- ~~draw on the walls~~
- clean the walls
- swim with sharks
- swim fast
- run now
- wear hats
- be in the sun

"He mustn't draw on the wall."

Lesson 3

1 Read.

Don't sit on that chair!

Imperatives (affirmative and negative); Let's

To give instructions or orders, we use only the verb of the action. It doesn't matter if we're talking to one person or many.

Listen!

To ask a person not to do something, we put **Don't** at the beginning of the sentence.

Don't eat in the classroom!

To suggest something to do with someone, we use **Let's** at the beginning of the sentence and before the verb of the action.

Let's have a picnic.

2 Write.

1 This is Suzie's birthday cake.   look (✔) touch (✘)
   Look! Don't touch!

2 I love this song.   listen (✔) shout (✘)
   _____

3 There's a lion.   run (✔) sit down (✘)
   _____

4 The road is icy.   walk (✔) run (✘)
   _____

5 I'm throwing the ball.   catch (✔) close your eyes (✘)
   _____

6 Grandma is here.   say hello (✔) play video games (✘)
   _____

42 UNIT 6

3 Write and match.

1 some / buy / let's / chocolate
   <u>Let's buy some chocolate.</u>

2 bed / let's / to / go
   _____

3 today / don't / out / go
   _____

4 the / let's / to / go / castle
   _____

5 now / the / box / open
   _____

a

b

c

d

e

4 Write.

buy a toy
draw a picture
~~go camping~~
go skiing
go to the park
wear warm clothes

1 I like sleeping in tents. <u>Let's go camping.</u>

2 It's freezing. _____

3 It's Uma's birthday. _____

4 That's a beautiful bird. _____

5 We must walk the dog. _____

6 It's snowing in the mountains. _____

LESSON 3   43

Review

1 Write.

1 He __isn't throwing__ the ball. (throw)

2 She _____. (fall)

3 Frank _____ a photo. (take)

4 They _____. (shout)

5 We _____ to bed. (go)

6 The boys _____ to the teacher! (listen)

2 Write.

1 you / do / homework
What are you doing?
I'm doing my homework.

2 they / make / snowman
_____
_____

3 they / play / baseball
_____
_____

4 it / wear / hat
_____
_____

3 Write *can* or *can't*.

1 __Can__ ants run fast? No, they __can't__ .
2 _____ you swim? Yes, I _____ .
3 _____ we go to the beach today? No, you _____ .
4 _____ you speak English? Yes, we _____ .

4 Write *must* or *mustn't*.

1 In winter, we __must__ wear warm clothes.
2 In summer, we _____ sit in the sun.
3 It's your friend's toy. You _____ take it.
4 It's ten o'clock. You _____ go to bed.
5 You are at school. You _____ shout in the classroom.

5 Circle.

1 Sit down! / (Don't sit down!)

3 Don't stand up! / Stand up!

2 Don't be good! / Be good!

4 Eat it! / Don't eat it!

6 Match.

1 It's raining.
2 I'm hungry.
3 It's Johnny's birthday.
4 This is my favourite cartoon.
5 Mum is very tired.

a Let's make a pizza.
b Let's buy a present.
c Let's help her.
d Let's watch it.
e Let's bring an umbrella.

7 Lesson 1

1 Read.

I want to be a doctor. My sister wants to be a dentist.

Present simple (affirmative)

We use the **present simple** to say that an action happens, or that a person does an action, *always, often, every day* or *usually*. In affirmative sentences, we use only the verb and the person.

I **go** to the park on Saturday.

The verb changes when we have **he/she/it**. We must put **–s** at the end of the verb.

I dance.
You dance.
He dance**s**.
She dance**s**.
It dance**s**.
We dance.
You dance.
They dance.

When the verb ends in **–sh**, **–ch**, **–o**, and we have **he/she/it**, we add **–es** to the verb.

Steve go**es** swimming on Saturday.

When the verb ends in a consonant + **–y**, and we have **he/she/it**, we drop the **–y** and add **–ies** to the verb.

Bob stud**ies** English on Tuesday and Wednesday.

Note: We use **prepositions of time** with the **present simple** to say when an action happens.

James rides his bike **in the morning / in the afternoon / in the evening**.
The children go to bed **at nine o'clock / at midday**.
Maria plays tennis **on Saturday**.

2 Write.

catch cry do fly go play say
speak study take think watch

−s	−es	−ies
plays	catches	cries

3 Circle.

1 I **go** / **goes** skiing in winter.
2 Mum **take** / **takes** lots of photos every day.
3 Tom's sisters **speak** / **speaks** French.
4 The doctor **give** / **gives** us biscuits.
5 My grandparents **watch** / **watches** TV at three o'clock.
6 The postman **arrive** / **arrives** at ten o'clock.
7 My brother **wear** / **wears** a baseball cap.
8 We **stay** / **stays** in a hotel every summer.

4 Say it!

Sally rides her bike on Saturday morning.

Lesson 2

1 Read.

I don't like dolls. I like robots.

Present simple (negative)

We use the **present simple** with **don't** (**do not**) or **doesn't** (**does not**) before the verb to say that an action doesn't happen, or that a person doesn't do an action, *always, often, every day* or *usually*. We use **doesn't** with **he/she/it** and we use **don't** with **I/you/we/they**. When we use **doesn't**, we don't put –**s**, –**es**, or –**ies** at the end of the verb.

He **doesn't play** the piano.
They **don't watch** TV at school.

When we speak, we usually use the short form.

I **do not** dance.	I **don't** dance.
You **do not** dance.	You **don't** dance.
He **does not** dance.	He **doesn't** dance.
She **does not** dance.	She **doesn't** dance.
It **does not** dance.	It **doesn't** dance.
We **do not** dance.	We **don't** dance.
You **do not** dance.	You **don't** dance.
They **do not** dance.	They **don't** dance.

2 Write *don't* or *doesn't*.

1 Children ___don't___ have lessons every day.
2 The twins _____ like ice cream.
3 He _____ have a computer.
4 Fiona _____ play football.
5 Paul's dad _____ ride a bicycle.
6 My friends _____ go swimming in winter.

3 Write.

1 John goes to school at eight o'clock.   six o'clock (✘)
   <u>He doesn't go to school at six o'clock.</u>

2 The twins eat pizza on Saturday.   pasta (✘)
   _____

3 We play basketball at the weekend.   tennis (✘)
   _____

4 Sally plays video games at night.   watch TV (✘)
   _____

5 I read comics in the afternoon.   books (✘)
   _____

6 My brother likes popcorn.   crisps (✘)
   _____

4 Write.

| help   like   ~~play~~   ride   sleep   work |

1 Jerry <u>doesn't play</u> tennis well.

4 He _____ in a school.

2 I _____ a bike to school.

5 She _____ her mum.

3 They _____ their dinner.

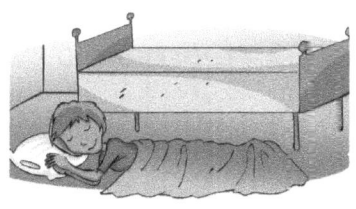

6 She _____ in a bed.

LESSON 2

Lesson 3

1 Read.

Present simple (questions and short answers)

To form a question with the **present simple**, we put **Do** or **Does** at the beginning of the question. When we use **does**, we don't put **–s**, **–es** or **–ies** at the end of the verb. We give short answers with **Yes** or **No**, the correct person and **do/does** or **don't/doesn't**.

Do I dance?	Yes, I **do**. / No, I **don't**.
Do you dance?	Yes, you **do**. / No, you **don't**.
Does he dance?	Yes, he **does**. / No, he **doesn't**.
Does she dance?	Yes, she **does**. / No, she **doesn't**.
Does it dance?	Yes, it **does**. / No, it **doesn't**.
Do we dance?	Yes, we **do**. / No, we **don't**.
Do you dance?	Yes, you **do**. / No, you **don't**.
Do they dance?	Yes, they **do**. / No, they **don't**.

Do you **work** at the weekend?
Yes, I **do**. / **No**, I **don't**.
Does Peter **listen** to music in the morning?
Yes, he **does**. / **No**, he **doesn't**.

2 Answer about you.

1 Do you watch TV in the evening?   <u>Yes, I do. / No, I don't.</u>
2 Does your mum work on Sundays?   _____
3 Does your teacher play video games?   _____
4 Does your dad have money?   _____
5 Do you want to be an astronaut?   _____
6 Do you and your friend go to the park at the weekend?   _____

3 Write.

1. astronauts / wear uniforms / (✔)
   Do astronauts wear uniforms?
   Yes, they do.

2. nurses / wear boots / (✘)

3. your brother / like video games / (✘)

4. you / play the piano / (✔)

5. your friends / watch TV / (✔)

6. your sister / snowboard / (✘)

4 Say it!

What's my job?

No, I don't

Yes, I do.

Do you wear a hat?

Do you love animals?

You're a vet!

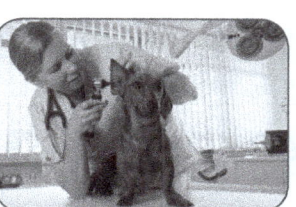

8 Lesson 1

I sometimes read books on my tablet.

1 Read.

Adverbs of frequency

We use **adverbs of frequency** to show how often something happens.
We use these words with the **present simple** and they always come before the verb.
Some **adverbs of frequency** are:

always
often
sometimes
never

He **sometimes** sees his friends.
He **never** plays football.

Note: When we use **adverbs of frequency** with **have got** and **to be**, these words come after **have** and **am**, **are** or **is**.

We've **often** got sandwiches with us.
Grandma is **always** happy to see us.

2 Write.

1 My best friend has got some money. (always)
   My best friend has always got some money.

2 The teacher arrives late for the lesson. (never)
   _____

3 I am hungry after school. (often)
   _____

4 Geoffrey does his homework at the weekend. (sometimes)
   _____

5 Vicky, Beth and Andy aren't at home. (always)
   _____

6 The postman has got a letter for me. (never)
   _____

3 Look and read. Write *T* for True or *F* for False.

	Lee	Mae
watch TV in the morning	■■□□	□□□□
answer emails on a smartphone	□□□□	■■■□
read books on a tablet	■■■□	■■■□
drink cold milk	□□□□	□□□□
play video games in the afternoon	■■■■	■■□□
eat cereal for breakfast	■■■■	■■■□

1 Lee never watches TV in the morning. **F**
2 Lee and Mae never drink cold milk. ☐
3 Mae never answers emails on her smartphone. ☐
4 Lee and Mae always read books on their tablets. ☐
5 Mae sometimes plays video games in the afternoon. ☐

4 Say it!

always   often   sometimes   never

I sometimes play football.

I never play football, but I sometimes play basketball.

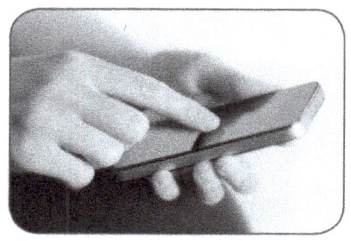

LESSON 1   53

Lesson 2

1 Read.

My tablet is smaller than yours.

Comparatives

To compare two or more people, animals or things, we use the adjective (the word which describes what a person is, e.g. tall, thin) in the **comparative**. To form the **comparative**, we put **–er** at the end of the adjective. Sometimes we use the word **than** after the adjective.

small → small**er than**

The blue car is **smaller than** the red car.

When the adjective ends in **–e**, we add only **–r**.

nice → nic**er**

My bag is **nicer than** your bag.

When the adjective ends in **–y**, we drop the **–y** and add **–ier**.

happ**y** → happ**ier**

Lucas is **happier than** Valerie.

When the adjective has got one syllable and ends in **consonant-vowel-consonant**, then we double the last consonant and add **–er**.

hot → hott**er**

My house is **hotter than** your house.

There are also adjectives which don't follow these rules and have their own word in the **comparative**.

good → better
bad → worse

My sandwich is **better than** yours.
My drawing is **worse than** your drawing.

2 Write.

fast   happy   small   sunny   ~~tall~~   warm

1 My brother is ___taller___ than my sister.

2 The cat is _____ than the dog.

3 Greece is _____ than England.

4 Number 3 is _____ than number 5.

5 Kim is _____ than Sim.

6 John is _____ than Mike.

3 Say it!

- fast
- funny
- happy
- old
- short
- ~~tall~~
- young

Akim is taller than Shelly.

Lesson 3

1 Read.

It's the best day of the year! It's my birthday!

Superlatives

To compare a person, animal or thing with many others, we use the adjective in the **superlative**. To form the **superlative**, we add –**est** at the end of the adjective and use **the** before the adjective.

small → **the** small**est**

Katharine has got **the smallest** doll.

When the adjective ends in –**e**, we add only –**st**.

larg**e** → larg**est**

Elephants are **the largest** animals in Africa.

When the adjective ends in –**y**, we drop the –**y** and add –**iest**.

happ**y** → happ**iest**

This is **the happiest** day of my life.

When the adjective has got one syllable and ends in **consonant-vowel-consonant**, then we double the last consonant and add –**est**.

big → bigg**est**

This is **the biggest** bike in the shop.

There are also adjectives which don't follow these rules and have their own word in the **superlative**.

good → best
bad → worst

My mum makes **the best** biscuits.
This is **the worst** game.

56 UNIT 8

2 Circle.

1 The teacher is the **oldest** / **youngest** person in the class.
2 My fish is the **biggest** / **smallest** animal in the house.
3 The whale is the **kindest** / **biggest** animal in the sea.
4 My baby brother is the **fastest** / **youngest** person in the family.
5 Koalas are the **cutest** / **worst** animals in Australia.
6 The giraffe is the **shortest** / **tallest** animal in Africa.

3 Write.

~~big~~   cold   pretty   safe   tall   warm

1 Baobabs are the ___biggest___ trees in Africa.

4 12345 isn't the _____ password.

2 This is the _____ butterfly in Brazil.

5 This is the _____ mountain in the world.

3 These are the _____ boots my dad has got.

6 This is the _____ day of the year.

Review

1 Write.

> like   play   read   wear   ski   ~~work~~

1 She ___works___ in a school.

4 He _____ tennis.

2 They _____ to play video games.

5 They _____ together.

3 She _____ a uniform.

6 She _____ with her mum.

2 Circle and write.

1 **(Do)/ Does** you like ice cream?   Yes, ___I do___.
2 **Do / Does** your teacher shout?   No, _____.
3 **Do / Does** the doctor give you chocolates?   No, _____.
4 **Do / Does** your friends have computers at home?   Yes, _____.
5 **Do / Does** your dad get up early every day?   Yes, _____.
6 **Do / Does** you eat your dinner at school?   No, _____.

3 Write.

1 Beth ____is always____ (be, always) late for school in the morning.
2 Mark and Lucas _____ (go, never) to the park together.
3 Kelly _____ (eat, always) her breakfast at eight o'clock.
4 Mum _____ (drive, often) us to school.
5 We _____ (watch, sometimes) TV in the evening.
6 Our dog _____ (be, never) quiet at night.
7 My big sister _____ (study, often) in the kitchen.
8 Dad _____ (wash, always) the car on Saturdays.

4 Circle.

1 This is the **better / (best)** video game in the world!
2 My cat is **cuter / cutest** than your cat.
3 My tablet is **bigger / biggest** than your smartphone.
4 My grandma is **older / oldest** than your grandma.
5 That is the **worse / worst** job in the world.
6 I have the **newer / newest** school bag in class.

5 Write.

| big   ~~old~~   sunny   tall   young |

1 Grandpa is ____older____ than Dad, but Grandma is the ____oldest____.
2 Dad is _____ than Grandma, but Mum is the _____.
3 Leopards are _____ than monkeys, but elephants are the _____.
4 Spain is _____ than England, but Greece is the _____.
5 Billy is _____ than Helen, but Patrick is the _____.

9 Lesson 1

1 Read.

I was at my cousin's house last weekend.

I was at home with my family.

Past simple: be (affirmative)

To talk about what people or things were like, or where they were in the past (yesterday, last year, etc.), we use the **past simple** of the verb **be**.

I **was**
you **were**
he **was**
she **was**
it **was**
we **were**
you **were**
they **were**

Some dinosaurs **were** very big.

Note: The **past simple** of **there is** / **there are** is **there was** / **there were**.

There were ten children at the party yesterday.

2 Circle.

1 *Tyrannosaurus Rex* **was** / **were** a dinosaur.
2 Max and Uma **was** / **were** at a bookshop.
3 The reporters **was** / **were** in England last week.
4 There **was** / **were** an old bridge near the castle.
5 It **was** / **were** rainy on Monday.
6 They **was** / **were** in a cave yesterday!
7 Leo **was** / **were** a beautiful baby.
8 There **was** / **were** a giant whale at the museum.

3 Write was or were.

Yesterday, Margot and Jules (1) __were__ at a very big parade. It (2) _____ at the Carnaval de Oruro, in Bolivia. There (3) _____ lots of people and there (4) _____ a lot of food. It (5) _____ fun! Margot (6) _____ happy because the music (7) _____ really good and there (8) _____ many people in colourful costumes. Jules (9) _____ angry because his smart phone and his camera (10) _____ at home!

4 Say it!

On Thursday, we were at the museum.

There was an elephant, a dinosaur and birds.

Thursday

Friday

Saturday

Sunday

Lesson 2

1 Read.

I wasn't at school last week.

Don't worry! There wasn't any homework.

Past simple: be (negative)

To form the negative of the verb **be** in the **past simple**, we put the word **not** after **was** or **were**. When we speak, we usually use the short form.

I **was not**	I **wasn't**
you **were not**	you **weren't**
he **was not**	he **wasn't**
she **was not**	she **wasn't**
it **was not**	it **wasn't**
we **were not**	we **weren't**
you **were not**	you **weren't**
they **were not**	they **weren't**

The boys **weren't** at school yesterday.

Note: The **past simple** of **there isn't / there aren't** is **there wasn't / there weren't**.

There wasn't any milk in the glass.

2 Circle.

1 Dinosaurs ___ friendly.
   a wasn't   (b) weren't

2 T.rex's teeth ___ sharp.
   a wasn't   b were

3 A long time ago, there ___ any people on Earth.
   a wasn't   b weren't

4 There ___ dinosaurs with wings.
   a was   b were

5 T.rex's food ___ vegetables.
   a wasn't   b weren't

6 T.rex ___ a very big dinosaur.
   a were   b was

3 **Write *wasn't* or *weren't*. Then match.**

1 There __weren't__ any vegetables for dinner.   a

2 It _____ a sunny day yesterday.   b

3 The teacher _____ in the classroom at nine o'clock.   c

4 The boys _____ in the garden in the afternoon.   d

5 There _____ any tea in Grandpa's cup this morning.   e

4 **Write.**

1 On Monday, Mario and Ana were at the museum. (school)
   __They weren't at school.__

2 On Tuesday, Leo was at school. (home)
   _____

3 On Wednesday, Mia and Lee were at the market. (park)
   _____

4 On Thursday, Chang and Mia were at the beach. (theatre)
   _____

5 On Friday, Tony was at school. (home)
   _____

6 On Saturday, we were at the beach. (forest)
   _____

LESSON 2   63

Lesson 3

1 Read.

Were you at school yesterday?

No, I wasn't.

Past simple: be (questions and short answers)

To form the question of the verb **be** in the **past simple**, we put **Was/Were** at the beginning. We give short answers with **Yes** or **No**, the correct person, and **was/were** or **wasn't/weren't**.

Was I ...?	Yes, I **was**. / No, I **wasn't**.
Were you ...?	Yes, you **were**. / No, you **weren't**.
Was he ...?	Yes, he **was**. / No, he **wasn't**.
Was she ...?	Yes, she **was**. / No, she **wasn't**.
Was it ...?	Yes, it **was**. / No, it **wasn't**.
Were we ...?	Yes, we **were**. / No, we **weren't**.
Were you ...?	Yes, you **were**. / No, you **weren't**.
Were they ...?	Yes, they **were**. / No, they **weren't**.

Were you with your friends on Sunday?
Yes, we **were**. / **No**, we **weren't**.

Note: The **past simple** of **Is there ...? / Are there ...?** is **Was there ...? / Were there ...?**
Was there a camera in the box?

2 Write about you.

1. Were you seven on your last birthday?   Yes, I was. / No, I wasn't.
2. Was it sunny yesterday?   _____
3. Was it rainy at the weekend?   _____
4. Were you in the park on Sunday?   _____
5. Was your best friend at school yesterday? _____
6. Were the shops open yesterday afternoon? _____

3 Write *was* or *were*. Then match.

1  __Were__ the boys naughty? — a Yes, they were.

2  _____ the dog hungry yesterday evening? — b No, he wasn't.

3  _____ they at home last night? — c No, it wasn't.

4  _____ it a good day for the beach yesterday? — d Yes, it was.

5  _____ Berto two years old yesterday? — e No, they weren't.

4 Say it!

 Brazil — January
 Brazil — February
 United States — March
 Canada — April

 Spain — May
 Spain — June
 Greece — July
 Greece — August

 Egypt — September
 Japan — October
 Japan — November
 Australia — December

Where were you in August?

I was in Greece.

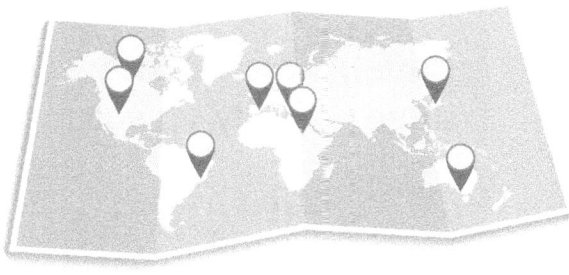

10 Lesson 1

1 Read.

I played tennis yesterday.

Past simple (regular verbs, affirmative)

When we want to say that something happened (and finished) in the past, we use the **past simple**. To form this tense with **regular verbs**, we add **–ed** at the end of the verb.

I play**ed**
you play**ed**
he play**ed**
she play**ed**
it play**ed**
we play**ed**
you play**ed**
they play**ed**

Yesterday, we **played** a game.

Note: When the verb ends in **–e**, then we add only **–d**.
clos**e**   clos**ed**

When the verb ends in a **consonant** + **–y**, we drop the **–y** and we add **–ied**.
stud**y**   stud**ied**

When the verb has only one syllable and ends in **consonant-vowel-consonant**, we double the last consonant and add **–ed**.
s**top**   stop**ped**

2 Write.

close   ~~cry~~   ~~dance~~   ~~pack~~   play
share   study   watch   worry

–d	–ed	–ied
danced	packed	cried

66 UNIT 10

3 Write.

~~climb~~   cry   pack   play   study   watch

1. Tommy __climbed__ a tree.
2. Jen _____ baseball.
3. Martha _____ all night.
4. Pablo _____ at school.
5. Mrs Evans _____ three suitcases.
6. The Smiths _____ a film.

4 Write.

On Saturday, we (1) __visited__ (visit) the Natural History Museum. We (2) _____ (arrive) in London by train. Then we (3) _____ (walk) through the park to the museum. At the museum, we (4) _____ (watch) a video about dinosaurs, and we (5) _____ (look) at all the old dinosaur bones. After that, we (6) _____ (listen) to the noises that whales make in the sea. I (7) _____ (love) the museum. Best of all, I (8) _____ (like) the dinosaurs.

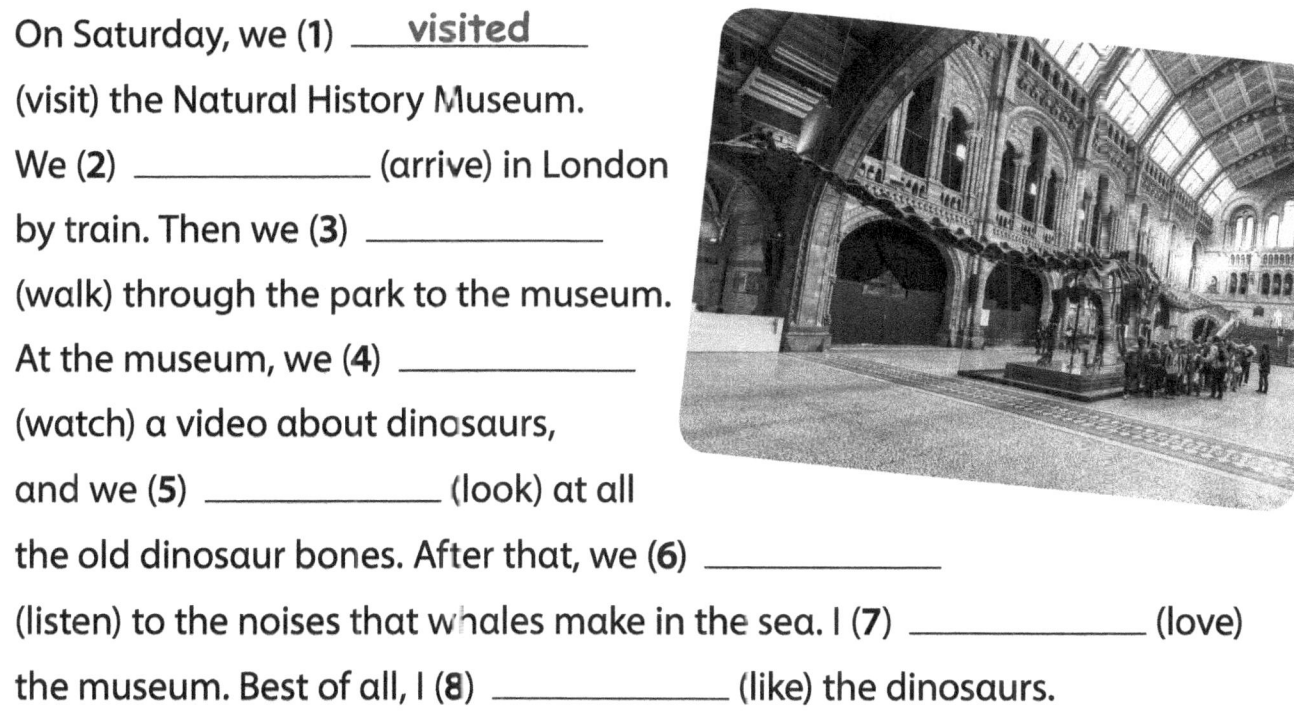

5 Say it!

cry   listen   play   study   visit   walk   watch

Last week, I visited my grandma.

LESSON 1

Lesson 2

1 Read.

I went to Egypt and saw the Pyramids!

Past simple (irregular verbs, affirmative)

There are **irregular verbs** which don't follow the rules that **regular verbs** follow.

build	built
buy	bought
catch	caught
drink	drank
eat	ate
find	found
fly	flew
get up	got up
give	gave
go	went
have (got)	had (got)
make	made
ride	rode
see	saw
take	took

Max **got up** at seven o'clock this morning.

2 Circle.

~~buy~~
catch
drink
eat
give
go
see
take

B	R	T	R	I	O	P	X
O	F	Y	G	J	A	L	A
U	T	C	A	U	G	H	T
G	O	H	V	T	H	N	E
H	O	Y	E	G	S	M	K
T	K	B	D	R	A	N	K
X	Y	D	F	T	W	T	X
Z	W	E	N	T	S	Y	X

68 UNIT 10

3 Write.

1 Sissi ___went___ (go) to Athens with her family.
2 Dad _____ (drink) all the orange juice yesterday.
3 My brother _____ (eat) my dinner last night!
4 We _____ (ride) our bikes to school last Friday.
5 Mr Brown _____ (see) the Pyramids in Egypt.
6 Last week, Dad _____ (fly) to the desert.

4 Write.

buy   eat   find   ~~give~~   have   make

1 Sally ___gave___ her mum some flowers.

4 Mum _____ a lot of chocolate yesterday.

2 Joseph _____ a spider in his bedroom.

5 In Canada, Ed _____ a snowman.

3 The twins _____ a birthday party.

6 Amy _____ too many sweets.

LESSON 2

Lesson 3

1 **Read.**

I didn't go to school today! It's Saturday!

Past simple (negative)

To form the negative of the **past simple**, we use **did not** (**didn't**) before the **verb**. When we speak, we usually use the short form.

I **did not** play
you **did not** play
he **did not** play
she **did not** play
it **did not** play
we **did not** play
you **did not** play
they **did not** play

I **didn't** play
you **didn't** play
he **didn't** play
she **didn't** play
it **didn't** play
we **didn't** play
you **didn't** play
they **didn't** play

We **didn't go** to Brazil last year.

2 **Write.**

Lee (1) __didn't have__ (not have) a good day. He (2) _____ (not sleep) well because his baby sister cried a lot. He (3) _____ (not like) the breakfast that his mum cooked. He (4) _____ (not bring) lunch to school and he (5) _____ (not like) the school lunch. In the afternoon, he (6) _____ (not watch) his favourite TV programme because the TV (7) _____ (not work). He (8) _____ (not ride) his bike because it was raining. But in the evening, he was happy! His mum made his favourite food for dinner: noodles!

3 Write.

1 Sara / go to school / yesterday
   Sara didn't go to school yesterday.

2 Sol / do her homework / on Monday
   _____

3 Billy and Eva / go to Japan / last month
   _____

4 Ahmed / win / a medal / in the Olympics
   _____

5 Asim / fly / to England / last week
   _____

6 I / buy / a book / for my friend
   _____

4 Write.

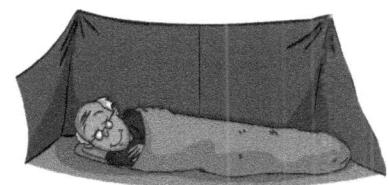

1 On holiday, Grandpa __didn't stay__ in a hotel. He __stayed__ in a tent. (stay)

2 Last night, Simone _____ pasta. She _____ pizza. (eat)

3 Yesterday, Tommy _____ a house. He _____ a car. (build)

4 On Saturday, the twins _____ to the park. They _____ to school. (go)

5 On her birthday, Dad _____ Mum flowers. He _____ her chocolates. (give)

6 On the boat, I _____ birds. I _____ dolphins. (see)

Review

1 Write *was*, *wasn't*, *were* or *weren't*.

1 There ___were___ many bananas.
There ___weren't___ any apples.

4 On Monday, Domenico _____ at school. He _____ in bed.

2 Yesterday, it _____ rainy.
It _____ sunny.

5 They _____ in the park.
They _____ at home.

3 Last year, Gaby and Sara _____ in London.
They _____ in Athens.

6 They _____ at school.
They _____ at the theatre.

2 Write.

1 ride ___rode___
2 eat _____
3 take _____
4 go _____

5 like _____
6 drink _____
7 build _____
8 see _____

9 get up _____
10 play _____
11 have _____
12 study _____

3 Write.

1 At the weekend, we didn't eat dinner at home. (a restaurant)
   We ate at a restaurant.

2 Last summer, Steve didn't ride a horse every day. (a bike)

3 Last night, my brother didn't study maths and history. (English)

4 Last Sunday, the girls didn't climb a mountain. (tree)

5 My parents didn't go to Tunisia. (Morocco)

6 My sister didn't drink milk. (water)

4 Write and answer about you.

1 ? / pasta / you / did / eat / yesterday
   Did you eat pasta yesterday?
   Yes, I did. / No, I didn't.

2 ? / to school / you / go / did / at the weekend

3 ? / last summer / you / in London / were

4 ? / to the park / go / you / did / yesterday

5 ? / tired / last night / your dad / was

11 Lesson 1

1 Read.

Did you walk to school today?

What time did you get to school?

Yes, I did.

I got to school at eight o'clock.

Past simple (questions and short answers)

To form a question in the **past simple**, we put **Did** at the beginning of the question.
We give short answers with **Yes** or **No**, the correct person and **did** or **didn't**.

Did I play …?	Yes, I **did**. / No, I **didn't**.
Did you play …?	Yes, you **did**. / No, you **didn't**.
Did he play …?	Yes, he **did**. / No, he **didn't**.
Did she play …?	Yes, she **did**. / No, she **didn't**.
Did it play …?	Yes, it **did**. / No, it **didn't**.
Did we play …?	Yes, we **did**. / No, we **didn't**.
Did you play …?	Yes, you **did**. / No, you **didn't**.
Did they play …?	Yes, they **did**. / No, they **didn't**.

Did the students help their teacher yesterday?
Yes, they **did**. / No, they **didn't**.

We use **What …?** with the **past simple** to find out what someone did.
What did Mike eat yesterday?
He ate pizza.

We use **What time …?** with the **past simple** to find out at what time something happened.
What time did Samantha leave?
She left at two o'clock.

2 Write and answer about you.

1 _Did_ you go to school yesterday?   _Yes, I did. / No, I didn't._
2 _____ your friend visit you yesterday? _____
3 _____ you eat pizza on Sunday?   _____
4 _____ it rain yesterday?   _____
5 _____ you and your friend walk to school yesterday? _____

3 Write and match.

1 ? / did / do / Tom / what / last / night
   <u>What did Tom do last night?</u>

2 ? / they / do / what / did / at the park
   _____

3 ? / go / they / did / what time / to bed
   _____

4 ? / Mae / did / yesterday / what / do
   _____

5 ? / see / who / they / did / on the train
   _____

6 ? / did / Ahmed / his dad / meet / what time
   _____

a They played tennis.

b They went to bed at ten o'clock.

c They saw their teacher.

d She rode a bike.

e He watched TV.

f He met his dad at six o'clock.

4 Say it!

What did you do on Monday?

I went to school.

on Monday

on Saturday

at the weekend

last night

on Tuesday

LESSON 1

Lesson 2

1 Read.

I'm going to pick up rubbish in the park. We're going to have a clean park!

Be going to (affirmative)

To talk about things or actions which we want to do in the future, we use **am**, **are** or **is** with **going to** and the **verb**. When we speak, we usually use the short form.

I **am going to** sleep
you **are going to** sleep
he **is going to** sleep
she **is going to** sleep
it **is going to** sleep
we **are going to** sleep
you **are going to** sleep
they **are going to** sleep

I**'m going to** sleep
you**'re going to** sleep
he**'s going to** sleep
she**'s going to** sleep
it**'s going to** sleep
we**'re going to** sleep
you**'re going to** sleep
they**'re going to** sleep

I**'m going to** watch a film tonight.

2 Circle.

1 We ___ to clean the beach.
   a are going   **b** is going

2 He ___ pick up the rubbish.
   a going to   **b** is going to

3 Simon and Mary ___ to save a life.
   a are going   **b** is going

4 Look! It ___ jump into the sea!
   a is going to   **b** going to

5 I ___ be a vet when I grow up.
   a is going to   **b** am going to

6 They ___ to sing a song.
   a are going   **b** going

76 UNIT 11

3 Write.

Next weekend ...

1 Greg ____is going to____ have a party.
2 Mum _____ do the shopping.
3 Misao and Aiko _____ climb Mount Fuji.
4 Dad _____ ride his bicycle in a race.
5 I _____ get a birthday present.
6 Hitomi and Miki _____ catch the train to Kyoto.

4 Write.

1 he / get / ill
   He's going to get ill.

2 Mum / open / a shop
   _____

3 I / find / my friends
   _____

4 Gaby and Berto / call / their dad
   _____

5 you / fall asleep / at the table
   _____

5 Say it!

At the weekend ...

- go to the park
- have a party
- play video games / basketball / tennis
- read a book
- visit my grandma / grandpa / friends
- watch TV / a film
- listen to music

At the weekend, I'm going to play tennis.

LESSON 2   77

Lesson 3

1 Read.

I'm not going to watch TV! I'm going to read a book.

Be going to (negative)

To say that we don't want to do an action in the future, we use **not** after **am**, **are** or **is**. Then we put **going to** and the **verb**. When we speak, we usually use the short form.

I **am not going to** sleep I**'m not going to** sleep
you **are not going to** sleep you **aren't going to** sleep
he **is not going to** sleep he **isn't going to** sleep
she **is not going to** sleep she **isn't going to** sleep
it **is not going to** sleep it **isn't going to** sleep
we **are not going to** sleep we **aren't going to** sleep
you **are not going to** sleep you **aren't going to** sleep
they **are not going to** sleep they **aren't going to** sleep

They **aren't going to ride** their bikes tonight.

2 Match.

1 Grandpa is old.
2 It's sunny.
3 It's raining.
4 The beach is clean.
5 Mum is working tonight.

a We aren't going to need our warm boots.
b She isn't going to cook dinner.
c They aren't going to go to the beach.
d I'm not going to drop litter.
e He isn't going to run fast.

78 UNIT 11

3 Write.

1 Sally is going to get up early. (late)
   She isn't going to get up late.

2 Ellie and Thomas are going to visit Japan. (China)
   _____

3 I'm going to swim in the sea. (pool)
   _____

4 We are going to write a story. (email)
   _____

5 It's going to rain tomorrow. (snow)
   _____

6 They are going to have a picnic in the forest. (party)
   _____

4 Write.

| buy   catch   clean   eat   sit   win |

1 He ___isn't going to catch___ the train.

2 She _____ any eggs.

3 She _____ the table.

4 Jo and Liz _____ _____ the race.

5 It _____ the fish.

6 We _____ _____ on this beach!

LESSON 3   79

12 Lesson 1

1 Read.

Are you going to eat that sandwich?

Yes, I am.

Be going to (questions and short answers)

To ask someone if they want to do an action in the future, we put **Am**, **Are** or **Is** at the beginning of the question. Then we put **going to** and the **verb**. We give short answers with **Yes** or **No**, the correct person and the verb **to be**.

Am I **going to** sleep …?	Yes, I **am**. / No, I**'m not**.
Are you **going to** sleep …?	Yes, you **are**. / No, you **aren't**.
Is he **going to** sleep …?	Yes, he **is**. / No, he **isn't**.
Is she **going to** sleep …?	Yes, she **is**. / No, she **isn't**.
Is it **going to** sleep …?	Yes, it **is**. / No, it **isn't**.
Are we **going to** sleep …?	Yes, we **are**. / No, we **aren't**.
Are you **going to** sleep …?	Yes, you **are**. / No, you **aren't**.
Are they **going to** sleep …?	Yes, they **are**. / No, they **aren't**.

Are you **going to** eat your biscuit?
Yes, I **am**. / No, I**'m not**.

2 Write and answer about you.

1 __Are__ you __going to__ play tennis tonight?
  __Yes, I am. / No, I'm not.__

2 _____ you _____ buy a robot?
  _____

3 _____ your mum _____ cook tonight?
  _____

4 _____ your teacher _____ draw a picture?
  _____

5 _____ your friends _____ go to a party?
  _____

80 UNIT 12

3 Write.

1  ? / going / he / is / swimming / to / go
   <u>Is he going to go swimming?</u>
   <u>No, he isn't.</u>

2  ? / she / to / is / going / baseball / play
   _____
   _____

3  ? / meet / going / is / to / she / a film star
   _____
   _____

4  ? / to the party / going / to / is / he / go
   _____
   _____

5  ? / the beach / clean / they / to / going / are
   _____
   _____

6 ? / vegetables / to / is / it / going / cook
   _____
   _____

4 Say it!

- go climbing
- ~~go swimming~~
- go to a party
- listen to music
- play football
- play tennis
- play the guitar
- read a book
- run
- take photos

Is Lee going to go swimming?

Yes, he is.

LESSON 1   81

Lesson 2

1 Read.

My family will go to Greece this summer!

Future simple (affirmative)

To show that an action will happen in the future, we use the **future simple**. We use the word **will** and the **verb**. When we speak, we usually use the short form.

I **will** open	I**'ll** open
you **will** open	you**'ll** open
he **will** open	he**'ll** open
she **will** open	she**'ll** open
it **will** open	it**'ll** open
we **will** open	we**'ll** open
you **will** open	you**'ll** open
they **will** open	they**'ll** open

We**'ll go** to the park later.

2 Write.

> be   buy   go   pack   stay   swim

1 On Friday, we ___will go___ on holiday.
2 Mum _____ our suitcases.
3 Dad _____ the tickets for the plane.
4 We _____ in the sea every morning.
5 It _____ hot and sunny every day!
6 We _____ in a hotel near the beach.

3 Write.

> be a clown   bring presents   eat crisps and pizza
> make a cake   play games   sing songs

It's my birthday tomorrow …

1 Dad ___will be a clown___ .

4 We _____ .

2 Mum _____ .

5 They _____ .

3 My friends _____ .

6 We _____ .

4 Say it!

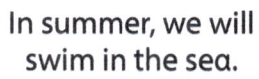

> In summer, we will swim in the sea.

Lesson 3

1 Read.

I won't play video games today. I'll read a book.

Future simple (negative)

To form the negative, we use **won't** (**will not**) before the **verb**. When we speak, we usually use the short form.

I **will not** open	I **won't** open
you **will not** open	you **won't** open
he **will not** open	he **won't** open
she **will not** open	she **won't** open
it **will not** open	it **won't** open
we **will not** open	we **won't** open
you **will not** open	you **won't** open
they **will not** open	they **won't** open

She **won't get up** at seven o'clock tomorrow.

2 Write.

1 In summer, it will be sunny. It ___won't be___ rainy.
2 On Tuesday, I'll go to the swimming pool. I _____ to the park.
3 On Thursday, I'll visit Grandma. I _____ my friends.
4 In Rio, we'll go sightseeing. We _____ shopping.
5 Dad will take his phone on holiday. He _____ his camera.
6 At the weekend, they'll walk in the mountains. They _____ on the beach.

3 Write.

1 When I grow up, I will be a teacher. (doctor)
   <u>I won't be a doctor.</u>

2 In 15 years, I will drive a car. (bus)
   _____

3 In summer, people will swim in the sea. (pool)
   _____

4 Tomorrow at school, I will play in the playground. (classroom)
   _____

5 For dinner, I will eat pasta. (pizza)
   _____

6 At the weekend, we will go to a museum. (theatre)
   _____

4 Write.

When my baby brother grows up, he (1) <u>won't drink</u> (not drink) milk all the time. He (2) _____ (eat) other food, too. I think he (3) _____ (like) pizza, just like me! And he (4) _____ (not like) eggs, just like me! When he is seven, I'm sure he (5) _____ (not play) with teddy bears. He (6) _____ (play) with robots, he (7) _____ (play) video games, and he (8) _____ (ride) his bicycle. He (9) _____ (not go) camping. He (10) _____ (be) just like me!

Review

1 Circle and match.

1 Did he **eat** / **ate** a sandwich?
2 Did you **ride** / **rode** your bike yesterday?
3 Did you and your brother **watch** / **watched** the football game?
4 **What time** / **What** did he go to school yesterday?
5 What **did** / **does** your brother do yesterday?
6 **Did** / **Do** you and your family go sightseeing in Athens?
7 **Did** / **Does** your cat open the fridge?
8 What time **did** / **do** you go to sleep yesterday?

a No, we didn't. We **watch** / **watched** a film.
b No, he didn't. He **eat** / **ate** an apple.
c Yes, I did.
d No, it **wasn't** / **didn't**. It was outside.
e Yes, we **did** / **do**. We went to the museum.
f He **walks** / **walked** to town.
g He **goes** / **went** to school at seven o'clock.
h I **went** / **was** to bed at eight o'clock.

2 Write and answer about you.

1 ? / pasta / you / did / eat / yesterday
   <u>Did you eat pasta yesterday?</u>
   <u>Yes, I did. / No, I didn't.</u>

2 ? / to school / you / go / did / at the weekend
   _____
   _____

3 ? / last summer / you / in Lisbon / were
   _____
   _____

4 ? / to the park / go / you / did / yesterday
   _____
   _____

5 ? / tired / last night / your dad / was
   _____
   _____

3 Write.

1 I _____'m not going to ride_____ (not ride) my bike on the beach.
2 My friends _____ (go) to Greece this summer.
3 Mr Nelson _____ (visit) his family in the USA next year.
4 We _____ (not have) lessons tomorrow!
5 The cat _____ (not sleep) under the table tonight.
6 I _____ (buy) a lovely present for my mum.

4 Circle.

1 Wear a coat! You **will** / **won't** be cold.
2 In summer it **will** / **won't** be sunny.
3 It isn't your birthday. You **will** / **won't** get any presents.
4 We are going to the desert. It **will** / **won't** be very hot.
5 The film starts at ten o'clock. The children **will** / **won't** be very tired.
6 I don't like tomatoes. I **will** / **won't** eat them.

5 Circle.

Last weekend, my grandparents (1) **visit** / **visited**. They (2) **gave** / **give** me a present. It (3) **is** / **was** a kitten. Its name (4) **is** / **was** Fede. Fede (5) **is** / **will be** a fun kitten. He (6) **likes** / **liked** to play with a ball. Tomorrow, we (7) **will go** / **went** to the park and play with the ball again! Next weekend, when I (8) **go** / **went** to visit my cousins, (9) I **will bring** / **bring** Fede with me. My cousins (10) **had** / **have got** a cat, but (11) it **ran** / **run** away last month. I'm sure they (12) **will be** / **are** happy to meet my kitten.

National Geographic Learning,
a Cengage Company

Wonderful World 2 Grammar Book, Second Edition

Vice President, Editorial Director: John McHugh
Executive Editors: Eugenia Corbo, Siân Mavor
Commissioning Editor: Kayleigh Buller
Head of Strategic Marketing EMEA ELT:
Charlotte Ellis
Product Marketing Executive: Ellen Setterfield
Head of Production and Design: Celia Jones
Content Project Manager: Melissa Beavis
Manufacturing Manager: Eyvett Davis
Art Director: Brenda Carmichael
Cover Design: Lisa Trager
Interior Design and Composition:
Lumina Datamatics, Inc.

© 2019 Cengage Learning, Inc.

ALL RIGHTS RESERVED. No part of this work covered by the copyright herein may be reproduced or distributed in any form or by any means, except as permitted by U.S. copyright law, without the prior written permission of the copyright owner.

"National Geographic", "National Geographic Society" and the Yellow Border Design are registered trademarks of the National Geographic Society ® Marcas Registradas

For permission to use material from this text or product, submit all requests online at **cengage.com/permissions**
Further permissions questions can be emailed to
permissionrequest@cengage.com

Grammar Book: Level 2
ISBN: 978-1-4737-6081-3

National Geographic Learning
Cheriton House, North Way
Andover, Hampshire, SP10 5BE
United Kingdom

Locate your local office at **international.cengage.com/region**

Visit National Geographic Learning online at **NGL.Cengage.com/ELT**
Visit our corporate website at **www.cengage.com**

Photo Credits

5(d) Marilyn Barbone; **13(mbl)** Marilyn Barbone; **15(3)** Halina Valiushka; **16(tl)** Ervin Monn; **35(br)** Image Source

©Corbis: 19(3) Corbis; **44(tl)** Thinkstock; **44(tr)** DigitalStock; **44(br)** DigitalStock; **58(br)** Cultura

© Alamy Stock Photo: 9(tml) Jupiter Images/Comstock Images; **15(a)** YAY Media AS; **58(bl)** Digital Vision

© Getty Images: 5(a) Stockbyte; **5(c)** PhotoDisc; **5(e)** PhotoDisc; **5(f)** Stockbyte; **7(bl)** Digital Vision; **9(tm)** PhotoDisc; **15(4)** Monkey Business Images; **29(mtl)** PhotoDisc; **51(tm)** Hill Street Studios/Blend Images; **51(bl)** PhotoDisc; **51(tr)** Stockbyte; **53(c)** PhotoDisc; **57(br)** PhotoDisc; **72(br)** Caiaimage/Martin Barraud

© iStockphoto: 15(c) Urilux; **19(2)** Joe_Potato; **26(tl)** Zoomstudio; **29(bl)** Peter Jobst; **39(tml)** EllenMoran; **39(tr)** Rich Legg; **58(tl)** iStockphoto

© Jupiter Images: 13(tl) Polka Dot Images; **13(ml)** Jupiterimages; **32** Comstock Images; **35(tl)** Creatas; **39(tmr)** BananaStock; **44(bl)** Comstock; **53(a)** Comstock; **76** Creatas

© Shutterstock: 5(b) Melory; **5(g)** Photobac; **5(h)** Shutterstock ; **5(i)** Venus Angel; **5(j)** ID1974; **5(k)** Elnur; **5(l)** AGfoto; **5(m)** Violetkaipa; **7(br)** TasfotoNL; **9(tmr)** Shutterstock; **9(tr)** Eric Isselee; **9(tl)** Rohit Seth; **9(bl)** Gelpi JM; **9(b)** BlueRingMedia; **11** Studio Chki; **12** DreamBig; **13(mtl)** Hwongcc; **13(bl)** Purino; **13(b)** Akiradesigns; **14** Yellow Cat; **15(1)** A Cotton Photo; **15(2)** Fotolistic; **15(5)** Margie Hurwich; **15(6)** Patrizia Tilly; **15(b)** Eric Isselee; **15(d)** Abramova Kseniya; **15(e)** DreamBig; **15(f)** FOTOCROMO; **15(g)** Mika Heittola; **15(h)** Serghei Starus; **15(i)** Javarman; **16(tr)** Mircea Costina; **19(1)** Pavel L Photo and Video; **19(4)** Tony Campbell; **19(5)** Rey Kamensky; **20** Ronald Sumners; **22** Saskia Wagenaar; **23** Bannykh Alexey Vladimirovich; **24** Drozdowski; **25** Wavebreakmedia; **26(tr)** Hortimages; **29(tl)** Shebeko; **29(ml)** Olga OSA; **29(mr)** Olga OSA; **29(mbl)** Valentina_G; **30** Elvetica; **31** Mahmuttibet; **35(bl)** MaszaS; **35(tr)** Maxslu; **36** MchlSkhrv; **37** Arbit; **38** Panda Vector; **39(tl)** IM_photo; **42** Jerrysa; **47(tl)** Gibsons; **47(tml)** Ruzanna; **47(tmr)** Trofimov Denis; **47(tr)** Levent Konuk; **47(bl)** Brocreative; **47(bml)** Ruzanna; **47(bmr)** Olga Utlyakova; **47(br)** Levent Konuk; **48** Charles Taylor; **51(tl)** Alexander Raths; **51(bm)** Wavebreakmedia; **51(br)** Olga Utlyakova; **53(b)** Szefei; **53(d)** Bloomua; **53(e)** Creativa Images; **53(f)** OlScher; **57(tl)** Nazzu; **57(ml)** Doug Lemke; **57(bl)** Azovtsev Maksym; **57(tr)** Rawpixel.com; **57(mr)** Vadim Petrakov; **58(ml)** AVAVA; **58(tr)** Bikeriderlondon; **58(mr)** Olesya Feketa; **61** Eduardo Rivero; **62** Frederick R. Matzen; **65(r)** Cienpies Design; **65(l)** Simo988; **68** WitR; **70** SAWITRE INTAYAM; **72(tl)** Aleph Studio; **72(ml)** Wavebreakmedia; **72(bl)** Tatiana Popova; **72(tr)** Rob Hainer; **72(mr)** LuckyImages; **67** Aivita Arika; **77** Zina Seletskaya; **85** ZouZou; **87** Anna Tkach

Printed in the United Kingdom by Ashford Colour Press Ltd.
Print Number: 05   Print Year: 2022

Helion & Company Limited
Unit 8 Amherst Business Centre
Budbrooke Road
Warwick
CV34 5WE
England
Tel. 01926 499 619
Email: info@helion.co.uk
Website: www.helion.co.uk
Twitter: @helionbooks
Visit our blog http://blog.helion.co.uk/

Text © Usman Shabbir and Yawar Mazhar 2023
Photographs © as individually credited
Colour artwork © Tom Cooper 2023
Maps drawn by George Anderson © Helion & Company 2023

Front cover artwork: A pair of F-104A Starfighters of the Pakistan Air Force (Artwork by Pablo Albornoz © Helion & Company 2023); front cover profile: A B-57C bomber of the Pakistan bomber of the Pakistan Air Force (Artwork by Tom Cooper).

Designed and typeset by Farr out Publications, Wokingham, Berkshire
Cover design by Paul Hewitt, Battlefield Design (www.battlefield-design.co.uk)

Every reasonable effort has been made to trace copyright holders and to obtain their permission for the use of copyright material. The author and publisher apologise for any errors or omissions in this work, and would be grateful if notified of any corrections that should be incorporated in future reprints or editions of this book.

ISBN 978-1-804510-17-9

British Library Cataloguing-in-Publication Data
A catalogue record for this book is available from the British Library

All rights reserved. No part of this publication may be reproduced, stored in a retrieval system, or transmitted, in any form, or by any means, electronic, mechanical, photocopying, recording or otherwise, without the express written consent of Helion & Company Limited.

We always welcome receiving book proposals from prospective authors.

CONTENTS

Abbreviations		2
Acknowledgements		2
Introduction		2
1	The Transformation	3
2	The Indo-Pakistan Air War of 1965	20
3	The Interlude	46
4	The Indo-Pakistan Air War of 1971	56
Epilogue		78
Appendices		80
I	1965 Indo-Pakistan Air War Kills and Losses	80
II	1971 Indo-Pakistan Air War Kills and Losses	83
III	Aircraft Tail Numbers: Supplement to Volume 1	87
Bibliography		88
Notes		89
About the Authors		92

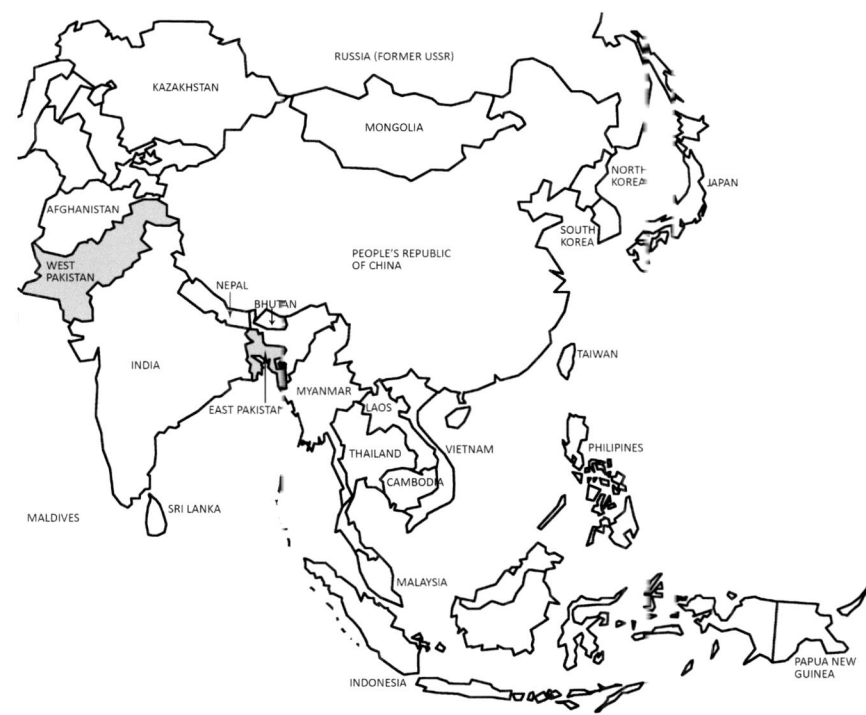

Note: In order to simplify the use of this book, all names, locations and geographic designations are as provided in *The Times World Atlas*, or other traditionally accepted major sources of reference, as of the time of described events.

ABBREVIATIONS

AAA	antiaircraft artillery	MOU	Mobile Observer Unit
AB	air base	MU	Maintenance Unit
ADA	air defence alert	NCO	non-commissioned officer
AFB	Air Force Base (USA)	OC	officer commanding
AGL	above ground level	ORP	operational readiness platform
AHQ	Air Headquarters	PAF	Pakistan Air Force
AoA	angle of attack	PIA	Pakistan International Airlines
AOC	Air Officer Commanding	POW	prisoner of war
ATC	air traffic control/controller	RAF	Royal Air Force (United Kingdom)
CAP	combat air patrol	R/T	radio transmission
CAS	close air support	RJAF	Royal Jordanian Air Force
C-in-C	Commander-in-Chief	RPAF	Royal Pakistan Air Force
CO	commanding officer	SAM	surface-to-air missile
ELINT	electronic intelligence	SAR	search and rescue
FAC	forward air controller	SNCO	senior non-commissioned officer
FLS	Fighter Leaders School	Sqn	squadron
GCI	ground control intercept	ToT	time on target
IAF	Indian Air Force	USAF	US Air Force
MDAP	Mutual Defence Assistance Program	VHF	very high frequency

ACKNOWLEDGEMENTS

The authors would like to thank a number of people whose support and help during the research and writing of the two volumes has been instrumental.

These include many PAF veterans who were generous with the time they devoted in responding to our queries and discussing various aspects and episodes of interest. Air Chief Marshal Jamal A Khan responded with great clarity and detail to our requests, he provided us with excellent insights and shared details from PAF's historical records which were invaluable. Air Commodore Kaiser Tufail has in recent years done excellent work on the 1965 and 1971 air wars and was very helpful in providing advice, data and insights he obtained in the course of his research. Similarly, Air Commodore Sajad Haider was always encouraging and forthright in sharing his own personal experience of a long and eventful career in the PAF. Others like Air Commodore Mansoor Shah and Rais Rafi shared with us their perspective arising out of the unique positions they held. Over the course of our research the authors have met or corresponded with dozens of PAF veterans, and it is not possible to acknowledge all of them individually in these paragraphs. A complete list is included in the bibliography, their help and responses were an essential part of our work and are thankfully acknowledged.

Equally important is the group of aviation enthusiasts who have been researching various aspects of PAF's history and were very supportive of our efforts. Mr Kamal Butt has made a commendable effort in researching PAF's markings and aircraft serial numbers related to its early years which he generously shared with us. Mr Fahad Arshad Siddiqui, an avid aviation enthusiast with a vast collection of literature was always at hand for his help and advice. Franciszek Grabowski, a Polish researcher on PAF has set up a page on Facebook related to the Royal Pakistan Air Force which was very helpful and allowed us to get in touch with families of several veterans and thus allowed access to unique information in some cases. Mr Murtaza Qasim has collected a unique library of F-86 Sabre pictures and Mr Zahid Husain shared with us pictures from his father's photo collection. The later included pictures from early PAF years when his father (Air Commodore F. S. Hussain) as a fighter pilot also catalogued the events through his camera. Mr Tom Cooper contributed the beautiful artwork included in the volumes and Jagan Pillarisetti was helpful with his work on the Royal Indian Air Force.

INTRODUCTION

In this second volume, we pick up the story from the last chapter of the first volume, where the Pakistan Air Force (having dropped its Royal prefix) under its first Pakistani Commander-in-Chief is on the doorstep of a transformative journey.

This volume covers the transformation of PAF into a modern tactical air force. PAF entered the period with the advent of the US Mutual Defence Assistance Program (US MDAP). By this time, the officers who were young and inexperienced at the time of the birth of the service had grown in confidence and had ambitions for a more capable air arm. These ambitions, in the initial stage, were more focused on the possible benefits of acquiring US technology which was considered better than what was available to date from the United Kingdom as detailed in Volume 1. As PAF entered this phase, the PAF leadership and its rank and file would realise that to make the best use of the material support provided under the MDAP, a wider transformation needed to take place.

PAF's first Pakistani Commander-in-Chief, Air Marshal Asghar Khan, would initiate wide-ranging changes in the service and can very aptly be considered as the father of the modern Pakistan Air Force. For PAF it was indeed a fortunate coincidence that a person as dynamic and competent as Air Marshal Asghar Khan would take over exactly when the possibilities of significant modernisation opened up. PAF would see a complete change in its training, operations, planning, support systems such as logistics, maintenance and flight safety. Even areas like administration and how policies pertaining to flying regulations or personnel were issued and maintained would undergo a sea change.

In less than 10 years, from Air Marshal Asghar Khan's taking over the command of the air force to the eve of the 1965 war with India, PAF saw its equipment from front line fighter aircraft to training and transport aircraft revitalised. While PAF's doctrinal concepts of air power always stressed the centrality of an independent air mission, issues relevant to how PAF could in practice fulfil its mission started to be addressed in earnest. PAF would be reorganised from the older Group structure with tactical units reporting through stations to a dedicated operations branch. A planning department would now focus on war plans, these would develop from the sketchy contingency planning of the early years to how the air force could be employed as an integrated whole over a range of missions. All of this was contextualised within the expected dynamics of a possible war. During this period, fundamental questions like the force structure of PAF, the total number of aircraft required, and the logistics needed for a conflict would start getting raised and thought through.

At the sharp end, pilots would be exposed to new fighter tactics and operational training would become better organised and structured. Maintenance and supply officers would be introduced to newer systems which would result in a robust support system for the air force. Adoption of this new way of doing things was a requirement under the US assistance programme, however PAF went much further with this. First, a large number of service personnel were sent for training courses to US Air Force-led courses. From an organisational perspective this helped PAF to manage resistance to change as more and more personnel started seeing the benefits of the change. PAF elected to be an active participant rather than just a recipient of the US assistance program and started building local training and other units so that not only the benefits were absorbed but a foundation was laid for future developments.

As a result, on the eve of the 1965 war PAF was well prepared for full-scale hostilities. The war itself would see a severely outnumbered PAF confident in its abilities and adopting an aggressive posture. It would out-perform the adversary in the air and would also provide excellent support to the Army.

This volume then moves to the intervening period between the 1965 conflict and the 1971 air war. This period was perhaps Air Marshal Nur Khan's finest hour as the second Pakistani Commander in Chief (C-in-C) of the PAF. He had taken over PAF just a few weeks before the start of the 1965 war and the conflict was largely fought with the team and the air arm he inherited from his predecessor. Air Marshal Nur Khan instead would face the challenges of US sanctions, and the need to rebuild the air force because of these sanctions, and the weaknesses highlighted in the preceding conflict. His command would see PAF multiply in size and infrastructure and the rebuilding of the force's strength from diverse sources, this time entirely on its own and with no support from a superpower.

He would leave the command of the air force to Air Marshal Rahim Khan, an indomitable leader who would command PAF most ably in the subsequent 1971 war with India. The larger national debacle at the time has meant that PAF's performance and Rahim Khan's contribution have been mostly overlooked. However, it was in this conflict that PAF came into its own element and again faced not only a much larger but far more determined Indian Air Force. PAF also faced this conflict constrained with a large part of its manpower not available. Political developments in the country meant that most East Pakistani manpower was removed from frontline duties and in some cases actively contributed and provided useful intelligence to India.

The book covers the 1971 war in detail and includes several accounts which have not been made public before. With the end of the war, we complete the first 25 years of PAF's history which sees us from its birth to it maturing as a world class tactical air force.

1

THE TRANSFORMATION

On 23 March 1956 the state of Pakistan's new constitution came into force and Pakistan would declare itself a republic and give up its dominion status. With this the Royal prefix would be dropped and Royal Pakistan Air Force would now be simply known as Pakistan Air Force. This change came around about the time of two other important changes in the history of PAF, the signing of the Mutual Defence Assistance Program (MDAP) with the United States and appointment of the first Pakistani Commander-in-Chief of PAF.

As mentioned in the previous volume, Pakistan had approached the US very early on for military assistance, however these early efforts did not yield any results. Both the new nations of India and Pakistan were considered valuable by the USA for different reasons and initial attempts were made to foster better relations with both. India's importance stemmed from the fact that it was the natural successor to the British Raj and the dominant state in South Asia.[1] On the other hand, Pakistan was considered the largest Muslim country allowing better conductivity with Middle Eastern nations and its Western Wing had significance due to its location, allowing reach to the Soviet industrial areas in the Urals, and also its proximity to the Persian Gulf. It thus had an important potential in any defence arrangement for the Middle East.[2]

The Truman Doctrine of containment to check the expansionist ambitions of the Soviets announced in March 1947, was initially focused on containing the communist threats in Greece and

Turkey. The focus on South Asia only came in 1949 after the end of the Chinese civil war and fall of the Chinese mainland into the communist sphere. Initial USA attempts were to use Pakistan and India to form a strategic bulwark against further communist expansion but the Indian stance of non-alignment along with their refusal to join any American-sponsored pact and failure to condemn the communist aggression during Korean War (25 June 1950 – 27 July 1953), presented Pakistan as more of a natural ally and a right-fit for an alliance. Pakistan's condemnation of the Communists as aggressors further solidified American inclination towards Pakistan.

A MDAP between Pakistan and the USA was signed in Karachi on 19 May 1954. The decision to extend military aid to Pakistan was made by the American president in February 1954 after prolonged considerations, and against strong Indian objections.[3]

For the United States, the overriding factor in extending military assistance to Pakistan was the belief: 'That by so doing, Pakistan could not only build up its own internal strength to resist any threat of communist aggression but could also make an effective contribution to the collective defense efforts of the free world.'[4]

The New Tools and the First Pakistani C-in-C

With the Supermarine Attacker's rather unsatisfactory career, the Pakistan government and Pakistani RPAF officers did not let go the quest for a better jet fighter. Mir Laiq Ali again submitted a detailed proposal in 1952 outlining numerous options including F-80s, F-84s, F-94s and F-86s. The Air Headquarters deliberated on the available options and ruled out the F-80 and F-84 for being out of production or nearing obsolescence. The F-94C was looked at more favourably for being an all-weather day and night interceptor but being still classified, not enough was known about its ground-attack capabilities. The F-86 was deemed more suitable, as it had proved its worth during the Korean War in both interceptor and strike roles and the associated operational and maintenance cost was also judged to be affordable for a developing nation such as Pakistan. Here too, the British officers of RPAF, to safeguard the interests of British aircraft manufacturing industry proposed numerous options, including Swifts (a further development of Attacker), Venoms and Meteors along with very favourable financial terms for all acquisitions. It was at this juncture that senior Pakistani officers of RPAF, notably Group Captains Asghar Khan and Nur Khan took a firm stand in favour of the F-86 and against the British officers trying to further their own commercial interests. This battle of wits is noted eloquently by Air Commodore M. Zafar Masud:

> They (Group Captains Asghar Khan and Nur Khan) were able to argue convincingly that both the Meteor and the Venom were unacceptable because by the time these were fully assimilated in the RPAF, they would be well on the road to obsolescence. The Swift, on the other hand, was ruled out because it was as yet untested and, being a successor to the Attacker of ill repute, could well pose the same type of protracted teething problems.

Perhaps at no other time during the 'British phase' did RAF-RPAF tension run so high, as the ding-dong battle raged for several months over this crucial issue – the choice of the RPAF's next primary weapon system. The RAF high command magnified the good features of the British products beyond all proportions; they tried to sweeten their proposals with more attractive commercial terms. Conversely, they down played the F-86's qualities and pointed up its financial penalty to Pakistan's precious dollar reserves. But the Pakistani officers stood their ground – they had had a bitter experience with the Attacker and were now determined to get their hands on a tried and proven system which would also remain current for at least a decade.[5]

The discussion reached an impasse and resulted in an unprecedented step, that of Air Headquarters writing to the

A scene from the crew room showing young officers Farooq Feroze Khan (later Air Chief Marshal), seated first from left and beside him is M.M. Alam, who would go on to become the only ace of the sub-continent. (Authors' collection)

PAF pilots pose with visiting RAF Hunter pilots. First from left is Alauddin 'Butch' Ahmad, later OC No. 18 Squadron during the 1965 War and third from left is Sarfraz Rafiqui, later OC No. 5 Squadron during the 1965 War. First from right is Flight Lieutenant Hamid Anwar. (Authors' collection)

Ministry of Defence for arbitration. The impasse resolved in early 1954 with the advent of US military aid in the shape of MDAP, which ruled out any non-US equipment. The British officers of RPAF now become mere observers as Pakistani government and senior Pakistani RPAF officers proceeded in active discussions with the USA.

It was strongly expected by the ranks that the new C-in-C after retirement of the fourth loaned British C-in-C, Air Vice Marshal Arthur McDonald, would be a Pakistani. Asghar Khan, a Second World War squadron commander, was chosen as the first Pakistani C-in-C of the PAF at a remarkable young age of 36 in July 1957.

The Bristol Freighters soldiered on into 1960 for airlift in the absence of enough replacement aircraft like C-130s. This example appears to have spray bars affixed beneath the port wing. (Authors' collection)

Asghar Khan, who enjoyed a stellar reputation owning to his pre- and post-independence service record, and a no-nonsense approach to leadership and as a stern taskmaster, was to reforge the PAF into a first-rate tactical fighting force over the next seven years. Even though the rank and file were unanimous that Asghar Khan was the right man for the job, including those who were senior to him, there was speculation in the crew rooms whether the new Pakistani C-in-C would be empowered enough to resist London's pressure on Pakistani government to induct UK-made aircraft and systems; 'The Pakistani airmen by that time were quite familiar with the vast differences between the products of American and British technologies and strongly hoped that PAF's leaders and aircrew would now have the last say on what was good for our Air Force.'6

The new C-in-C began by giving PAF its first doctrinal edict, which until then had been popularised by his outgoing RAF predecessors; 'Are You on the ball', a slogan-like truism. This was replaced with an operational template and a more realistic and practical dictum 'Train to fight outnumbered.'7

The major constraints faced by the previous C-in-Cs were financial but with the commencement of US military aid, the new C-in-C had at least one fewer challenge to address. In addition, only American-made or held weapons were to be supplied under the programme, freeing the PAF from its reliance on British industry.

The commitment of United States military aid to Pakistan was outlined in an aide-mémoire which was concluded between the two governments on 21 October 1954. This aide-mémoire was the result of long discussions and repeated requests from Pakistan, strongly supported by then United States ambassador Horace Hildreth. The initial program proposed by the United States government was estimated at $171 million, spread over three to four years

A pilot walks towards his Sabre for a routine sortie. (Authors' collection)

and included six squadrons of aircraft. Out of these, three were to be in the Fighter/Bomber category (16 aircraft each), one in the category of Fighter/Interceptor (16 aircraft each), one Light Bomber (20 aircraft) and one Transport (20 aircraft). These numbers were later revised with F-86F filling the Fighter/Bomber and Fighter/Interceptor category and each squadron consisting of 24 aircraft along with six reserves. Since mid-1953 PAF had been in search of its first jet trainer, and after evaluating various options such as the de Havilland T-11, Gloster Meteor and T-33, settled on the latter as it was to be readily available via the impending American aid programme. The first four T-33s were delivered to PAF in May 1955 and were inducted in No. 2 Fighter Conversion Squadron, replacing their Tempest and Furies. Six RT-33As, were also delivered in 1957 and formed the first tactical reconnaissance squadron of PAF.

Confusion has persisted over the years about the total number of F-86F Sabres delivered, with some stating 102 and others 120. To keep the count close to the numbers originally supplied, it was a normal practice of the American MDAP that the US replaced aircraft that were lost due to unavoidable reasons.8 This was done only where possible. The replenishment would not work if no planes could be spared or were no longer on the USAF's inventory or, if parked in the boneyards, were not recoverable within the budget authorised for the concerned country. However, compared with some other MDAP allies, the PAF enjoyed a high reputation for its professionalism and most of its replenishment needs were accepted and met.

Fortunately for the PAF, most of the planes it had were available from within USAF stocks (or from other allies), making it possible for the PAF to be given its attrition replacements after following a closely supervised and controlled process. Much paperwork preceded the approval, and many months would pass before the PAF would be asked to pick up a few replacement planes from Europe or were told if they would be shipped to Pakistan instead.

The initial group of Sabre pilots completed their combat crew training on the Sabres in Texas and Arizona (Williams Air Force Base) before delivery of the first lot of 30 F-86Fs, which were delivered in July 1956 and the remaining portion of the 120 F-86s were delivered by March 1958. Thirty more F-86s were delivered subsequently – in small batches of twos and threes – between April 1960 and March 1965, when the last six were delivered. Thus, the total F-86Fs that the PAF added to its inventory were 120 in the initial batch, plus 30 over five years to replace attrition losses. The PAF would go on to acquire an additional 90 German F-86Es via Iran after the 1965 War.

The F-86Fs supplied under the MDAP were a mix of subvariants including -25NA, -35NA and -40NA. The most significant difference between these sub variants were in the wings of the aircraft, with the later -40NAs adopting longer chord and extended wingspan along with leading-edge slats. In the case of PAF, later retrofits meant that all subvariants ultimately had these wings which aided aircraft manoeuvrability. For F-86Es, the aircraft retained the original wing form of the Sabre F.Mk 6 which had the shorter wingspan but included the leading-edge slats.

One reason that the numbers were revised upwards was the growing requirement of training, not just for the PAF but also allied forces of the Middle East who were approaching Pakistan for this purpose. The United States was supportive of a scheme by Pakistan to develop in-country capability to train regional air forces of the Middle East, as well as generating income to the government of Pakistan.[9] During 1957–58, PAF had already begun training Jordanian personnel which included three officers, 10 flying cadets, six maintenance technicians, two electricians and four mechanics. The planned input of Jordanian pilots was 10 flying cadets every six months and along with PAF's own pilot production of 30 pilots in FY 1958 with a planned increased to 38 in FY 1959, it became apparent that additional aircraft would be required.[10]

The American deliveries of equipment under the 1954 agreement were completed by FY 1958 with the major exception of a light bomber squadron, which was programmed for FY 1960. The make and model of the light bomber to be supplied was left to be decided later. During a state visit to the United States by President Ayub Khan in April 1958 to accelerate the military aid, among others he was accompanied by Air Vice Marshal Asghar Khan – then C-in-C of PAF – and it was at one of these meetings with American

Ground crew work on an F-86F Sabre at Mauripur. (Authors' collection)

Table 1: Aircraft delivered as part of MDAP

Year of Delivery	Type	Quantity	Category	Remarks
1956	Lockheed T-33A	10	Trainer	Later at least 33 additional delivered, mostly during 1967–1968
1956–58	F-86F Sabre	120	Fighter	Additional 30 delivered over time as attrition replacements
1957	Lockheed RT-33A	6	Recce	
1958	Martin B-57B/C Canberra	26	Bomber	24 B-57B & 2 B-57C
1962	Martin RB-57 Canberra	2	Recce	Modified B-57s from original lot
1960–62	Sikorsky S-55	8	Helicopter	
1962	Lockheed F-104A Starfighter	12	Fighter	2 additional delivered as attrition replacements
1962	Lockheed F-104B Starfighter	2	Fighter	
1957–58	Grumman HU-16A Albatross	4	ASW	
1963	Lockheed C-130E Hercules	4	Transport	One L-100 civilian version of C-130 was also transferred to PAF by Pakistan International Airlines
1963	Cessna T-37B	25	Trainer	
1964	Kaman HH-43B Huskie	3	Helicopter	

President Ayub Khan is briefed on the B-57 and its armament by by senior PAF officers. (Authors' collection)

representatives held on 29 April and led by Mansfield D. Sprague, Secretary of Defense, that Air Vice Marshal Asghar enquired to the type of light bomber the United States had in mind.[11] He was informed that they were of the B-57 type. Air Vice Marshal Asghar Khan considered the B-57 obsolete and was not enthusiastic about the idea. In his view, the B-66 was better suited to PAF needs and should be the primary candidate for the light bomber role. Even though the discussions dragged on, the American side was adamant on the B-57 as the only type that they could offer. They arranged a trip to an active B-57 base so that Air Vice Marshal Asghar Khan could have a first-hand look and any obsolescence or maintenance concerns could be addressed.

The first B-57 Bombers started arriving in Pakistan during November 1959, and all 24 B-57Bs and two B-57Cs were delivered by March 1960. The aircraft were ferried to Mauripur airbase to form 7th and 8th Bomber Squadrons as part of the 31 Bomber Wing. The United States could not make slots available for initial pilot training in the USA and accomplished this in Pakistan using a Mobile Training Detachment. Conversion training for pilots and navigators was conducted at No. 31 Wing usually lasting three weeks.

For Search and Rescue (SAR) operations, rotary and fixed wing assets were also provided. These included four (later renamed HU-16B), for which the Pakistani aircrew consisting of four transport pilots and four navigators proceeded to West Palm Beach AFB, Florida, for their four-month-long flying training and conversion course in August 1957.[12] The training involved non-stop long flights of up to 18 hours by two sets of crews, and water landings practised in the sea close to the Miami coast and sometimes in various lakes across Florida State. The first SA-16 was ferried by USAF aircrew to Pakistan during December 1957.

As part of a wider security understanding, Pakistan had allowed basing rights to the US at Peshawar for U-2 and RB-57 for reconnaissance and ELINT missions against the Soviet Union. In

A trio of B-57s perform a fly-by. (Authors' collection)

Table 2: F-104 Model Numbers and USAF Tail Numbers[13]		
Model	Tail number	Date received
F-104A-20	56-802	05 August 1961
F-104A-20	56-803	05 August 1961
F-104A-20	56-804	05 August 1961
F-104A-20	56-805	05 August 1961
F-104A-20	56-807	05 August 1961
F-104A-25	56-868	05 August 1961
F-104A-25	56-874	05 August 1961
F-104A-25	56-875	05 August 1961
F-104A-25	56-877	05 August 1961
F-104A-30	56-879	05 August 1961
F-104A-15	56-773	08 June 1964
F-104A-20	56-798	01 March 1965
F-104B-10	57-1309	05 August 1961
F-104B-15	57-1312	05 August 1961

This photograph taken on 14 August 1956 shows a lineup of 80 Sabres, T-33, and Bristol Freighters at Mauripur. (Authors' collection)

A USAF F-100 Super Sabre seen at an airshow, possibly during a CENTO training event. The Americans had offered this type to Pakistan but it was not considered suitable and was rejected. (Authors' collection)

All the aircraft were ex-USAF Air Defence Command and were equipped with the 20mm M61 Vulcan Gatling gun besides being able to carry AIM-9B Sidewinder air-to-air missiles on wingtips. All aircraft delivered were also equipped with the C2 upward firing ejection seat and higher thrust General Electric J-79-GE-11A engines.

The first three pilots selected to undergo type conversion in the United States included Squadron Leader M. Sadruddin, Flight Lieutenant Mervyn Middlecoat, and Flight Lieutenant Alauddin 'Butch' Ahmed. Squadron Leader Sadruddin was sent to George AFB, California (east of Los Angeles) and spent time with 434th TFS, 479th TFW. This was part of "on the job" training as an executive officer for a squadron for 6–7 months. Towards the end of the stay, he transitioned to F-104s and flew about 22 hours on the aircraft while in the USA (4–6 hours dual, and the rest solo). Since the F-104As in American service were nuclear weapon capable, the USAF considered stripping the aircraft of this equipment before allowing Squadron Leader Sadruddin to go solo but later decided against this. During this timeframe Squadron Leader Sadruddin also became the first Pakistani to fly at Mach 2. The other two pilots went to an Air National Guard unit in South Carolina for type conversion. The fully assembled aircraft were sent by ship to Pakistan where they arrived at Karachi harbour in August 1961.[14]

May 1960, during one of these missions, a U-2 aircraft piloted by Gary Powers staging via Peshawar, was shot down over the Soviet Union. It was after this incident and subsequent Soviet threats to Pakistan that the United States government agreed to provide Pakistan with higher performance fighter aircraft. The choice ultimately settled on F-104As after PAF's refusal to accept an American offer of F-100 Super Sabre aircraft.

Initially Pakistan tried to secure a commitment for 30 F-104s but costing $40 million in addition to spares, and a very substantial yearly maintenance cost, this was ruled out as being too expensive. A total of 12 F-104 Starfighter aircraft were transferred to Pakistan, including 10 A and two B models. The model numbers and USAF tail numbers (retained by PAF) are given in Table 2.

Before these newly delivered Starfighters could scream through Pakistani skies at Mach 2, they had to undergo a more mundane journey i.e., travel on Karachi's roads from the harbour to PAF Station Drigh Road (now called PAF Base Shahra-e-Faisal). This was done by towing the aircraft with tractors during the night, with pilots sitting in the cockpit during this journey to apply aircraft brakes if necessary. The time also marked the arrival of USAF test pilot Major Swart Nelson who checked out the three PAF pilots after which the aircraft were ferried to PAF Station Sargodha (now PAF Base Mushaf).

Late Wing Commander Mervyn L. Middlecoat, described the arrival of Starfighters at Sargodha in these words:

All set for another training sortie, PAF pilots converse with a colleague before heading to the flight lines. Sporting sunglasses in the middle is Flight Lieutenant Rashid A. Bhatti, Mauripur (Authors' collection)

At about 1500 hours on 15th September, 1961 two silver streaks were seen moving across the Sargodha sky leaving behind them thick white contrails. Covering over 15 miles a minute the streaks turned to specks and then faded altogether. Suddenly, the silence was broken by two thunderous bangs shaking window-panes and doors. Three minutes later, the specks reappeared, this time at tree-top level flying along the length of the runway. The specks turned to streaks which suddenly went into near-vertical climbs and within seconds, had changed back into specks leaving behind their tell-tale contrails.

At Sargodha these aircraft reequipped PAF's No. 9 Squadron (Griffins, who today fly F-16s). In 1961 the squadron was still flying Sea Fury aircraft while all other PAF squadrons had converted to jets. Perhaps to compensate its oldest squadron for such neglect, it was decided by Air Headquarters to re-equip it with the first Mach 2 capable jet in PAF's inventory. Squadron Leader M Sadruddin took over as the squadron commander of the reequipped No. 9 Squadron with Flight Lieutenant Alauddin Ahmed as his flight commander. Other early joiners included Flight Lieutenant Jamal A Khan, Flying Officer Farooq F Khan, Flight Lieutenant Hakimullah, Flying Officer M. M. Khalid, Flight Lieutenant Arif Iqbal, Flight Lieutenant Hashmi, Flying Officer Amjad Hussain and Flying Officer M. Akbar. The squadron was at the same time joined by two United States Air National Guard pilots, who along with the already converted first three PAF pilots helped convert other PAF pilots to F-104s. That PAF senior commanders literally lead from the front is demonstrated by the fact that the Air Marshal Asghar Khan (PAF C-in-C at the time) and some other senior officers attended the relevant ground school and undertook

Visiting RAF personnel pose with PAF aircrew during a visit to a B-57 squadron at Mauripur. (Authors' collection)

The first Starfighter at Drigh Road. Notice the tail number is not applied yet. (Authors' collection)

Many PAF pilots had flown Hunters during their training in the UK. Here an RAF team visiting with Hunters joins a PAF team with Sabres for a group photo. (Rod Dean)

Squadron Leader Mervyn Leslie Middlecoat briefs the President and C-in-C on Starfighters at Sargodha. (Authors' collection)

C-in-C Air Marshal Asghar Khan shakes hands with Squadron Leader M. Sadruddin, the first OC of the F-104 Squadron at Sargodha. (Authors' collection)

a number of familiarisation flights on the aircraft. The conversion course included 2–3 weeks of academic classes followed by a few rides in F-104Bs and final check rides in a single seater. Once the pilot was qualified, an initial training period consisting of 40–50 sorties commenced. This included navigation, formation flying, gunnery, air combat manoeuvring and interceptions.[15]

F-104s clearly surpassed the F-86F Sabres in the PAF inventory in terms of performance and represented the cutting edge of aviation technology at that time. Although the Sabre was loved for its beautiful handling and manoeuvrability, the Starfighter's performance remained unmatched until the induction of F-6 and Mirage aircraft later in the decade.

The PAF lost two Starfighters from induction to the start of the September 1965 war. On 11 November 1963, Flying Officer Asghar Shah while flying an air-to-air cine training mission in F-104A (S/N 56-802) ejected after entering a spin. The mission leader, Flight Lieutenant Farooq Umar recalls the nose of Asghar's aircraft pulling up followed by oscillation with the Auto Pitch Recovery system kicking in but failing to prevent spin entry. The second aircraft (S/N 56-803) was lost on 3 September 1964 when Flight Lieutenant Tariq Masood entered a dive at a steep angle while practicing ground strafing; the pilot pulled hard to recover the aircraft and though the nose of the aircraft cleared, its tail hit the ground – this time the crash was fatal.[16] The aircraft were replaced under the Mutual Aid Program by aircraft with tail numbers 56-773 and 56-778.

The Training and Indoctrination

Under the MDAP, to support the large-scale induction of F-86 Sabres, batches of cadets usually consisting of 20 each were selected

Ground crew work on Sabres on the tarmac at Mauripur. (Authors' collection)

This F-86 on jacks is seen undergoing maintenance outside, though it may be a trainer airframe given the coating on the canopy. (Authors' collection)

The pilots appear to have most commonly mounted their Sabres without ladders. Note also the retained American markings just beneath the forward canopy, though the "U.S." portion of "U.S.A.F." has been removed. (Authors' collection)

and sent to the USA for an Undergraduate Pilot Training (UPT) course. The training was based on the existing UPT syllabus of the USAF, which consisted of primary and basic flying training. Aircraft used were the T-34, T-37 and the T-33 – in that order – with approximately 30, 110 and 100 hours respectively in each aircraft. The syllabus allowed a maximum of 10 hours of dual flying before going solo. This was followed by conversion to the F-86F at one of the F-86-equipped bases, usually at Luke AFB, Arizona, which was the home of the USAF fighter conversion school. The syllabus called for a total of approximately 40 hours of flying which included, besides conversion, weapons training in air-to-ground and air-to-air as well as air combat training.

After completing flying training and conversion in the United States, the pilots would be posted to one of the operational F-86F Sabre squadrons, either at Mauripur (now Masroor) or Peshawar airbase. From the early 1960s onwards, Sargodha (now Mushaf) air base, being built with American assistance, also housed three F-86F, an F-104, an RT-33 Recce and a helicopter squadron along with all the necessary support units, resulting in a large number of newly converted pilots as having this as their first posting station.

Air Vice Marshal (retd.) Sadruddin Hossain, who was posted to Sargodha as a F-86F pilot in November 1962, recalls:

> There were about 60 pilots in the base, most of them in their 20s. The base had a large air-conditioned officers' mess which was the centre of all social activities since the small rural town of Sargodha had very little to offer. For larger events there was Lahore some 120 miles away.
>
> We were some 15 pilots in our squadron, more than half being from the same course. So, most of us were course mates which made life very interesting as well as challenging. There was fierce competition amongst us as I recall and everyone was trying their best to excel the other, and the supervisors very much encouraged such healthy competition.[17]

This is where perhaps the most important facet of PAF's transformation into a modern and competent air force started taking place. For the first time PAF's fighter conversion training stepped up significantly and a large number of pilots started getting exposed to a structured and well thought out training program. Pilots were provided with a comprehensive ground school on the aircraft, introduced to new techniques and procedures and comprehensively evaluated on the same. The days of brazen attitudes towards flying with showmanship in the air being the focus were now numbered. Pilots now would follow a graduated approach to fighter training and were greatly helped with training aids.

The difference in the American approach and what was available before is best illustrated by comparison of the conversion to Attackers and Sabres. The Pilot's Notes provided to a pilot for the Attacker consisted of approximately 70 pages with brief comments on various aircraft systems and similarly brief instructions and procedures for aircraft handling. Compared to this the equivalent publication (called Technical Order 1 F-86-1, or Dash One for short) for the Sabre was 416 pages long and was one of several handbooks available to the crew. The handbook was the gold standard for such material and its basic structure is followed for similar material for modern aircraft even in the twenty-first century. The Dash One would provide a pilot with a sound understanding of the aircraft's technical systems which were explained in accessible detail. Different techniques and procedures were explained in a logical manner and illustrated as required. Instead of a perfunctory understanding of the aircraft, a pilot was now provided with detailed performance charts which could also be used to understand and determine the aircraft's performance for various missions and flight conditions. This thought out approach to training methods and aids meant that even a junior pilot who had just completed his conversion to the aircraft had a very thorough understanding of the aircraft and the system he

To sharpen the pilot skills and showcase them, PAF routinely held aerial displays. This 16-ship Sabre formation set a world record of 16-aircraft loop in front of 20,000 spectators at Mauripur airbase, led by Wing Command M Z Masud on 2 February 1958. (Murtaza Qasim)

was operating in and with. Gone were the days of 'gut', raw talent, and personal experience. A not insignificant consequence was in the quality of mission planning and briefing in the squadrons. Now briefings and debriefings would take place on a common ground of thorough academic and technical understanding of the subject and what worked or did not work could be evaluated by established and thought out standards.

Contrary to popular belief, novelty in fighter flying is not something to be strived for. Instead, what is valued is knowledge, a deep understanding of what and why, well trained responses, brutal evaluation of mistakes and relentless repetition. The deep knowledge base and common and well thought out standards created the ground for this.

While the paragraphs above illustrate the step-up PAF had by illustrating a comparison between two fighter aircraft types, the same difference also started appearing in general flying with more robust procedures being adopted. This change even started extending to how PAF would establish and disseminate its policies and procedures; instead of being delegated, this process was now centralised, which meant that any contradiction between one policy with another was more easily identified and rectified. While earlier, a unit in the field was informed of changes in a policy or procedure, there was little control over how this would extend through the system. The prevailing "cut and paste" methodology even meant laborious insertion of handwritten new texts between printed lines. This was now superseded by a replacement system, where specific pages of a handbook or manual would be replaced by a new set of pages thus ensuring common changes across all units and all relevant material being uniformly updated. Following the USAF example now, all briefings and work practices were standardised, and a work-by-checklists culture was adopted for the PAF.

A canvas target on a gunnery range shows the results of engagement during training. Some holes have been marked, possibly from a prior pass. (Authors' collection)

Fighter squadrons were now also provided with training aids like handbooks on various fighter maneuvers and a young pilot was no longer just left to his own devices. Briefings and debriefings of missions now had a thoroughness which was missing before. This effort was supported by another very significant effort by PAF which was setting up of the Fighter Leaders School.

With the addition of significant new capabilities, Air Marshal Asghar Khan also sought in 1958 to maximise the force potential through a training school of higher learning for its middle-tier combat leaders, in the increasingly complex air operations. He directed that a Fighter Leaders School (FLS) be established at Mauripur (Masroor) AFB. The FLS would function as an F-86 operational squadron in peacetime. For its commanding officer and instructor pilots, Asghar Khan chose Wing Commander M. Zafar Masud (a DFLS graduate from England, as was Asghar Khan) and Flight Lieutenants Wiqar Azim and Jamal A. Khan. The latter two had recently returned as distinguished graduates from the Fighter Weapons Schools of the USAF and the RAF. Masud a professionally reputed and experienced commander and his two deputies quickly formulated the academic and flying syllabi of the FLS.

Each course of six students (resources did not allow a larger course size) underwent intensive training for three months. They would first learn the latest destructive characteristics of modern munitions and how they could be delivered most accurately, utilising appropriate offence/defence tactics suited to a given combat environment. Under observation by their accompanying instructors, they would lead both dawn and dusk strike missions, employing low-low-low and high-low-high altitude profiles. Each student would learn to drill his younger pilots in all the basic and more complex fighter manoeuvres in the air defence/air combat phase. Subsequent exercises in simulated air combat were designed to develop in them a clear understanding of time-space dynamics and the proper use of energy that resulted in gaining advantageous positions over an adversary. In the live weapons phase, the students attacked ground targets using rocketry, bombing and gun attacks and, after each sortie, were asked to analyse their scores and errors. In the air-to-air attack segment, they fired their guns at towed targets and similarly debriefed the mistakes after scoring the target. During each phase of training, the student leader also acted as an instructor because he was required to explain to his formation members (assumed to be less experienced juniors) the theoretical side of the manoeuvres, tactics and the weapon delivery calculations that went into his planning for the mission.

Since all the students came to the FLS straight from leadership positions in their flying units, the emphasis was not only on doing a flawless job of thorough preparation and leadership in the air, but equally on their role as a trainer in both the tactics and weapon delivery modes applicable to a particular mission. Questions by a formation member (coparticipant) or the accompanying FLS instructors (who roleplayed as junior pilots) had to be satisfactorily answered.

For the next four years, the FLS (under succeeding commanders) produced over one hundred graduates. Those dozens of squadron leaders and flight lieutenants the FLS returned to the operational units became the squadron commanders and flight commanders for the 1965 war.

Between courses, the FLS staff regularly visited the squadrons to see its graduates' work, and also ran many condensed weapon delivery and air tactics courses for junior pilots. They also carried out tactical evaluation visits of the combat squadrons and organised several PAF-wide armament competitions.

During the first few years of MDAP, PAF's focus was on the fighter squadrons with the Flying Training College at Risalpur continuing on old systems. This is partially explained by the fact that Risalpur's collaboration with RAF Cranwell meant that the college's training program was considered quite robust. However, in time Risalpur's turn would also come, especially with the expected induction of T-37 basic jet trainers.

In the early 1960s, C-in-C Air Vice Marshal Asghar Khan had invited a USAF team to come and assess the training syllabus and methodology at Risalpur Flying Training College and come up with their recommendations.[18] The USAF team wrote a detailed report on what they saw and highlighted several deficiencies, the major one being that not enough was being put down on paper and recorded – with most things done on an ad-hoc basis, resulting in no lessons learned and missing the objective and know-how the following year. This was a weakness inherited from the British system.

In conformity with the observations made by the USAF team, PAF made considerable efforts to update the syllabus and refresh the entire training apparatus. The new syllabus encompassed both the ground as well as the flying journey for students. Each sortie was now planned with an objective in mind instead of just instructing the students on a blackboard and asking them to fly up to step x; they were now handed a complete mission profile with clearly stated objectives that needed to be achieved. Once the syllabus and training processes were overhauled by late 1962, the USAF team was invited again for another assessment, which this time met their criteria and conveyed satisfaction.

Maintenance and Infrastructure Development
Under the MDAP, the infrastructure across various airfields was also to be improved. A budget of $32.5 million for various construction projects in Pakistan for FY 1956 and $26.7 million in FY 1957 was granted. Most of these projects were related to the Pakistan Army (such as the Kharian cantonment), but for PAF, the work carried out by the United States Army Corps of Engineers in collaboration with local vendors involved in upgrading the facilities at Mauripur, Drigh Road, Peshawar and Sargodha.

The construction at Mauripur Station involved strengthening the existing runway; extending it from 6,100 to 9,000 feet; adding lighting for the field; and installing two tanks for jet fuel, each with a 10,000-barrel capacity. Since the Sabre came equipped with a radio compass, lots of radio beacons were installed and an extra few were also put up to be used as let-down aids or markup points. The first runway barrier was also installed on 5 January 1957.

Mauripur at this time was an extremely busy station and a hive of activity. Even though the expansion works were in progress and the main 200ft wide concrete runway (direction 09/27) was being constructed, the station housed most of the PAF's squadrons, operating from the extended secondary (direction 04/22) runway, as they were being converted to Sabres. The F-86s had started arriving by the second half of 1956, and by early 1957, 56 aircraft had been delivered. Some were flown in, but more than half were delivered by ship. No. 11 and 14 Squadrons had converted to Sabres by early 1957 and soon thereafter other squadrons No. 5, 15, 16, 17, 18, 19 and 20 also started forming and acquiring their aircraft at Mauripur. The pilot conversion to Sabres was being overseen by No. 2 Squadron which had its own element of T-33s and F-86s.[19] After having flown 200–220 hours on the T-6G at Risalpur, the pilots would be converted on jets after logging 80 hours on T-33A during a three-month course, followed by another three-month course on Sabres, where they would log 50 hours.

As strength increased, so did confidence, with the Base Commander (Group Captain S.A. Yusaf) deciding to fly all 56 Sabres delivered by then during the 23 March Republic Day flypast at Karachi. This was against the advice of the local American MDAP representatives, who believed it to be an impossible task as only 56 to

Ground crew prepare to tow a Sabre. (Authors' collection)

58 pilots were available, and that not all 56 aircraft could be brought online. All 56 Sabres managed to get airborne and participate in the flypast, with some pilots having logged only two and half hours on Sabres by then.

A similar feat was repeated at Mauripur in February 1958, watched by King Zahir Shah of Afghanistan and thousands of spectators, when a 16 Sabre loop was performed, along with a firepower demonstration and additional aerobatics, coupled with a lineup of over 100 Sabres, T-33s and Freighters on the secondary 04/22 runway presenting an impressive sight.

The majority of the upgrades at Mauripur were completed by July 1958.[20] Near the end of 1957, work was also started to strengthen and extend the runway at the Drigh Road airfield; and parallel work began at Peshawar and Sargodha. Sargodha had an old derelict runway from British days along with a few old buildings. It was judged to be an ideal location for a new Major Operational Base (MOB) as its location would allow sufficient on-station time for aircraft providing close air support to Pakistan Army units, but was far enough away not to be overrun by the Indian Air Force or Indian Army. The decision to develop Sargodha as an MOB was taken in 1953 and initial plans also called for a radar site on the close-by Kirana Hills along with dug-in aircraft pens.[21] At first, PAF officers found it difficult to convince the Americans of the importance of Sargodha; the Americans preferred that PAF focuses on the communist threat with greater emphasis on Peshawar and Quetta; but they eventually warmed up to the idea and agreed to its development.

Most of the infrastructure had been completed under the supervision of Wing Commander R.D. Rollo to make Sargodha ready to receive its first flying squadrons by November 1959. The main runway was ready by December 1958, and the first two F-86 Sabres from No. 16 Squadron, piloted by Squadron Leader M. Sadruddin and his wingman Flight Lieutenant Sajad Haider, conducted the initial tests by landing on the newly constructed runway at 1130hrs on 3 December 1958, eagerly watched by the Station Commander along with the welcoming groundcrew and others near the touchdown point of Runway 14.

Over the next year, along with the new black-top runway, parallel taxi track, Operational Readiness Platforms (ORP) and required hangars and workshops were also constructed. Even though by April 1960, three squadrons equipped with F-86F aircraft were already deployed to Sargodha under the supervision of Group Captain Salahuddin as the first base commanding officer, the accommodation to house aircrew with their families was not ready. There were only a few Bachelor Officer Quarters (BOQ) available, and the rest were housed in 'E' type requisitioned bungalows. By late 1961 to early 1962, the domestic accommodation was also completed along with a very large Officers Mess and messes for NCOs.

By September 1961, the only Mach 2-capable F-104 squadron (No. 9) was also moved to Sargodha. The base by January 1962 housed three F-86F squadrons (No. 5, 11, 15), one F-104 squadron (No. 9) and one RT-33 photo recce squadron (No. 20) along with two rescue helicopters. The Sabre and Starfighter squadrons had 12 aircraft each on strength and the photo recconnaissance squadron operated with six aircraft. These assets comprised No. 33 Wing.

Other than refurbishing and expanding the bases, work also concurrently began on upgrading maintenance procedures and the supply chain to support these newly acquired assets. At the centre of this process was the PAF Base Drigh Road (later Faisal), which supported three Maintenance Units (MU) led by Wing Commander rank officers. These three MUs were No. 102, responsible for third- and fourth-line maintenance, No. 101, responsible for the supply of technical spares to all of the PAF, and No. 107 MU, which was responsible for all radio and radar maintenance.

No. 102 MU was one of the oldest units; well before partition in 1932 it was known as Aircraft Repair Depot and was tasked with repair/overhaul of airframes and engines in addition to various other components. In January 1953 a project was initiated to set up the first Gas Turbine Section (GTS) for the overhaul of Rolls Royce Nene engines – which powered the Attacker aircraft – with the help of Rolls Royce engineers. The project was completed in eight months making this the first facility of its kind in the region and brought with it new methods of repair/overhaul techniques in addition to machining processes and inspection methods.[22]

The Engine Repair Section (ERS) at No. 102 MU during the mid-1950s had on its strength a large number of British SNCOs along with representatives from Bristol for the repair/overhaul of Bristol Centaurus and Hercules engines. PAF was interested in replacing these personnel at the earliest opportunity with Pakistani SNCOs and was successful in doing so progressively over time.[23] As the American hardware started flowing in under MDAP, they also assessed the existing technical facilities and knowhow, intending to set up a regional hub that could also cater to other CENTO nations.[24] Since PAF already operated such facilities and were deemed to have the 'knowhow', they won the race, and the existing depot repair and overhaul facilities were expanded and developed further.

The GTS at No. 102 was expanded with a new jet engine testing house along with various accessories to support the new types of

With pilots strapped in the cockpit, the ground crew perform final checks before a training sortie. (Authors' collection)

A rare picture of a PAF Sabre with wing fences. This aircraft is an F-86F-25NA without the later wing modification. (Authors' collection)

engines and aircraft. Technical officers and aircrew were either trained onsite by American teams or sent to the USA for initial training. A team from No. 102 was sent to Tinker Air Force Base, Oklahoma, for their initial training on repair and overhaul of J-47 engines and this team on their return set up facilities for the overhaul of various American engines such as General Electric/Allison J33 (T-33), General Electric J-47 (F-86F) and Wright J65 (B-57). By 1959 other programmes such as IRAN (Inspect, Repair As Necessary) for T-33 and F-86F aircraft were also up and running. Repair and servicing facilities for various pneumatic and hydraulic components were also set up along with electrical parts and aircraft instruments.

Before the flow of American hardware in great numbers, being a much smaller force and equipped with simpler aircraft, the RPAF had relied on an orthodox servicing organisation. The technical wing provided second-line maintenance to squadrons based on the station, while the first-line maintenance remained the responsibility of individual squadron commanders. The squadron commanders and servicing personnel took great pride in upkeep of the aircraft and keeping the aircraft serviceability high, but it was evident that with the induction of more complex aircraft in greater numbers and with the raising of new squadrons, the centralised maintenance model based on American concepts had to be adopted.

Another major difference between the new American approach to maintenance, compared to the existing British inspired approach, was the concept of "repair by replacement". This concept meant an entire defective component was to be replaced; an approach the Americans could well afford due to their large industrial capacity and which was also better suited to support a larger and more diversified fleet where individual repair of components would be considered time consuming and hence also cost prohibitive. The same approach in PAF to maintain high availability of aircraft would have required a well-stocked depot which could supply such replacement components in a timely fashion. In the event of these components being unavailable at a local depot, there would usually be a long waiting period to have it shipped from the USA, severely impacting the aircraft serviceability rate. Under the terms of US aid, local repair of components was not permitted. At the beginning of the American aid flow PAF tried to adhere to this concept as well, but soon discovered that with long waiting periods for spare part components it was not feasible. This fallback to inhouse repair seems to have started at Drigh Road as well, where a Sikorsky S-55 helicopter was grounded for eight months awaiting some minor spare to be flown in from the US. The then base commander Group Captain A. Majeed Khan, who took over command of Drigh Road in April 1958, after discussing the unserviceability of helicopter with his technical team reached out to the then C-in-C Air Marshal Asghar Khan, seeking his permission to repair the defective component locally. The permission was granted within three hours and the defective component was repaired within an hour. The

Flight Lieutenant Mazhar Abbas steps into the cockpit of his F-86F at Peshawar. Note the Freighter, B-57s, and Vickers Viscount in the background. (Authors' collection)

With Pakistan part of the South East Asian Treaty Organization (SEATO), and CENTO, exercises with visiting RAF and US aircraft were common. Here a visiting RAF Canberra taxis backs to the tarmac at Mauripur after a training flight. (Authors' collection)

Even after becoming a republic and severing the formal association with Britain, PAF retained close ties to the RAF for training. Here visiitng British officers stand before the 31 Wing headquarters building. (Authors' collection)

helicopter was test flown and accepted back into the service the same day.[25]

Encouraged by this success, a component repair scheme emerged, and similar efforts were carried out to clear the bottlenecks in aircraft serviceability. One of these was the IRAN for F-86s, which was also well behind the schedule of handling four aircraft each month and had a backlog of 12 aircraft. The US Military Assistance Group was pursued to streamline delivery of spares to increase spare stocks at No. 101 MU and along with an inhouse repair of components scheme, the backlogs were cleared within a month with all 12 Sabres delivered back into service. Even though the Americans did not approve this inhouse repair of components scheme, they decided to look the other way, accepting it as a PAF necessity. This innovative scheme of inhouse component repairs was to stand PAF in good stead after the 1965 war, when the American arms embargo was imposed.

The change to a centralised maintenance model did not come without its challenges. Aircraft serviceability rates

A scene from the crew room showing young officers ready to respond to their country's call. Third from right is a smiling Flight Lieutenant Rashid Bhatti and to his right is Flight Lieutenant Saif-ul-Azam. (Authors' collection)

Squadron Leader Farooq Feroze Khan poses for the camera in front of a Starfighter at Sargodha air base. (Authors' collection)

Squadron Leader M.M. Alam shakes hands with his wingman, Flying Officer Masud Akhter, beside his Sabre, reflecting his multiple kills. (Authors' collection)

dropped during the transition period, before recovering. An ambitious flying target based on 25 hours per aircraft was set, which was achieved after considerable efforts, but saw a considerable spike in Special Occurrences (S.O.R.s) being reported.[26] This was judged by leadership to be due to excessive pressure on maintenance units and once the flying target was lowered, the S.O.R.s also dropped. The Officer Commanding (OC) Maintenance Wings were allowed to determine how many aircraft snags they could rectify during a normal working day and from then on, only given tasks which could be achieved during routine work hours. Much of the maintenance work was kept to day working hours, and the culture of working at nights to meet unrealistic targets was discouraged. The reduced workload on maintenance units resulted in the quality of work increasing, with higher serviceability rates, and considerable decrease in post-flight snags. To demonstrate the high serviceability rates, Sargodha air base once flew all 12 F-104s in formation over Air HQ, and had no fatal accidents during 1962–1963.[27]

Flight Safety and the Changing Mindset

The PAF's flight safety programme remained in close conformity to the British model, slowly improving accident statistics. Yearly reviews of each squadron's safety performance and the award of a trophy to the top performer added another incentive. The adoption of the RAF's standardised accident classification, definitions, investigation methodology and the popularisation of its air safety-related publications greatly assisted the Pakistani commanders, even in their less developed flying environment. The accumulating statistical data on accidents, especially those caused by avoidable lapses and inadequacies, helped avoid repetition of past mistakes. Air Headquarters also used that information to introduce a two-volume compendium of Command Flying Orders and Local Flying Orders. The first book was issued directly by Air Headquarters. The second was written and enforced by individual air bases, focusing on additional procedures uniquely applicable at an air base and warnings to aircrew about local hazards to safe flying operations. Each wing and squadron maintained copies of the two volumes in an updated state. All aircrew read and signed those two books for strict compliance, immediately upon arrival at their new unit, or whenever the base issued a new local order.

The new nation's tight budgets and the rudimentary work environment continued to impede the comprehensive availability of a safe flying infrastructure and professional expertise resembling that of the RAF. The PAF still lacked the full range of machinery and test equipment to determine the specific environmental or human deficiencies contributing to accidents. It could also not accurately determine the physical and psychological state of the personnel involved in an accident. Above all, the PAF needed urgently to set up a group of qualified experts for identifying the activities, locations and units that had become the likely candidates of future accidents, so that the anticipated mishaps could be prevented with timely interventions.

That opportunity came when Air Marshal Asghar Khan (1957–65) introduced a major expansion in both the structure and span of the PAF's flight safety programme. He studied, adapted and then enforced an enhanced version of the best parts chosen from the safety programmes of the RAF, the USAF, the US Navy and US Marine Corps and some other air forces. He also extended that programme to include units operating ground-based machinery such as expensive radars, vehicles and other mechanised equipment.

The USA-Pakistan MDAP agreement removed many of the new air chief's resource hurdles. This enabled the PAF rapidly to train (with the benefit of scientific expertise, analytical techniques and newly acquired forensic and other test equipment) air and ground Flight Safety Officers, Quality Assurance Specialists, Safety Inspectors and Flight Surgeons (aviation-qualified doctors and psychologists). Together, these skilled officers' work greatly assisted the squadron commanders in bringing down the loss rate of aircraft, aircrew and equipment operators. The Flight Safety Directorate was setup in PAF, and an initial team led by Squadron Leader P.D. Callaghan was sent to Norton Air Force Base to learn more about American concepts of flight safety. The team spent a month at Norton AB, going through all their records of F-86 and T-33 mishaps. There was no formal education in Flight Safety available within the USAF, just a lot of reading of mishap reports. The team also visited other air bases in the country to learn more about their flight safety concepts.

After the team returned, Callaghan wrote a report for Air Headquarters (AHQ), emphasising the formal training of officers in flight safety at the University of Southern California, which was the only institution within the country at the time offering this education to USAF officers.

During 1959, the Air Investigation Board was also set up. Formal training for members of an initial Air Investigation Board was provided at the Air Investigation Branch (AIB) London, which was a civilian organisation. The course was the Senior Officers Flight Safety Orientation Course, which was a more practical, hands-on course where engineers and pilots involved in actual air crash investigations would share photographic or material evidence to discuss and draw conclusions.

The Central Medical Board (CMB), Pakistan's aircrew medical test and certification unit, was upgraded to an Aero-Medical Institute (AMI) with foreign-qualified doctors. Simultaneously, the air chief launched a 'hearts and mind' campaign among all the commanders of flying units to channel and assess the performance of their men by a more precisely defined responsibility toward flight safety. The PAF would still judge them by their air combat competency, gunnery, rocketry and bombing scores, but henceforth also equally by what they did to avert accidents by shunning the old attitudes, misplaced overconfidence or foolhardy risks. The 'attitude problem' also started to diminish, but it took several years to bring down the accident rate to a tolerably low figure.

PAF's learning curve for flight safety is reflected best in a narration by Air Commodore P.D. Callaghan who was deeply involved in PAF's flight safety journey:

> We had a T-33 which pranged on take-off from Mauripur. An accident investigation report was done which went to AM Asghar Khan. The chief walked into the Flight Safety Directorate offices visibly angry and threw the report saying – I do not want to see all the algebra and the graphs in the report, tell me what happened in the cockpit. Basically, he rejected the report and we were in a fix, ultimately, we decided to send the report to the University of Southern California who were the knowledge base on flight safety issues for the USAF. USC endorsed our report and its findings and so did the C-in-C begrudgingly.[28]

What this anecdote illustrates is the development of institutional knowledge within PAF on flight safety and also generally. It took the organisation significant time and effort to understand that flight safety was much more than finding a culprit who committed a mistake and a whole system approach within the context of flight theory needed to be adopted.

Turn of the Tide

Within a few years of the MDAP with the USA and Air Marshal Asghar Khan taking over as the first Pakistani C-in-C, the PAF stood completely transformed. The professional methods of late 1940s to mid-1950s had now become distant memories.

PAF's order of battle had changed completely by the eve of 1965 war with India – it was now an all-jet force and its equipment was comparable to its likely adversary. PAF's command structure had been changed and instead of a particular Group being responsible for operations, PAF was now organised on a functional basis with central functions under an Assistant Chief of Air Staff position being responsible for competencies. These positions included Operations, Training, Maintenance and Administration. This organisation set

These 'hero pictures' offer a look at the AIM-9B installation on the F-86. Provided during the period of dalliance with the Americans, PAF sustained these air-to-air missiles for more than a decade and did well with them in the 1971 war despite their onsolescence. (Authors' collection)

Two Sabres taxi out for a routine training sortie at Mauripur. (Authors' collection)

Table 3: Summary of squadron re-equipment under MDAP				
Sqn	Formation date	Equipped with	Location	Remarks
No. 2	April 1956	T-33A	Mauripur	Raised with T-33 as Fighter Conversion Unit
No. 4	January 1958	SA-16 & Bristol Freighter	Mauripur	Initially equipped with 2 x SA-16 on raising, the squadron strength was increased to 4 SA-16 and 4 Freighters on 15 August 1959. On 8 July 1960, the strength was reduced to 2 SA-16 and 2 H-19D helicopters
No. 5	August 1947	F-86F	Sargodha	Equipped with Tempest Mk II at raising, the squadron was reequipped with Hawker Fury in early 1950s and subsequently with Sabres
No. 6	August 1947	C-130	Chaklala	Squadron was equipped with C-130 during 1963. After independence it initially operated Dakota and then Freighter transport aircraft
No. 7	June 1960	B-57B/C	Mauripur	At raising the squadron had 10 x B-57B and 1 x B-57C on strength
No. 8	August 1960	B-57B/C	Mauripur	
No. 9	August 1947	F-104A/B	Sargodha	Initially equipped with 8 Tempest aircraft at independence, the squadron was reequipped with F-104 in March 1961
No. 10	August 1959	B-57B/C	Mauripur	Initially raised to train B-57 aircrew, the squadron was number-plated on 1 March 1960
No. 11	January 1949	F-86F	Sargodha	The squadron was number-plated in February 1949 and raised again in June 1951. Initially equipped with Supermarine Attacker aircraft, the squadron converted to F-86F on 18 January 1958
No. 12	March 1950	F-27	Chaklala	Equipped with 8 Halifax bombers on raising, the squadron later operated various VIP transport aircraft and then SA-16 in sea rescue role during early 1957. The Squadron was equipped with Fokker F-27 aircraft on 9 July 1960
No. 14	November 1948	F-86F	Dacca	The squadron started converting to F-86F in late 1956 and was initially based at Mauripur. The squadron was permanently moved to Dacca on 7 October 1964
No. 15	June 1956	F-86F	Sargodha	Initially based at Mauripur, the Squadron was moved to Sargodha in October 1963. The squadron received the first F-86F on 20 July 1956
No. 16	April 1957	F-86F	N/A	Raised in 1957 and equipped with F-86F, the squadron was disbanded in 1963. The squadron was reactivated again on 13 April 1970 at Mauripur and once again it was equipped with F-86F
No. 17	April 1957	F-86F	Sargodha	Raised at Mauripur and with multiple deployments to Dacca prior to 1964, the squadron was based at Sargodha during the 1965 war
No. 18	February 1958	F-86F	Sargodha	Raised at Mauripur and equipped with F-86F during June 1958, the squadron was largely deployed at Sargodha during the 1965 war
No. 19	February 1958	F-86F	Peshawar	Raised at Mauripur and equipped with 12 F-86F on 1 February 1958, the squadron was deployed to Dacca from 1962-1963, and moved to Peshawar in October 1963
No. 20	March 1956	RT-33	Mauripur	

Table 3: Summary of squadron re-equipment under MDAP (*continued*)				
No. 23	May 1961	Fury	Kohat	The squadron was number-plated on March 1964 after Fury aircraft were phased out from service. The squadron was reactivated at Sargodha on 8 February 1966 and equipped with Chinese F-6 (MiG-19) aircraft
No. 24	December 1962	RB-57B	Peshawar	Equipped with specially modified RB-57B and RB-57F (US owned), the squadron had a specialist surveillance and ELINT role

up was not only necessary on account of adoption of USAF systems for operations, planning and maintenance but also encouraged standardisation and best practices through an organisation created around these competencies. Along with these changes, PAF in late 1961 created a dedicated planning department at AHQ under a Director. Its function included the responsibility for all operational planning including emergency planning, war plans, development planning, inter-service joint plans and international plans and treaties. With this change PAF would have a more robust capability to develop war and force development plans.

The new equipment and capabilities along with a renewed organisation structure meant that PAF's war plans changed accordingly. From the sketchy war plans of the 1950s, which essentially called for a defensive posture focused on survival of the force, plans now called for taking the offensive to the adversary. The whole gambit of air operations was now included, the ethos was explained by the following remarks made by Air Marshal Asghar Khan when queried on what may appear as a mundane matter of moving the AHQ from Mauripur to Peshawar:

> The government had decided to move to Islamabad and I thought Mauripur would be too far away; a lot of work at AHQ is about dealing with the government and we needed to be reasonably close. I did not want to move the AHQ to Rawalpindi as I thought we would be swamped by the Army given the General Head Quarters was there. At the time Army had not gotten it out of their system that the air force was an adjunct to the Army. Being at Islamabad or Rawalpindi would have compounded that problem and affected the growth of the Air Force. We would have lost our individuality. I do not share the view that an air force is an adjunct to the Army and provide ground support; it is just a subordinate role. An air force must have control of the skies and that is its first role.

While these few years saw a marked increase in PAF's capabilities in many respects the service was still very much in a growth phase. Training standards across the service had improved, especially for the air crew, nevertheless the majority of squadron air crew were still young and needed more experience and the number of aircraft was insufficient compared to the adversary. Infrastructure was perhaps the weakest when it came to main and forward operating bases with significant reliance on one major operating base covering the likely land battle theatre. Similarly, the air defence network – especially for low level warning – was woefully inadequate.

Strong confidence in its abilities, thanks to the hard work in the preceding years and a 'can do' aggressive attitude (what the early PAF veterans call the Battle of Britain spirit) is what PAF would take to the full-scale hostilities just on the horizon.

2
THE INDO-PAKISTAN AIR WAR OF 1965

The Opposing Forces

At the start of the 1965 war, PAF had a total of 119 F-86F Sabres, 12 F-104A/B Starfighters, and 24 B-57B/C Canberra aircraft in service. The Sabres, divided among seven squadrons (Nos. 5, 11, 14, 15, 17, 18 and 19), had a serviceability rate that hovered around 83 percent during most of the war. On 6 September, 91 Sabres were in serviceable condition, and as the war progressed, nine additional Sabres which were off-line in periodic inspections or other maintenance, were brought online. The 12 Starfighters equipping No. 9 squadron had a 100 percent serviceability rate, and the two B-57 squadrons (Nos. 7 and 8 squadrons) also had all their 24 B-57s on strength. Twelve serviceable T-33s were also available, along with a handful of RT-33s for recconnaissance roles. No. 6 Squadron had 5 C-130s, including a civilian version transferred by PIA (Pakistan International Airlines) on strength. A further 25 T-37s, and 32 T-6G were also serviceable and available for second tier roles such as mail and communication or to harass lightly defended targets at night.

Table 4: PAF Combat ORBAT during September 1965[1]				
Station	1 September 1965		6 September 1965	
	Type	Number	Type	Number
Mauripur	F-86F	35	F-86	16
	F-104	-	F-104	2
	B-57	22	B-57	14
	T-33	9	T-33	5
Sargodha	F-86F	30	F-86	44
	F-104	12	F-104	10
	T-33	1	T-33	6
Peshawar	F-86	14	F-86	20
	B-57	2	B-57	10
	RB-57	1	RB-57	1
Dacca	F-86F	12	F-86	11
	T-33	1	T-33	1
Totals: F-86 = 91, F-104 = 12, B-57 = 25, T-33 = 12				

It was not unusual to have 100 percent serviceability in the F-104s, B-57s and T-33s, especially if some advance warning was available to speed up the recovery of planes undergoing Periodic Maintenance. Before the 1965 war, the PAF was still free of any American weapon embargos so spare parts were well stocked, which also partly explains the high serviceability rates. However, those

F-104As at Sargodha prior to the 1965 war. (Authors' collection)

Pilots pose in front of a F-104 Starfighter at Sargodha. First from right is Squadron Leader Alauddin 'Butch' Ahmed, who commanded No. 18 Squadron during the 1965 war. (Authors' collection)

rates would have been impossible to attain without a competent force of engineers and technicians and this particular credit is often omitted because it is taken for granted.

The F-86's serviceability was kept at 83 percent throughout the 1965 war as it was more maintenance-heavy due to its multi-role profile. There was hardly any problem with spares, but high-value parts, such as wings, tailplanes, gunsights and engines, could not be acquired and held in large numbers as a reserve owing to their high cost. All spares for US-supplied planes had to be stocked from within the yearly budget allocated to the F-86 weapon system under the MDAP.

As the war progressed, squadrons were moved around and most of the Sabres from Nos. 17 and 18 Squadrons, which had 12 aircraft each on strength and comprised No. 32 Wing under the leadership of Wing Commander M A Sikander, were moved from Mauripur to Sargodha between 4 and 6 September to be used as a specialised strike wing to provide close air support to Army units. Two F-104s were also stationed at Peshawar each night to be available for any operations in the northern sector. The B-57s also rotated between Mauripur, Sargodha, and Peshawar.

The war was conducted from Theatre Air Ops at Air HQ, but the air defence was entrusted to Air Officer Commanding (AOC) Masroor Hussain, who was based at Sakesar, which was the eyes of the Northern Sector with its set of American-made FPS-20 surveillance and FPS-6 height finder radars. A second set of the same types of radars at Badin provided coverage for the south. The AOC Air Defence had a reserved pool of aircraft (out

Table 5: IAF Combat ORBAT of combat units on 1 September[2]				
Type	Number of Squadrons	Squadron Numbers	Total Aircraft	Remarks
Mystère IVA	5	1, 3, 8, 31, 32	80	All deployed in Western Sector
Hunter	6	7, 14, 17, 20, 27, 37	96	Three deployed in West Pakistan and three in East Pakistan
Gnat	5	2, 9, 18, 23, 15	80	Four deployed in West Pakistan
Toofani (Ouragan)	3	4, 29, 47	48	All in East Pakistan
Vampire	6	24, 45, 101, 108, 220, 221	80	One deployed in West Pakistan
Canberra	4.5	5, 16, 35, JBCU, 106	72	
MiG-21	1	28	10	Deployed in West Pakistan
Total			466	

of available serviceable aircraft) dedicated for air defence tasks, and which could not be tasked for any other mission by the base commanders, with only the C-in-C having the authority to override him. As part of Joint Operations Center (JOC), a team reporting to Air HQ but based at GHQ was entrusted with close air support coordination with the Army.

The IAF was divided into three Air Commands; Western, Central and Eastern as shown in Table 5.

Unlike PAF where most squadrons were made up of 12 aircraft each, the IAF as a standard had 16 aircraft per squadron (with some exceptions). Another strength variation between the two forces was the concept of aircraft in reserve. While the PAF was modelled on the American operational concept and had all the aircraft on the service line or under maintenance, with no aircraft kept in reserve, the IAF was still following the British model had a handsome number of reserve aircraft that could be utilised to replace losses in combat units. The PAF intelligence assessment at the start of the war estimated 496 operational aircraft in IAF units, with 188 kept in reserve.[3] The same intelligence assessment also believed that more than 10 MiG-21s were delivered before or during the war. The IAF notes 106 aircraft being held in reserve including those going through regular maintenance.[4]

Air Marshal Nur Khan goes through preflight checks before a familiarisation sortie in a Starfighter at Sargodha. (Authors' collection)

A trio of Sabres conduct a training flight while fitted with underwing tanks. (Murtaza Qasim)

Flying Officer Rahim Yousafzai poses for the camera before a flight. (Author's collection)

Indian early warning was provided by a high-powered mobile Russian P-35 radar deployed in the vicinity of Amritsar city. The mobility, unlike the fixed US-made FPS-20/6 radars of the PAF, afforded it a higher level of protection.

The Prelude

Since independence, even though there had been regular flareups and skirmishes – largely over the simmering issue of Kashmir – these were localised to the Ceasefire Line (later known as Line of Control), and both air forces were largely kept out of action after the first Kashmir war. Despite all their differences, the political and military leadership on both sides understood that the involvement of airpower could quickly escalate and lead to an all-out war. Even as caution prevailed, both air forces did carry out limited electronic- and photoreconnaissance missions occasionally, to keep an up to date ORBAT of their foe.

During one such photoreconnaissance mission on 10 April 1959, PAF managed to bring down an intruding English Electric Canberra PR-7 when two F-86Fs belonging to No. 15 'Cobras' Squadron were scrambled from Peshawar. IAF Canberras had carried out such incursions in the past, mostly confident in the fact that no operational PAF fighter (Starfighters were yet to enter service), could reach their operational ceiling of 50,000ft.

Being an Eid day, it was a public holiday and PAF stations were maintaining a skeleton crew.[5] PAF Station Peshawar kept two F-86F on the ORP (Operational Readiness Platform), with ADA (Air Defence Alert) duties assigned to two young bachelors, Flight Lieutenants Naseer Butt and M. Yunis, allowing the more senior crews to be with their families enjoying the Eid festivities. An order to scramble came early in the morning via Sector Operations Center (SOC) when a vintage Type 15 radar deployed at Wegowal (close to Sargodha) belonging to 223 Squadron and manned by young Pilot Officer Rab Nawaz detected the incoming bogey.[6]

The pair of Sabres led by Flight Lieutenant Naseer Butt took off from the ground in a maximum rate climb and were vectored by the young air defence controller into visual contact with the bogey. Flight lieutenants Butt and Younis spotted the double trails of the bogey way above them while at 20,000ft, initially thinking it to be two Hunters. The Marconi Type 15 radar lacked height-finding facility but since the Sabre pilots had acquired visual, and could see the bogey much higher, they kept climbing and at 41,000ft finally identified the bogey as an English Electric Canberra on a northerly heading at approximately 50,000ft.[7]

The Sabre leader requested permission to shoot and the young controller after a quick consultation with his Squadron Commander, Flight Lieutenant S.A. Rahman, gave the goahead. By this time both the Sabres had jettisoned their drop tanks and while the wingman kept a steady height and heading, the leader tried to bring down the Canberra using a mix of energy climbs, followed by a burst of gunfire and stall out sequence. While the leader was making repeated attempts, Cranwell-trained Flight Lieutenant Yunis, who had studied the flight characters of the Canberra closely during his training days in the UK, remembered that it would lose height while in a turn, perhaps providing them with a better opportunity. Thinking that the Canberra, which was still oblivious of the chasing Sabres, would turn east towards the friendly border as soon as it spotted the threat, decided to ease off to the right. Flight Lieutenant Yunis recalls:

> The leader has given me the okay to have a go if I could, but I could see I was still too far below the target. Presently the Canberra did turn right and then, as if he had spotted me, quickly reversed. On that side, he must have spotted Butt, for he seemed to panic and tightened his turn, which of course caused him to lose height rapidly. I saw my chance and put a bead on his right engine – just in time I remembered my Hunter wingspan setting and quickly ranged on half the Canberra's span – immediately I could see my bullets impacting on his right engine. I traversed the bead to the left engine and back to the centre, not letting go of the trigger till the guns stopped – due to over-heating, as it turned out. But I had fired 1,200 rounds by then and the doomed Canberra whipped into a spiral.[8]

Group Captain Massroor Hussain is seen in the cockpit of the crashed IAF Ouragan. (Authors' collection)

The Canberra crew, Squadron Leader J.C. Sen Gupta and Flight Lieutenant S.N. Rampal from the IAF's No. 106 Squadron managed to eject and were captured. After a short period of captivity, both were released and repatriated to India.

Tensions between the two regional rivals spilled over into armed conflict with the Rann of Kutch dispute in April 1965.[9] This was also the first time when PAF F-104s saw operational duties with a detachment of two F-104s sent to PAF Station Mauripur to reinforce the existing F-86F and B-57 squadrons.

To avoid escalation, PAF only undertook combat air patrols (CAP) well on its side of the border. During this period PAF made two interceptions of intruding IAF aircraft. The first interception on 24 June involved an armed IAF Ouragan (known as Toofani in IAF service) believed to be on a recconnaissance flight, where the pilot seems to have become disoriented and ended up almost 50 miles inside Pakistan. The pilot, Flight Lieutenant Rana Lal Chand Sidda of 51 Auxillary Squadron, had taken off from IAF Jamnagar and after seeing the warning pass made by the two Sabres,[10] which were scrambled from Mauripur, decided to lower his undercarriage and land at an open field, damaging the undercarriage in the process. The pilot was taken as prisoner and was released as a goodwill gesture on 14 August (Independence Day).

The second interception of an IAF recconnaissance Canberra was made by a PAF Starfighter north-east of Sargodha. In this case the pilot visually tracked the intruding aircraft for 10 minutes but was under orders not to fire.

Starting in August 1965, the cease fire line between Indian-held and Pakistani Kashmir started heating up. At 0330hrs on 1 September, Pakistan Army, led by Major General Akhtar Hussain Malik, launched Operation GRAND SLAM with the aim of capturing Chhamb and then subsequently the bridge on Akhnur to sever the only Indian land link to Kashmir. By evening of 1 September, hard-pressed and in complete disarray, the Indian Army requested that the air force provide air support to stem the Pakistani advance. The

A Sabre armed with two Sidewinders rolls down the runway at Sargodha for another mission. (Authors' collection)

orders to IAF were given at 1710hrs and the first sortie was over the battlefield at 1800hrs, but due to lack of communication between their Brigade HQ, ended up attacking both Pakistani and their own armour.[11]

These were the first sorties by the IAF in support of their ground forces and are described vividly by Bhupinder Singh:

Commander 191 Infantry Brigade had asked for air support at 11 a.m. The demand for air support reached the Army Headquarters without any delay. The IAF was ready for taking off but the Government of India took some time to arrive at the decision for using the IAF. Ultimately at 6 p.m., four Vampires and four Mysteres were over the battlefield. The IAF support did not prove to be of much use to the Indian ground forces, as it did not do any harm to the Pakistanis. On the other hand, their planes engaged Indian troops. The Vampires circled over 3 Mahar localities and strafed their positions. There were, however, no casualties in the Battalion. All four Indian planes were knocked down by PAF aircraft over 3 Mahar area in area Uparla Batala within sight of the Battalion. IAF planes also engaged Indian gun areas and armour destroyed all their ammunition lorries of artillery, one lorry of tank ammunition, three AMX tanks and one armoured recovery vehicle. Consequently, no ammunition was left in the sector for Indian tanks and artillery. The Brigade and Corps Commanders later regretted having asked for air support. The IAF fired on Pakistani tanks already knocked out by Indian ground forces. However, the appearance of Indian aircraft served as a deterrence to the Pakistani tanks whose attack was slowed down. The IAF did not appear in Chhamb sector again for two days.[12]

The opening close air support sorties of the IAF, did not cause much damage to Pakistan Army ground units, other than damaging a 155mm howitzer of 28 Medium Regiment and the dispersal of an infantry battalion (13 Punjab),[13] but the consequences for the attackers were fatal.

Due to the escalating tension with India since the Rann of Kutch skirmishes, PAF had been maintaining a higher state of alert. On the morning of 1 September as Pakistan Army crossed the Line of Control, pilots from No. 15 Squadron were on air defence alert duties at Sargodha. The duties were being shared across different squadrons and dawn to afternoon alerts were entrusted to No. 15 Squadron and afternoon to dusk to No. 5 Squadron led by Squadron Leader Rafiqui. The crew rooms were already abuzz with excitement and high anticipation of seeing some action, and pilots were jostling to get spots for air defence duties.

Imtiaz Bhatti, then acting Flight Commander of No. 15 Squadron, taking full advantage of his current position, had programmed his pair as No. 1 to scramble and waited anxiously till about noon, when they were to be relived of duties by No. 5 Squadron. As pilots from No. 5 started pouring into the standby hut to take over the air defence duties, Bhatti approached Rafiqui with a request to let him stay on as No. 1 for scramble. Rafiqui, who had been Bhatti's instructor during the F-86 conversion and later also his Flight Commander, agreed with the condition that he takes his wingman from No. 5 Squadron.

Bhatti takes up rest of the story:

… We waited till 4 in the evening and nothing happened. Sqn. Ldr. Rafiqui rang up Ground Liaison Officer and told him to come to the standby hut to brief the pilots about the latest situation. It was then that the things started developing and I was told to fly a patrol mission. As we were leaving for the aicraft, Sqn. Ldr. Rafiqui decided to lead the mission with myself flying as his No. 2. It was about 5 O' clock when we took off and headed towards the battle area. After take-off we were told that enemy aircraft were straffing our troops. Soon we were slicing through the cool evening air of Chhamb (War Sector) and the beautiful valley lay sprawling below us. We were scanning the sky around us for enemy aircraft. Suddenly I spotted a speck and called out 'Bogie left 9 O' clock low'. Sqn. Ldr. Rafiqui immediately acknowledged 'contact'. As the speck came nearer, we recognised it as two Vampires in close formation. They were now 6000 feet below us. We jettisoned our fuel tanks. The leader rolled in for attack and I realizing that we will be fighting outnumbered, pulled up to give top cover. While I was covering the leader's tail, I spotted two Canberras about 9000 feet towards our left. I reported their position and was about to ask his permission to go for them, when to my chagrin I saw two more Vampires trying to get behind the leader. After ensuring that the area is clear, I instinctively, positioned myself behind these two. In the meantime, Rafiqui had trained his sight on the No. 2 of the first pair of Vampires. Soon after I saw a flash – the Pakistan Air Force has opened its account with an Indian aircraft. I felt excited and yelled out 'leader well done.' Rafiqui was now chasing the other Vampire which manoeuvred fast to dodge him but he was following him as if glued to his tail. Meanwhile, I trained my gun sight on the second Vampire pair No. 2. I restrained my finger on the trigger as Rafiqui's aircraft was in my line of fire. I shifted my sight away and gave a small burst to make my presence felt but the Vampires continued their pursuit. Now the Vampires I was chasing had closed in on Rafiqui dangerously. "Leader break left" I yelled on the radio. Simultaneously I saw the Vampire ahead of Rafiqui burst into flames. Rafiqui broke left then reversed the turn and called 'two tail clear'. By this time, I had opened fire on my quarry on whom I already had my guns trained. Flashes all over his fuselage and no mistake. The Vampire caught fire at once. Tongues of flames escaped intermittently from his punctured tanks licking the fuselage and the booms. I had scored my first kill. My first emotion was of that satisfaction – satisfaction at a job adequately done. In aerial battles death is swift and fast. A fighter pilots has none of the personalised emotions of a soldier, handed a rifle and bayonet and told to charge. His emotions are of a duellist – cool, precise and impersonal. He is privileged to kill and to kill well. For, if one must either kill or be killed as one must in a battle, it should, I feel be done with dignity. Death should be given the setting it deserves, it should never be pettiness, for a fighter it can never be. I shifted the sight on to the last Vampire. During the chase we had lost lot of height and were flying too close to the ground. As I opened fire the Vampire in front of me ducked and hit the ground. Leader and myself joined in battle formation, checked each other's tail clear and looked for the other aircraft which apparently had made best use of the time and disappeared. The first encounter between the two air forces was fought in full view of our troops in Chhamb (War Sector) and they saw all the four enemy Vampire aircraft exploding into flames and crashing into the ground.

Frankly speaking our scores astounded us. Luck might have been on our side. However, in terms of fighting efficiency we had trained comparatively harder and proved more skillful.[14]

The Vampires on which Rafiqui and Bhatti had pounced belonged to No. 45 Squadron and were the second of three formations, launched with 10 minute intervals from Pathankot to provide CAS to their hard-pressed ground troops.[15] The IAF admitted to the loss of three Vampires in this engagement, with one making it home to tell the tale.[16] Another Vampire from the first formation is believed to have been shot down by AAA, though it is disputed by whose, as no Pakistan Army unit made a claim and hence it could well have been a case of fratricide. This swift and sharp engagement led to the IAF withdrawing the Vampires and Ouragons (Toofani) from frontline operations, reducing the IAF strength by about one third.[17]

2 September was a quiet day as PAF maintained vigilance and flew 24 CAP missions – 18 by F-86Fs and six by F-104s – without making any contact. Two CAS missions were flown from Sargodha to soften-up the Indian positions in the Akhnur area. The first

In a display for the cameras, the pilots demonstrate a scramble towards their Sabres. (Authors' collection)

mission consisting of four F-86s took off in the morning mist at 0530hrs led by Squadron Leader M.M. Alam, OC No. 11 Squadron, followed five minutes later by another formation of three F-86s, led by Flight Lieutenant Yousuf Ali Khan.[18] The formation led by Alam, unable to sight any worthwhile targets in the bad light, emptied their full load of 28 rockets each into an orchard where they believed the enemy might be hiding and were rewarded by the sight of military vehicles breaking cover to get away from the area. The second formation had no trouble in spotting the enemy tanks and soft skin vehicles, and made three attacks each, claiming five tanks and one carrier, along with 20–25 other vehicles damaged or destroyed. An RT-33 escorted by two F-86s carried out reconnaissance afterwards for battle damaged assessment.

After the first engagement and with the loss of three pilots and four aircraft to Sabres, the mood at Pathankot Air Base was grim and sullen.[19] The IAF flew in Gnat detachments to Pathankot from Ambala and Halwara belonging to No. 23 Squadron. The Gnat detachment led by Squadron Leader Johnny Green was tasked to shoot down the Sabres, which they planned to do the next morning by flying a formation of Mystére aircraft at high altitude to draw in the Sabres and then to ambush them with no fewer than eight low-flying Gnats, which would be outside the PAF's high altitude radar cover.[20]

Starting at dawn on 3 September, two Sabres and one F-104 were on CAP, to make their presence felt and to deter the IAF from interfering in the ground operations in the Chhamb area. At 0700 PAF radar at Sakesar picked up four bogeys at approximately 36,000 ft and headed towards the Chhamb-Akhnur battle area. Considering these to be a threat to the ground forces, the radar controller Flight Lieutenant Farooq Haider vectored the two Sabres on CAP from Sargodha piloted by Flight Lieutenant Yousuf Ali Khan and Flying Officer Abdul Khaliq towards the incoming bogeys. Noticing the four Gnats at 11 o'clock and a bit higher, Yousaf called contact and instructed his wingman to drop his tanks. The radar controller confirmed that they wanted to commit – considering that they were up against four bogeys – and received an affirmative from Yousaf, asking him to keep the area clear. As Yousaf closed in, he noticed two Gnats peeling off, which he decided to ignore and comfortably settled behind the other two. As he was about to press the trigger to fire the Sidewinder, Yousuf heard the thuds of bullets landing on his Sabre.[21] Unknown to Yousuf, Khalid's drop tanks had failed to jettison, and while he was concentrating on his switches, had lost

The damaged Sabre of Flight Lieutenant Yousuf Ali Khan at Sargodha. The aircraft was repaired within a few days and put back into action. (Kamal Butt and Authors' collection)

visual with his leader, and even worse, had failed to radio and notify Yousuf that he was out of the fight. With no wingman and a damaged aircraft, Yousuf maneuvered hard for the next 10 minutes, going in circles seeing Gnats all around.[22] Haider had by now instructed the scramble of an F-104 piloted by young Flying Officer Abbas Mirza from Sargodha to the aid of Yousuf, followed closely after by the scramble of another F-104 piloted by Flight Lieutenant Hakimullah.

Abbas Mirza takes up the story:

> I was on air defence alert with the rank of Flying Officer in the cockpit (aircraft number 877) when I got the order to scramble. The weather was very hazy. The visibility on the ground was about 2 miles and, in the air, it got worse reducing to about a mile or so. There was no cloud. In other words, an ordinary September day.
>
> I was airborne within 2 minutes and made an accelerated climb to 15,000 feet and 500 knots IAS. The GCI (Ground controlled radar) directed me to head immediately towards the Sialkot Sector as two F-86s were engaged in air combat against six IAF Gnats. The F-86 pair was led by Squadron Leader Yousuf Ali Khan and his wing man was Flight Lieutenant Khalid. Yousuf asked his wing man to return to base as on Khalid's aircraft one drop tank had failed to jettison. Yousuf was now alone against the six Gnats.
>
> GCI urged me to accelerate to 600 knots as the situation against Yousuf was getting increasingly precarious. I must add that the brilliant maneuvering of Yousuf had kept the Gnats at bay for over 10 minutes inspite of being damaged in the vertical fin and rudder area. I was asked to descend to 12,000 feet and then 10,000 feet and was informed that I was about five miles away from the fight and advised that the fight was taking place 12 O' clock to me. In the meanwhile, another F-104 was scrambled with Flight Lieutenant Hakimullah in the cockpit and was fast approaching the area. Suddenly, just ahead, about a mile or so I saw below me the F-86 in a tight turn to the right followed by the six Gnats. The lead Gnat was about 1,000 feet behind Yousuf and the rest in a line astern formation. I initially thought the Indian aircraft were Hunters but when I saw them a bit closer, they turned out to be Gnats.
>
> Unfortunately, since I was doing in excess of 500 knots when I had initial contact with the fight while the dogfight was around 200 or so I could not slow down fast enough to engage the enemy immediately, instead I decided consciously to pass in front of the F-86 to show Yousuf to hold on and to the Indians that reinforcements were on hand. I shut down my afterburner and simultaneously pulled up in a classic yo-yo maneuver to maintain the height advantage and also to slow down so as to keep the enemy in sight. The Gnats upon seeing me entering the melee immediately broke away from Yousuf and headed back towards the border. In the meanwhile, Flight Lieutenant Hakimullah had been maneuvered into the area and he was close to Pasrur airfield (disused by PAF) which was about five or six miles away from the area of engagement. One of the Gnats (Birjpal) saw the second F-104 as well and decided against taking up a fight against two F-104s and landed his aircraft at Pasrur airfield. Had he known that neither Hakimullah nor I had visual contact with him till he was about to land he may have got away safely but I guess personal safety got the better of him. In the meanwhile, as I reached the top of my yo-yo (16,000 feet) and began to descend, I lost contact with the Gnats because of very poor visibility and also because the Gnat is an extremely small aircraft and difficult to spot from a distance even in good visibility. I stayed in the area

A T-bird rolls down the runway at Sargodha after a sortie. (Authors' collection)

for another 30 minutes under the guidance of GCI but no other Indian aircraft entered to engage me.[23]

As the Gnats scattered on the sight of the diving F-104, Yousuf took the opportunity to disengage and head back to Sargodha for a straight-in approach. The aircraft had suffered damage to the elevator and aft area, losing the braking hydraulics and some electricals in the process but still somehow managed to stay aloft. The Sabre engaged the barrier at landing, but no further damage was done. The Sabre (S/N 55-3870) was repaired within a few days and saw action again.[24]

One of the Gnats flown by Squadron Leader Brijpal Singh Sikand got separated from the others and with F-104s lurking about, made a hasty decision to land at the Second World War landing strip at Pasrur.[25] As he disembarked the cockpit, he was quickly apprehended by troops from No. 210 Mobile Wireless Observer Wing, a unit of which was deployed in the vicinity to provide early warning. As news of an Indian aircraft landing at a Pakistani airstrip spread, locals started flocking to the airstrip hoping to catch a sight of it. At Sargodha, Squadron Leader Saad Hatmi, who had flown Gnats during his training in the UK was tasked by Station Commander Group Captain M. Z. Masud to proceed to Pasrur and inspect the aircraft.

At Pasrur, Hatmi recalled meeting the Gnat pilot:

I met Sikand when he was brought to the airfield. He was a smart Sikh pilot but without the usual long tresses. During our friendly chat he confessed that he was unsure of his position but the presence of an F-104 overhead had helped him into a quick decision to land at Pasrur. For a pilot, who handed over a perfectly serviceable aircraft to the enemy, he was too cocky. He thought it was a big joke when I told him that I was going to fly the Gnat to our base. According to him the Gnat was complex and difficult to start let alone to fly.[26]

A smiling Hakimulah poses with the captured Gnat. (Authors' collection)

On 6 September, escorted by two Sabres, Hatmi flew the Gnat to Sargodha. The Gnat was testflown extensively after the war and eventually found its place as a war trophy at PAF Museum Karachi, where it still resides.

After the aerial air skirmish on 3 September, PAF reassessed its strategy and decided to increase the strength of each CAP formation to four Sabres and two Starfighters to reduce the enemy's numerical superiority. The Sabres were to maintain CAP around 20–25,000ft with Starfighters keeping lower altitude.[27]

On 4 September, the PAF was to suffer its first combat loss. When conducting a CAS mission in the battle area, Flying Officer Nasir Mahmood while exiting at low level and trailing 2,000ft behind his formation was hit. Butt was in the third formation of Sabres belonging to No. 15 Squadron – with each formation consisting of four Sabres – that were in the area to strike any targets of opportunity. It was initially believed that he was brought down by friendly AAA, but IAF sources credited Flight Lieutenant V. S. Pathania, whose formation of four Gnats led by Squadron Leader Johnny Green from IAF No. 23 Squadron, had managed to sneak in behind the Sabre undetected.

On 5 September, Pakistani forces captured the town of Jaurian, some 14 miles inside Indian controlled territory. With the fall of Jaurian, Pakistani forces came across the main defences of

Akhnur. PAF mounted 16 sorties using Sabres and Starfighters, from Sargodha and Peshawar, to ensure IAF did not interfere with Pakistani ground forces. Indian artillery gun positions in the sector were strafed by a pair of Sabres led by Squadron Leader M.M. Alam along with his wingman Flight Lieutenant Jilani who were on a visual reconnaissance mission.

The Balloon Goes Up
At 0300hrs on the morning of 6 September, the Indian Army's XI Corps launched the invasion of West Pakistan across the Lahore–Kasur sector. As part of Operation Riddle, units from the Indian 7th and 15th Divisions, brushing aside the Rangers deployed at forward border posts, made quick progress on three axes to secure the eastern bank of BRBL canal.[28] The approaches to Lahore were not well guarded since Pakistan Army's 10th Division, which since its creation had the assigned task to defend Lahore, was yet not forward deployed. 10th Division had vacated its well-prepared defensive positions after the Rann of Kutch conflict as the agreement required both countries to withdraw their troops from the border.[29]

As reports of the Indian invasion started coming in and Pakistan Army units were rushed to their forward positions, PAF was called into action. The Indian 3 Jats and 15 Dogras battalions, which were the leading elements and had made good progress, were at the receiving end. This initial strike is recorded in the *History of the Regiment of Artillery, Indian Army*:

> At 0700 hours, the PAF appeared and carried out intensive air strikes with rockets and machine guns on 3 Jats and 15 Dogras, inflicting considerable casualties. This air strike came just when the second phase of the brigade's plan required the Dogras to pass through the Jats and advance rapidly in a bid to capture the bridge over the Ichogil canal at Dograi.[30]

The above strike is believed to have been conducted by a four-ship Sabre formation from Sargodha but finds no mention in the official PAF history book. Sabres from Peshawar too were soon to join the action with devastating results.

On the morning of 6 September, No. 19 Squadron – based at Peshawar and led by Squadron Leader Sajad Haider – was tasked to provide CAS to silence the Indian artillery guns deployed close to Sialkot Sector. Taking off at 0900hrs, as the six-ship Sabre formation was heading for their target, the Air Defence HQ rerouted them to Lahore sector to seek and destroy the advancing Indian Army units.[31] After crossing the border at Wagha, the leader picked up the tank tracks close to the Grand Trunk road, and following those soon discovered numerous tanks and armoured vehicles trying to climb onto the GT road from the banks.[32] Identifying the tanks by their saffron roundels, the leader dived into the attack, releasing his 5-inch rockets in pairs. As the No. 5 and 6 of the formation climbed to 7,000ft to keep an eye out for the enemy aircraft, the other four Sabres carried out multiple attacks, to pick off any visible target. A Starfighter piloted by Squadron Leader Mervyn L. Middlecoat soon arrived overhead, and leaving the lookout role to the sole Starfighter, the two other Sabres also joined the fray. After spending 17 minutes over the target and running out of rockets and nearly depleting all their gun ammunition, the Sabres headed to Sargodha for a quick refuelling stop before proceeding to their home base. According to numerous Indian historians, at the receiving end of this strike was the fighting echelons of two infantry battalions, 3 Jat and 15 Dogras. The 3 Jat lost all its recoilless guns, the artillery observation party from 34 Light Battery was written off, and the reserve artillery officer (OP) was also killed.[33] A troop of tanks from 14 Horse in support of 3 Jat was also destroyed.

Throughout the day additional strikes were launched from Sargodha. One of these by four Sabres struck the main body of Indian units at 1100hrs, destroying a mortar platoon truck and another at 1330 by six Sabres, attacked the Indian convoy for 35 minutes causing more casualties.[34] During all these attacks by the PAF, there was no interference from the IAF. Other than the lack of air support from the IAF, the Indian division was also lacking its air defence artillery allowing the Sabres to push home their attcks, with only small-arms fire to contend with. By end of the day, the Indian advance was stemmed by a combination of effective artillery fire and PAF strikes, which bought enough time for Pakistan Army units to rush and occupy their forward positions. This sector was to see further action till the end of the ceasefire with various positions changing hands, but the Indian Army never regained the initiative, after losing it on 6 September.

It was also on 6 September when a F-104 on an early morning CAP, piloted by young Flight Lieutenant Aftab Alam, claimed a Mystére with an AIM-9B Sidewinder when he intercepted a formation of IAF aircraft attacking a passenger train near Rahwali.[35] The first day of hostilities later saw two F-104s conducting a visual recconnaissance over Adampur and Halwara airbases in India to verify the presence of IAF aircraft as a prelude to PAF's counter-air strikes later in the day.

Now or Never
As the Indian Army launched its attack across the international border, the PAF leadership believing that the initiative now rested with the Indians, expected full-fledged attacks by

A lineup of Sabres at Mauripur. (Authors' collection)

the IAF to tie it down, denying it any chance to interfere with the ground battles. Up against a much numerically superior enemy, PAF was under no illusions that in such a scenario, fully occupied with counter-air operations and in keeping the IAF off the heads of Pakistan Army troops, it would not be able to provide the Army with any ground support. This was a point that had been emphasised repeatedly by the PAF leadership to their Army counterparts during numerous wargaming sessions.

Prior to 6 September, even though both air forces had flown CAS sorties across the Ceasefire Line (CFL), any action across the international border was avoided. Pakistan Army leadership might not have anticipated the launch of Operation Grand Slam leading to a full war, but PAF leadership had no such illusions. Anticipating an escalation in hostilities, PAF had been at a high state of readiness since May 1965. Dispersion and concealment of various assets along with activation of various forward airstrips for aircraft recovery was already planned. Heavy ground equipment and stores were also dispatched to various operational stations to support the ORBAT.[36] Airmen released during the last two years from the Ground Combateer trade were recalled, as were the Armament Fitters.

A Starfighter cuts a sleek figure at Sargodha. The Kirana hills are visible in the distance. (Authors' collection)

Aircrew rush towards their Sabres still in Luftwaffe colours. (Authors' collection)

One important preparation that was to pay handsomely was the construction of dummy aircraft to be placed at various air bases. This decision was born out of Second World War experience and was the brainchild of Air Commodore Haider Raza. A reconnaissance pilot on the Burma front, Raza had remembered one particular mission against an abandoned Japanese airstrip, where each squadron pilot after returning from his attack had claimed destroying a truck: the same truck. Understanding the human psyche to go after what might be easier and visible during a stressful situation, a lot of effort was spent in the concealment of actual aircraft in camouflaged pens, while wooden dummies were spread across the airfields at eye catching positions. Group Captain Mansoor A. Shah who was to head the ad-hoc (war time only) Joint Operations Center during the 1965 war, got an eagle-eye view of the camouflage at Sargodha and narrated the following to authors:

> Just before the 65 war I flew over Sargodha base and was pleasantly surprised to see almost nothing on the ground there except the runways and taxi tracks. No airplanes or vehicles or apparently anything else of value was visible. I knew that about 80 fighter planes were supposed to be there, so I looked more closely and after some careful searching was rewarded by seeing the nose and faint outline of a shiny but heavily camouflaged F-104. A little later I spied another one. On landing I went to my old friend, the base commander, (Group Captain Mitty Masud) and told him that his base camouflage was excellent but not perfect because I had seen two F-104s. He asked where I thought I had seen those F-104s. I told him, so Mitty and I piled into his jeep and Mitty drove quickly to the first location. The 104 was indeed there but from so close up, it became obvious that it was only a dummy. The same went for the other so called F-104 that I saw. This was PAF Sargodha's state of preparedness as far as camouflage went in 1965.[37]

The PAF war doctrine, carefully prepared under Air Marshal Asghar Khan, called for grabbing the initiative, by striking the IAF on the ground in strength, in well-coordinated strikes to reduce the force imbalance right at the start. With the Indian Army crossing the border, and the IAF absent from the battlefield, the PAF was now in a race to grab the initiative, and do to the IAF, what it had failed to do to the PAF – strike the first blow, as soon and as hard as it could. All the Squadron and Station commanders were briefed of this plan at Air HQ during early June 1965, and the finer details of mission planning were left to individual squadron commanders.

Now with a full-blown invasion at hand, the President during an early morning Cabinet meeting permitted the C-in-C to use the PAF as he deemed fit. To be able to strike the IAF bases at the same ToT (time on target), the tasking orders had to be dispatched to bases no later than 0900 PST, permitting them enough time to prepare the required aircraft with the right configuration. Between the time the President gave his goahead and the tasking orders were issued, there seems to have been a delay, caused by a debate at Air HQ. The new C-in-C Air Marshal Nur Khan, who has just returned from a long deputation to PIA six weeks earlier, perhaps needed more time to weigh the pros and cons of these dusk strikes. The debate over mounting the strikes was settled at 1100 PST, leaving two hours less than required for optimal preparations, and accordingly the targets were also adjusted.[38]

The modified plan called for strikes on four IAF airfields and three radar stations. The airfields at Adampur and Halwara were to be attacked by two formations of eight Sabres each from Sargodha. Pathankot was to be attacked by eight Sabres from Peshawar and a similar number of Sabres from Mauripur were to take care of Jamnagar. The primary IAF P-35 radar site close to Amritsar was to be tackled by six Sabres from Sargodha accompanied by an ELINT RB-57 acting as a pathfinder. The Ferozepur and Porbunder radars, believed to be lightly defended, were to be attacked by four T-33s each, from Sargodha and Mauripur respectively. The ToT was set to 1705hrs, which was to be followed by B-57 raids to keep up the pressure throughout the night.

Sargodha, which had been at the forefront of generating most of the sorties since 1 September to support ground troops, and which was to mount the main effort for upcoming strikes, could only muster eight Sabres in time with the required configuration. This seems to have been due to various operational and logistical reasons, such as the delay in turning around the aircraft that were returning from ground support missions, reloading of ammunition, or the delay in the movement of 12 additional aircraft that were to be flown in from Mauripur to increase the pool of serviceable aircraft. The Sargodha Station Commander, Group Captain Zafar Masud, popularly known as Mitty Masud, after informing the C-in-C about the availability of aircraft, had requested postponement by 24 hours, and being denied that requested that all effort (eight Sabres), be directed at one base, either Halware or Adampur. This too was turned down, and with that, PAF was poised to strike with whatever it had at hand.

The original plan to task eight F-86s against each enemy airfield and six against the Amritsar radar was set at the minimally optimum number of F-86s. The force calculation was based on professional 'weapon effectiveness and employment' data, globally used by all air forces. The planners factored in the probability of each group of eight being intercepted by the IAF. In that event, one half of that group (four F-86s) would jettison its external tanks to become more agile and protect the other half against enemy interference until it had completed its attack on the parked aircraft. The strikers would then join the other four in the ongoing air battle and make their way back, following the standard exit tactics. It is not difficult to see why a lesser number of Sabres would jeopardise both strikes, particularly if the surprise element were lost for any reason.

Towards Glory
OC No. 19 Squadron Sajad Haider received the tasking order to strike Pathankot airfield from the Peshawar Station Commander at 1230hrs.[39] The strike was to be conducted by eight F-86 aircraft, using guns only. Pathankot being on the outer fringes of the Sabres' endurance, each was to carry two 200-gallons drop tanks, which along with full internal fuel provided just enough legs to make the round trip. Two additional Sabres, equipped with Sidewinders were added as escorts. Like clockwork, all 10 Sabres rolled down the Peshawar runway on time. To confuse the Indian radar at Amritsar about their direction and intended target, the formation initially flew a high-level profile at 25,000ft towards Gujranwala. After

About one quarter of the PAF Sabres during the 1965 war were wired to carry Sidewinders. Here the ground crew get ready to install Sidewinders on the Sabres. (Authors' collection)

getting closer to Gujranwala the formation hit the deck and changed their approach sharply towards Pathankot.

The PAF planning staff was not certain if the base was still occupied as no recent photo intelligence was available.[40] As the formation led by Haider pulled up over Pathankot at precisely 1710hrs, they were excited to find the airbase brimming with aircraft. While the two escorts provided top cover, the eight Sabres went to work, making multiple passes to pick out various aircraft spread all over the base. With light antiaircraft fire and no aerial threat to contend with, the No. 19 Squadron pilots had a free run on their targets, as if they were on a gunnery range. After making multiple passes, the formation safely egressed and recovered at Sargodha. After debriefing, the pilots were credited with destroying seven MiG-21s, five Mysteres and one Fairchild C-119 on the ground. The Indians, for their part, initially claimed that no MiGs were destroyed, claiming them to be in fact Mysteres.[41]

While everything had gone as planned for No. 19 Squadron; at Sargodha the two four-ship Sabre formations, earmarked for striking Adampur and Halwara were already running well behind schedule. As happens on a particularly terrible day in some military operations, one F-86 each out of the two foursomes that finally started engines had to abort with technical failures. These last hard blows resulted in the two F-86 formations finally proceeding with just three – rather than eight – planes each, crossing into enemy territory to attack heavily defended airfields. Three of the six pilots that got airborne were the PAF's highest regarded squadron commanders.[42] Significantly, the formation members of the two woefully skimpy formations that took off against Adampur and Halwara were also well aware of the flawed decision process while they stoically pressed on with their missions.

In the fast-fading dusk light the three Sabres from No. 11 Squadron, led by Squadron Leader M.M. Alam, headed towards Adampur at low level. South of Amritsar and 30 seconds short from their final IP (Initial Point), the formation saw four Hunters slightly above them and crossing at almost 90 degrees in close attack formation.[43] As the the Sabres had already been warned by the radar at Sakesar of enemy aircraft in close vicinity and probably believing these Hunters to be the base's air defence formation, Alam decided to go after them.[44] As Alam ordered his formation to punch tanks, so did the Hunters and both formations turned into each other for combat. Skimming treetops at 200 knots, Alam quickly settled behind No. 4, who after a brief burst flicked and hit the ground in a great ball of fire.[45] The air battle lasted for five to six minutes during which Alam took shots at another Hunter, as did his formation members Squadron Leader Alauddin 'Butch' Ahmed and Flight Lieutenant Hatmi, who also claimed a Hunter each.[46] As the battle was taking place close to Adampur, worried about reinforcements, Alam ordered his formation to disengage and head for home.

To strike Halwara the last formation of three Sabres from No. 5 Squadron led by Squadron Leader Sarfraz Rafiqui, along with Flight Lieutenants Cecil Chaudhry and Yunus Hussain as his No. 2 and No. 3 took off from Sargodha in the fast-fading light. While crossing the border at low level, the formation crossed paths with that of Alam, which was returning from the abortive strike on Adampur. In the fast-deteriorating light conditions where it had become difficult to identify ground features even at low level, the formation pulled over what it believed to be the general airfield area. While orbiting at 200ft to pick out the airfield for a good five minutes unsuccessfully, Rafiqui spotted a pair of Hunters a few hundred feet above them and in a left-hand turn. Deciding to go after the two orbiting Hunters, Rafiqui picked the lead Hunter, which was on his left, while Yunus was to tackle the one on the right, with Cecil keeping their tails clear. Rafiqui slipped behind the lead Hunter with ease, and getting a tail-clear call from Cecil, made quick work of his quarry which exploded and crashed. While Rafiqui was tackling the lead Hunter, Yunus also hit and brought down the second. These two Hunters on CAP belonged to IAF No. 7 Squadron and were being piloted by Flying Officers P.S. Pingale and A.R. Ghandhi. Rafiqui had hit Pingale, who only noticed the Sabres when bullets had started striking his aircraft. As Pingale ejected successfully merely 100ft above ground, Gandhi was also simultaneously hit and managed to eject just in time.[47]

Two Hunters from IAF No. 27 Squadron which were patrolling further north were also vectored towards the Sabres. In the ensuing skirmish, Flight Lieutenant D.N. Rathore, who was the flight leader, claims to have seen a Sabre on a strafing run, which he managed to hit at 500 yards, and saw it crashing six miles from the airfield.[48] Rathore's wingman, Flying Officer V.K. Neb, managed to catch up to Yunus's Sabre and shot it down, after it had pulled up sharply. As the Sabre formation had not been able to locate targets on the ground in bad light, and there were no published reports of any target hit on the ground, Rathore and Neb might have mistaken the Sabres orbiting at low level trying to locate the airfield – or their gun flashes from shooting down Pingale and Gandhi – as being a strafing run. Cecil was the only member of the formation to successfully disengage and make it back to Sargodha.

The airfield strikes had brought PAF mixed fortunes. Pathankot was struck hard and without any loss and the Adampur strike, even though aborted, still did not result in any PAF loss. Over Halwara, the PAF lost two of its finest pilots. With the PAF being a small tightknit force, where all the officers knew each other, the loss of Rafiqui and Yunus was felt deeply and for years to come, left that 'what if' debate surrounding these initial strikes.

The four-ship Sabre formation that was to strike the Amritsar radar took off from Sargodha at 1740hrs led by Wing Commander Anwar Shamim. Their pathfinder RB-57, flown by Squadron Leader Rashid, which was to lead them to the target developed a fault midway and the mission had to be aborted. PAF knew the general location of the mobile and well camouflaged P-35 radar close to Amritsar but needed the ELINT RB-57 to pinpoint the location allowing the Sabres to deliver their attack. As another RB-57 from Peshawar, flown by Squadron Leader Iqbal, headed towards the target, two of the Sabres after quickly refuelling also got airborne. As the RB-57 approached closer to Amritsar, intense antiaircraft fire knocked out one of the engines. With the RB-57 damaged and the darkness now making it difficult to visually pick up the target, the strike was aborted again.[49]

The two four-ship formations of T-33s sent to hit the lightly defended auxiliary radar units at Ferozepur, believed to be housing a less capable type TPS-1DM radar, and that at Porbunder, which PAF had doubts even existed, fared no better. Unable to find anything at Porbunder the T-birds emptied their guns on the deserted Bhuj airfield.

To keep up the pressure on the IAF throughout the night, the B-57s were detailed to strike Jamnagar, Halwara, Adampur, and Pathankot after the F-86Fs' dusk strikes. Nos. 7 and 8 Squadrons, which were equipped with B-57s and made up No. 31 Wing, were deployed at Mauripur during peacetime. In anticipation of hostilities, four B-57s had already moved to Peshawar on 2 September and the rest were also ordered to be moved to Peshawar on 6 September. The last six B-57s which were about to leave for Peshawar were ordered at 1630hrs to cancel the move, most likely due to the abortive Sabre strike earlier on Jamnagar, and were tasked instead to attack Jamnagar at 1800hrs.

The night strikes at Jamnagar were to be carried out by a section of six B-57s led by OC No. 31 Wing, Wing Commander Hamid Qureshi leading the pack with Flight Lieutenant Akhtar as his navigator. The aimed ToT was 1853, which would be last light.[50] Taxiing out at 1800hrs, with ground crew lined up at the side of the taxiways waving goodbye, the stream of B-57s armed with four 1,000 lbs bombs, 56 x 2.75" rockets, and four 20mm cannons, rolled down Runway 27 at an interval of seven seconds. To make a stealthy approach the plan was to approach Jamnagar at a low-level from the sea, giving as little reaction time and warning to the enemy as possible. Skimming over the waves and using the Jamnagar radio beacon which the Indians had forgotten to turn off, the B-57s planned to pull up along the coastline and align themselves with the runway after doing a left wing-over and deliver bombs on the main runway followed by targeting any exposed aircraft.[51] As the lead B-57 pulled up to 8,000 ft over the target, right on time at 1853hrs, and delivered his bombs hitting the far-left edge of the runway, the other B-57s quickly followed and dropped their bombs during single passes, targeting various sections of the runway and technical areas. The lead followed up with a second pass and emptied his rockets on a hangar. The B-57s had met no opposition and crews did not even notice antiaircraft artillery (AAA). All the aircraft managed to recover safely at Mauripur. As the aircrews enjoyed a light dinner, the aircraft were turned around by the ground crew. From then on, Jamnagar airfield was to be kept under pressure with a stream of single B-57 attacks. Squadron Leader Alam Siddiqui, along with his navigator Squadron Leader Aslam Qureshi, who was to mount the last raid of the night, failed to return from their mission.[52] They had taken off at 0335hrs and it was Siddiqui's third mission of the night. On the way to the target he was warned about low cloud cover in the area by Squadron Leader Rais Rafi, who was egressing after his strike. Initially, due to the absence of the Indian

Ground crew move into position to assist disembarking B-57 aircrew. (Authors' collection)

Ground crew refuel a B-57. (Authors' collection)

claim of shooting down the B-57, doubts lingered about how it was lost. It was only decades later, after new research was conducted by the IAF and Indian researchers, that it became known that the aircraft was brought down by AAA while it was conducting a second bombing run on the airfield and crashed 10 miles from the base. India accepted four Vampires being damaged at Jamnagar in these B-57 raids.[53]

A similar effort was mounted against Adampur, Halwara, and Pathankot by B-57s from Peshawar. OC No.7 Squadron, Squadron Leader Najeeb Khan, led the four-ship formation carrying four 1,000lb bombs in the internal bombay only, against Adampur with a planned ToT of 1730hrs. The lead had no difficulty in locating the airfield as all the base lights, including the runway lights, were on. Spending eight minutes over the target, Squadron Leader Najeeb dived and dropped one 1,000lb bomb during each pass to maximise accuracy and have a greater impact. A novel technique had been developed by the Squadron Leader to cut down the throttle while diving which permitted a steeper angle of attack, resulting in higher accuracy. After delivering the bomb, Squadron Leader Najeeb would throttle up and climb over the AAA umbrella.[54] So impressed were the IAF officers by this technique, that even though they were at the receiving end of it, they nicknamed the pilot "8-Pass Charlie".[55] All the B-57s were recovered safely at Peshawar by 2100hrs. The number two B-57 in the formation had a close call as the ground crew discovered a 40mm hole in the left wing between the fuselage and engine that seemed to have missed all the vital parts. Two MiG-21s which were preparing to launch had been caught on the ORP and one was admitted as being destroyed and the second as being damaged.[56]

As Squadron Leader Najeeb's formation was landing, another formation of four B-57s was taking off for Pathankot, led by Wing Commander Mahmood Akhtar, the operations officer of No. 31 Wing. Making single passes, three of the B-57s managed to drop their load of eight 1,000 lbs bombs on the airfield runway, while one B-57 after failing to find the target had dropped its payload on dead reckoning. Halwara was struck by a single B-57 piloted by Flight Lieutenant Alvi just before dawn, as an earlier planned strike with three B-57s was aborted due to bad weather. Anticipating incoming IAF raids against a very crowded Peshawar the next morning, Alvi recovered at Samungli.

The Fight for Sargodha

The PAF anticipated that the IAF would strike hard at Sargodha, which housed most of the fleet. It was at 0530hrs (PST) that the first IAF strike on PAF's Sargodha air base was detected when the formation of six IAF Mysteres were already pulling up to attack the airfield. The Mysteres had made a perfect approach, undetected by radar or the various belts of the MOUs (Mobile Observer Unit). Most of the aircraft at Sargodha were well camouflaged and in their protected pens, but four F-86Fs and two F-104s were on ORP, refuelled and awaiting orders to scramble. The Mysteres exited after making a single high-speed pass, first emptying their rockets,[57] and then firing their guns at the empty tarmac area, completely missing the six manned and fully fuelled aircraft on the ORP.

An F-104A flown by Flight Lieutenant Amjad Hussain Khan, which was maintaining the pre-dawn CAP, was vectored by GCI to intercept the raid. Amjad picked up the two Mysteres which were exiting on a heading of 120 degrees at about 100ft AGL. Soon after making visual, Amjad let go an AIM-9B at one of the Mysteres, which impacted the ground well short of the target. Closing in at high speed he fired at the Mystére with his gun and saw hits on the aircraft. The second Mystére, meanwhile, broke towards the Starfighter, forcing Amjad to make a high-speed yo-yo and attack again. The Mystére turned into him again, forcing another yo-yo with afterburners engaged. The Starfighter climbed to 13–15,000 feet and then dived to make another attack on the Mystére. This time the Mystére pilot did not see the F-104, with the Starfighter diving and closing in at 540 knots and opening canon fire at a range of 3,000ft. The Mystére exploded when the range was 1,000–1,500

Starfighters on the flight line at Sargodha. (Authors' collection)

ft and before the Starfighter could pull up to clear the explosion, it flew through the resulting debris. The F-104's controls froze, and the aircraft stopped responding, going into a left bank. At this point about 75–100ft AGL, Flight Lieutenant Amjad Hussain ejected from the aircraft and landed near a village, receiving a hero's welcome from the villagers, and eventually made it back to Sargodha safely.[58] The Mystére downed by Hussain was flown by Squadron Leader Devayya, who perished in the encounter.[59]

Following this strike, two pairs of Sabres and an F-104 were launched to maintain CAP. One of the Sabre pairs were led by M.M. Alam with a young Flying Officer Masud Akhter as his wingman, and the second pair was led by Flight Lieutenant Imtiaz Bhatti, with Flight Lieutenant Sadruddin Hossain as his No. 2. The F-104, which was maintaining station at 15,000ft, was piloted by Squadron Leader Arif Iqbal.

Sadruddin Hossain was to witness what was about to transpire and takes up the story:

A number of aircraft were scrambled from PAF Base Sargodha on the morning of 6 September to intercept the incoming IAF attack on the base. The main tactics was to get the enemy on their way out. We were to circle and hold close to the airfield but out of the friendly ack-ack range. As I remember, two pairs of F-86Fs and a lone F-104 was in the air at that time. One pair was led by Squadron Leader M.M. Alam with Flying Officer Masud as his wing man. The other was led by Flight Lieutenant Imtiaz Bhatti with myself as his wing man. Initially the two pairs were on different radio frequencies controlled by separate ground controllers. We had visual contact with the enemy aircraft as they pulled up for the attack and the ack acks opened up. I witnessed a rather hasty, half-hearted attack on the part of the enemy aircraft, and they seemed to be in a great hurry to exit and get away.

We picked up at least six Hunters exiting as we informed our controller of our intentions and we were cleared for the attack. We were to drop our external fuel tanks as we roll in for the attack but unfortunately one of the drop tanks of my lead aircraft would not drop even by the alternate emergency method and in that condition it was virtually impossible for us to pursue the enemy aircraft effectively. We informed our controller of the situation who asked us to discontinue the attack and change to a new radio frequency. The controller then informed us of the presence of Alam's flight nearby pursuing the same target with the lone F-104 giving us top cover. As we visually established contact with these aircraft our flight was asked to support Alam as he pursued the attack. We were therefore in a very good position to observe the entire proceedings. Given the fact that I also had to look around to keep our tails clear, I saw Alam destroy at least three aircraft. Our aircraft speed was limited as a result of the hanging fuel tank. Unable to keep up with Alam's aircraft, we soon lost contact and returned to the base.[60]

Alam had caught up to escaping Hunters, and while diving down on the last pair, and being outside the gun range, fired a Sidewinder which impacted the ground well short of the target. Alam let go his second Sidewinder when he noticed the Hunters pulling up to avoid high tension wires. Even though Alam did not claim to see the result of the strike, he noticed the Hunter missing its canopy as he overtook it and saw the pilot descending by parachute.[61]

With unspent gun ammo and plenty of fuel, Alam decided to push on, hoping to catch the rest of the escaping Hunters. After crossing the Chenab river, Alam's wingman Akhtar called "Contact – Hunters 1 o'clock", and soon Alam also picked up the five Hunters flying in battle formation. As Alam dived on the low flying (100–200ft) Hunters, they all broke in one direction climbing and turning steeply to the left, putting them into loose line astern.[62] Turning very tightly and in excess of 5g, and at the limit of the Sabre's A-4 radar-ranging gunsight, Alam claims to have fired and hit all four Hunters. As the IAF was not forthcoming with its side of the story after the war, unnecessary controversy prevailed for decades about the actual number of aircraft hit in this short and sharp engagement. It was only decades later, when fresh research,[63] shed light on how so many Hunters filled the gunsight of Alam that day. While Alam was chasing the Hunters from the IAF's No. 27 Squadron which were egressing after their attack, another formation of five Hunters, belonging to No. 7 Squadron from Halwara and led by Wing Commander Toric Zachariah was ingressing towards Sargodha. This ingressing formation, after noticing the Sabre pair flown by Flight Lieutenant Imtiaz Bhatti and Flight Lieutenant Sadruddin Hossain, which were on the port side of Alam, called off their planned attack and turned left, placing them right in front of Alam. Alam had indeed hit all four Hunters he had aimed at. Squadron Leader D. S. Jog and his wingman Flight Lieutenant T.K. Choudhry, both from

No. 27 Squadron, managed to land back safely with badly holed Hunters. Squadron Leader Suresh B. Bhagwat and Flying Officer Jagdev Singh Brar, from No. 7 Squadron, were not so fortunate and were killed in action. The bodies of both the IAF pilots, along with the wreckage of their aircraft, were later found by Pakistani authorities.

Even before the war, Alam had developed a reputation for excellence in air-to-air combat and gunnery with above-average scores. Being a bachelor, the flight lines seem to have been his home, allowing him to grab every opportunity to fly. Such was his reputation, that not long before the war, one senior pilot sitting outside the crew room at Sargodha, and seeing Alam disembark from a Sabre, turned towards his colleagues and quipped 'Who is going to survive him!'. The ground crews also fondly recall Alam as being the one who always handed in the most detailed Form 781 after each sortie.[64]

A F-86F Sabre parked in its blast pen. (Authors' collection)

Flight Lieutenant M. Akbar dismounts from his Sabre. (Authors' collection)

The IAF put in two additional raids that day, both by Mysteres. The third raid of the day, which was detected by the outer belt of MOUs consisted of four Mysteres which pulled up for attack around 0945hrs and managed to catch an F-86F on the ORP, whose pilot Flight Lieutenant A.H. Malik, busy in preflight checks, managed to disembark for cover just in time. This was the only PAF aircraft to be lost on the ground for the entire duration of the war. The IAF claimed to have destroyed over seven aircraft during this raid.[65] The PAF investment in concealment and dummies had paid off handsomely.

The fourth and the last raid of the day, which was again detected by the MOUs, was over Sargodha at 1545hrs, and after making a quick pass, exited towards India. Two Sabres on CAP, one of which was being piloted by Flight Lieutenant A.H. Malik, were directed towards the fast-egressing Mysteres. Catching up to the tree-hugging Mysteres, Malik fired a Sidewinder after hearing the growling sound indicating lock-on. Flight Lieutenant U.B. Guha went down with his aircraft. Malik gave chase and fired on the other Mystére, which managed to escape unscathed. With one confirmed kill in the bag, Malik had managed to avenge his beloved Sabre before the day was out.

After suffering a high attrition rate, losing five aircraft along with their pilots in the effort to knock out Sargodha, the IAF seemed to reevaluate its plan and Sargodha was not subjected to any further daylight raids. The IAF also seems to have wasted effort in mounting strikes against various unused airfields such as Rahwali, Chander, Gujrat, and Pasrur. Even at Sargodha, some of the strikes had targeted various abandoned Second World War landing strips believing them to be part of the Sargodha airfield complex.

No. 19 Squadron, which had been flying CAS sorties throughout the day, mounted a strike against Srinagar airfield around 1600hrs, destroying two Dakota aircraft, one of which belonged to the IAF and the other to the Indian Airlines Corporation. A Caribou belonging to the United Nations Military Observer Group also went up in flames. The strike formation managed to recover safely at Peshawar without any damage.

While the PAF was stemming the IAF onslaught in the West, in East Pakistan, the lone sabre squadron was to mount its own little war, bringing carnage to the Indian Central Air Command (CAC).

The Action in the East
Prior to the 1960s, as no permanent squadron was deployed in East Pakistan, various squadrons had rotated through Dacca, including a flight from No. 14 Squadron.[66] When a decision was made in the early 1960s to house one jet fighter squadron permanently in East Pakistan, the honour fell to No. 14 Squadron. The squadron until then had been based at Mauripur after converting to Sabres during late 1956. At Mauripur the squadron had participated in numerous CENTO-organised exercises, honing their interception skills against hordes of raiding USAF and RAF bombers. The squadron also managed to lift the much-coveted Perry-Kerry Inter-Squadron Armament Competition Trophy in March 1964.

PAF No. 14 Squadron, then led by Squadron Leader Shabbir Hussain Syed, was permanently deployed to Tejgaon airfield in

Dacca on 7 October 1964 with its 12 F-86F Sabres and their 12 pilots.[67] No. 14 Squadron, flying from a single airfield with a single runway, was to face the Indian Central Air Command (CAC), spread over eight different Second World War-era airfields, with Kalaikunda being the main hub housing four squadrons.[68]

No. 14 Squadrons had received the alert and instructions from AHQ for dispersal and concealment of aircraft on 2 September. From then onwards the squadron also started maintaining twice a day CAPs by a pair of Sabres.[69] It was during one of these CAP missions, on 4 September, when Flight Lieutenant Hassan Akhtar ejected safely after his aircraft suffered a bird strike. Now left with only 11 Sabres, the odds for the lone squadron had become worse just before the showdown.

The six .50-cal machine guns of the F-86 were a powerful punch at the time the type was introduced but grew progressively less effective against more modern combat jets. (Authors' collection)

As war broke out in the West, the squadron was ordered by AHQ at 0800hrs to be ready for conducting immediate strikes, along with the caution to wait for clear-cut instructions before proceeding. The squadron mounted CAPs throughout the day expecting IAF strikes but made no enemy contact. The time difference of one hour between the two wings of Pakistan had precluded the dusk strikes in the East, so it was decided that No. 14 Squadron would instead strike at dawn. While No. 14 Squadron was gearing up for striking Kalaikunda, the Indian EAC and CAC were also preparing to attack and tackle the lone sabre squadron. At Kalaikunda, on the evening of 6 September, discussions were taking place between the visiting Air Officer Commanding CAC Air Vice Marshal Shivdev Singh, the base commander Group Captain M.B. Naik and the squadron commanders on how to carry out the offensive operations in the Eastern sector.[70] OC of the resident Canberra squadron, Wing Commander Peter Wilson, was tasked to strike Chittagong, while OC No. 14 Squadron Wing Commander La Fontaine, equipped with Hunters was tasked to hit Jessore. The EAC with its HQ at Shillong had planned to strike Kurmitola, a yet to be completed airfield north of Dacca, which IAF intelligence believed to be housing Sabres. The strikes and sweeps carried out subsequently against various unoccupied airfields or desolate landing strips provided little value. Two Sabres, one of which was being flown by Flight Lieutenant A.T.M. Aziz, were scrambled at 0537hrs on the morning of 7 September. Aziz announced contact with a Hunter, but nothing further was heard from him. It is believed that due to bad visibility and perhaps while concentrating on cockpit switches, his aircraft cartwheeled into the ground.[71] Now left with 10 aircraft and 10 pilots, the odds for the lone squadron had gotten even worst.

As words of IAF strikes on numerous unused airfields reached the squadron, a worried OC Squadron Leader Shabbir telephoned the top brass requesting permission to attack Kalaikunda. Assured of the squadron's readiness and preparations in carrying out the long-distance strike, approval was granted at 0525hrs.[72] After moving to East Pakistan, the squadron had changed its training philosophy with a higher emphasis on low-level strikes at extended

A ground crew tends to a Sabre's .50-cal guns. (PAF Museum)

ranges. To achieve the extreme ranges at the outer edge of the Sabres' endurance, flight profiles with four external tanks were flown leaving only the six 0.5-inch Browning guns for the attacks. Sluggish and a lot less manoeuvrable with the four tanks, this was not the favourite configuration of any Sabre jockey but considering this as a necessity, and with enough training sorties before the war, the pilots got comfortable with it.

Seven minutes after getting the goahead, the five-member Sabre formation was hurling down the runway at Tejgaon. Assembling in a tight arrowhead formation after take-off with Flight Lieutenant Tariq Habib Khan and Flying Officer M. Afzal Khan on the port side of the leader, and Flight Lieutenant Abdul Baseer Khan and Flight Lieutenant M. Abdul Haleem on his starboard the formation headed towards Kalaikunda at 200–300ft AGL. To give as little warning as possible the strike formation had planned their approach from over the sea. Struggling against heavy downpours and low cloud cover on the way, the formation reached close to Calcutta as the weather also cleared up. Using the big Hora Bridge on the Hugli river as a

Equipped with four external tanks, this F-86 was probably intended for a patrol mission. Note the different designs of the inboard and outboard tanks. The pilot is Squadron Leader Shabbir Hussain Syed, OC No. 14 Squadron at Dacca during the 1965 war. (Authors' collection)

Another strike against Kalaikunda to be conducted by a four-ship formation led by Flight Lieutenant M.A. Haleem was ordered by the Base Commander, Group Captain Ghulam Haider around 1030hrs. Haleem, a graduate of Fighter Leaders School, had joined the squadron in 1959 after completing his flying training in the USA and bagging the Top Gun award at William Air Force Base, Arizona.[75] Haleem suggested another target as Kalaikunda after being struck just four hours earlier would be on alert and would have dispersed the aircraft by now. His suggestion was overruled, and the heavy configuration four-ship Sabre formation led by Haleem with Flight Lieutenant Abdul Baseer, Flight Lieutenant Tariq Habib, and Flying Officer Muhammad Afzal Khan set course for Kalaikunda. Following the same route as during the previous strike and battling against the heavy downpour, the formation pulled over the airfield to deliver their attack. This time the Indians were ready. In the ensuing low-level air combat, Flying Officer Afzal perished after his aircraft was shot down by a Hunter flown by Flight Lieutenant Alfred Cooke.

reference point, the formation followed the railway tracks for the rest of the way. As the leader pulled up, finding the bustling airfield below, so did the rest of the formation one behind the other, calling contact. Squadron Leader Shabbir started the ball rolling with his No.2 in tow, by diving after the Canberras on the tarmac that seemed to be being armed or refuelled. Setting up a pattern and after each formation member had delivered multiple attacks, some as many as three, the formation exited the area. During the attacks, Flight Lieutenant Haleem had spotted four Hunters flying above, but for some unexplained reason, they never engaged the attacking Sabres and failed to give a chase on exit. After battling the bad weather on the way back, as well and keeping a good lookout for enemy aircraft, the formation landed safely at home base at 0744hrs.[73] The formation claimed to have destroyed 10 Canberra and two Hunter aircraft along with damage to a further five Canberras.[74]

As Haleem and Baseer exited the area, and while providing maximum cross-over support to each other, they had to do a hard turn to throw off a Hunter that was placing himself for an attack. The attacking Hunter, unable to cope with the turn and after crossing from left to right at a low level, did a 'split-S' manoeuvre, and unable to recover from it crashed into the ground towards the north.[76]

Tariq Habib, who was No. 3 in the formation, also managed to fight his way out of the area. After being intercepted by the Hunters, Tariq had punched his four tanks, but one had failed to jettison and

Pilots approach their flight-ready Sabres fitted with external tanks, Dacca. (Authors' collection)

Flight Lieutenant Tariq Habib poses in front of his Sabre. (Authors' collection)

An F-86F about to touch down on the runway at Dacca after a sortie. (Authors' collection)

during the ensuing combat, his flaps also got stuck in the down position. Tariq still managed to fight his way out of the trouble and landed back at Dacca with a damaged aircraft.[77] During this second raid, the formation claimed to have destroyed a further three Canberras, one C-119 and damaged two Hunters.[78]

Not content with the havoc it had caused at Kalaikunda, No. 14 Squadron turned its attention to other IAF airfields within reach. Baghdogra, an airfield in the 30km-wide Siliguri corridor that separated Nepal and East Pakistan, was stuck by a formation of four Sabres led by Squadron Leader Shabbir Hussain on 10 September. The strike claimed the destruction of four enemy aircraft along with damage to the airfield facilities such as hangars and the ATC building.[79]

On 14 September, Barrackpore and Agartala airfields were also attacked. Three aircraft were claimed as destroyed at Barrackpore, out of which the IAF admitted the loss of one C-119 and one Dakota. Discovering no worthwhile targets at Agartala, the ATC building was strafed, killing the civilian ATC officer.[80]

The IAF CAC and EAC by now had thrown in the towel, with many of the aircraft moved to deeper bases to keep them safe, and content with mounting CAPs only.[81] No offensive missions were undertaken by IAF in the East after the initial 26 sorties that were wasted on abandoned airfields.

As the word of the Baghdogra strike reached the GOC of the Eastern Command, Major General Fazl-e-Muqueem, and worried that the squadron's actions might result in a land invasion of East Pakistan for which the Pakistan Army was ill prepared, he advised the squadron to curtail their offensive operations. As the Base Commander failed to agree, it was suggested to send a message to GHQ. Instruction was received from AHQ around 16–17 September, "no more offensive operations; carry out defensive operations only".[82] For the remainder of the war, only air defence operations were carried out without any further enemy contact. No. 14 Squadron was to fight against even heavier odds against a much better-prepared foe in the 1971 war.

The Versatile Fighter

The F-104, due to its thin and stubby wings, was ill suited for the type of air combat that had taken place so far; slow turning fights at low to medium altitudes. The IAF pilots had accorded healthy respect to the F-104, disengaging and scattering whenever it had entered the battle area but other than utilising the F-104 as a bouncer to beef up the F-86 CAPs, PAF also had to find other novel ways of fully utilising this Mach 2 engineering marvel.

In the West, after the initial airfield strikes, PAF had been trying to keep the IAF on the backfoot with streams of night raids conducted by B-57s. IAF for its part, and after suffering high attrition rate during the initial day raids, had also entrusted its much larger fleet of Canberra bombers to disrupt PAF operations.

The F-104's radar-based fire control system meant that it was the only fighter in PAF's inventory which could take up the role of a night interceptor against IAF Canberras with any degree of credibility. In this role too, the F-104s were limited by lack of a comprehensive low-level radar network and the technology limitations of its onboard radar which suffered from ground clutter and limited search area. While most F-104s operated from Sargodha, a pair was deployed every night to Peshawar to provide night air defence over northern Pakistan.

The night intruding IAF Canberras were warned of the F-104s' presence by the Indian ground control radar at Amritsar and its own tail warning radar. On warning of an approaching F-104 the

A lineup of Starfighters at Sargodha prior to the 1965 war. (Authors' collection)

IAF Canberras would resort to sudden change in height making it difficult for F-104s to keep track of the target. The usual IAF method was to approach Pakistan at a medium altitude of 25–30,000ft and then descend to low level to approach the target. Close to the target the IAF Canberras would pull up to 8–10,000ft to avoid flak and then egress at low level climbing up to medium level after crossing into India. Given PAF's own night counterattack missions, IAF had deployed its Canberras at airbases deeper inside India and therefore range considerations were important while flying the hi-lo-lo-hi mission profile just described. PAF's counter to this tactic was to extend the arc F-104s would patrol at, hoping to intercept the Canberras as they climbed to medium altitude while egressing from Pakistan. CAPs of one or two F-104s and F-86 Sabres were flown against each wave of intruding Canberras. It was hoped that the Sabre, although lacking any night capability, could act as a deterrent using GCI and the infrared-homing heads of its Sidewinder missiles to detect and attack the Canberras at night.

The first positive contact between an F-104 and a Canberra took place on the night of 13–14 September, when Squadron Leader Middlecoat fired a Sidewinder on a Canberra in a blind intercept. An explosion was seen at a range of 4,000ft but no confirmation was possible as the encounter took place over Indian territory. A confirmed kill was obtained on the night of 21 September, when Squadron Leader Jamal A. Khan made radar intercept of an egressing Canberra and shot it down with an AIM-9B Sidewinder. In this engagement the IAF Canberra had climbed earlier than usual, perhaps due to fuel considerations, and failed to switch on its tail warning radar while climbing. The pilot managed to eject successfully and was captured.

One F-104 was lost on 17 September when Flying Officer G. O. Abbasi landed short of the runway during a dust storm at Peshawar airbase; miraculously the pilot still strapped in his seat was thrown clear of the crash and survived without any major injuries.

In another incident Flight Lieutenant Amjad Hussain intercepted an IAF Canberra near Lahore and positioned himself neatly behind it, only to experience short circuiting of the gun-missile selection switch rendering both weapons unusable. Amjad then flew alongside the Canberra with the IAF pilot looking at him. Other squadron pilots recall watching a long gun-camera film of this incident.[83]

Another supporting role was found for the F-104 in the reconnaissance arena. PAF's reconnaissance fleet consisted of RT-33 aircraft which were ill suited for any recconnaissance missions in a high threat area, therefore F-104s were used to escort any such recconnaissance missions and a pair of F-104s had to crisscross the slower RT-33 to maintain formation. On at least one such mission the PAF formation came across an IAF Hunter formation which appeared to be returning to its base. The IAF Hunter formation promptly scattered, and the PAF F-104s being deep into Indian territory with an RT-33 to escort, decided not to pursue matters. An innovative solution to the recconnaissance problem was found when two-seater F-104Bs were used as recconnaissance birds with the pilot in the back seat holding a handheld camera. The F-104B would fly extremely low, pulling up slightly near the target airbase and go inverted, allowing the pilot in the back seat to get a better view for recconnaissance photos.

That the IAF had nicknamed the Starfighters as "Badmash" (meaning scoundrel) shows the healthy respect it had for the aircraft. This respect was well demonstrated by the unchallenged sweeps the F-104s flew over Indian territory on a more or less standard basis. A number of PAF pilots reported that they hardly saw any IAF activity on such missions and when they did make contact with IAF aircraft they would promptly disengage and not rise to the bait. Most of these pilots now admit that such audacious missions were foolhardy as a single F-104 deep inside Indian territory would have had little chance against a well-planned and well flown interception.

On one occasion a faint sign of what might have been an ambush effort by the IAF was seen. On 11 September, Flight Lieutenant Hakimullah was orbiting over Indian territory, low on fuel he was about to turn for Pakistan when PAF radar at Sakesar, monitoring

Squadron Leader Jamal A. Khan prepares to step into his Starfighter at Sargodha. (Authors' collection)

IAF transmissions, reported two sections of IAF fighters reporting visual contact with the Starfighter. Flight Lieutenant Hakimullah spotted two Gnats below him and as he was placing his sights on one of the Gnats, he noticed that he was outside the firing parameters of AIM-9B missile. This necessitated a bit more repositioning, as he heard the missile tone, PAF radar warned him of two more contacts diving at him. He looked up and saw two MiG-21s diving at him, Hakimullah broke into them which took him further inside India. Given his fuel state, he broke in the opposite direction and engaged afterburner. Egressing he saw two more MiG-21s approaching him head-on. Diving down with afterburners engaged he broke the sound barrier, although the MiGs tried to pursue, the Starfighter was able to outrun the MiGs. Crossing over to Pakistan, Flight Lieutenant Hakimullah zoomed upto 25,000ft and reduced power. It was obvious that the Starfighter would not make it back to Sargodha with the remaining fuel, and the pilot elected to make a power-off approach to the disused airstrip at Risalwala. The Starfighter made a touch down at Risalewala with the engine flaming-out as the aircraft turned off the runway.

More decisive engagements between later model Soviet aircraft and the F-104 had to wait for December 1971 when India and Pakistan were again engaged in full-scale hostilities. The 1965 war ended with No. 9 Squadron flying 254 sorties of which 246 were day and night air defence, four escort and four counter-air missions.

Trading Blows
After dropping a total of 89 tons of bombs on the opening night of 6–7 September against the four IAF forward bases, the B-57s started a nightly milk run for the remainder of the war to keep the IAF on its toes. In total the B-57 force flew 195 missions, primarily targeting the IAF bases and radar installations, but some sorties were also flown in support of ground forces and were conducted during daytime, with Sabres providing top cover. During the first night of raids, many of the crews had flown three missions but for the remainder of war only two missions per night were allowed.

One problem faced by the PAF was the lack of any night reconnaissance capability to assess the damage being caused by the B-57 raids. The RT-33As being slow were deemed too vulnerable even when escorted by the F-104s for airfield reconnaissance. Visual reconnaissance conducted by an F-104 of Halwara after 6 September found the runway serviceable and this resulted in PAF high command deciding to broaden its airfield targets to include installations as well as runways.[84]

PAF lost its second B-57 of the war over Ambala on the night of 14 September when Flight Lieutenant Altaf Sheikh and his navigator Flight Lieutenant Bashir Chaudhry were shot down by heavy AAA. This was the 13th war mission for Sheikh, who had taken off from Peshawar around 2200hrs and was making his second diving run on the airfield, as during the first run the bombs had failed to release. Both the crew managed to eject safely and ended up as the first PAF POWs.

Another B-57 was lost in a landing accident on the night of 17–18th when Flight Lieutenant Mehmood Butt and his navigator Flight Lieutenant Khalid crashed while on finals to land at Risalpur. Mehmood is believed to have misjudged his approach due to disorientation caused by poor visibility.[85] This was the final loss of No. 31 Bomber Wing.

Table 6: Delivered B-57 bomb tonnage against various IAF targets during the 1965 war[86]

Target	Bomb load (in tons)
Halwara	134
Jodhpur	98
Adampur	85.5
Pathankot	77
Jamnagar	66.5
Sirsa	12
Jammu	10.5
Srinagar	7
Close Air Support	77.5
Beas Bridge	10.5
Amritsar Radar	14

The IAF also tried to use its substantial fleet of Canberras to target PAF airfields during the night raids. The IAF Canberras mostly delivered their payloads from higher altitudes, starting from 30,000ft at the start of the war and later from 8–9,000 ft staying clear of the intense AAA. This seems to have offered them safety from AAA but at the cost of accuracy. During the entire war, only two bombs out of an estimated 90 tons delivered by the Canberras targeting Sargodha came close to causing any substantial damage. One of the 1,000lb bombs landed 100ft from the main runway intersection without damaging the runway and the other, a Second World War vintage 4,000lb landed very close to the main fuel storage tank but failed to explode. On one occasion when an IAF Canberra pilot did push home his attack by delivering a 4,000lb 'block-buster' from 4,000ft over Peshawar on the night of 13–14 September, the luck seems to have gone PAF's way. The bomb landed in soft soil losing some of its blast impact and a small building took rest of the brunt, shielding 16 fully armed and fuelled B-57s. The most successful raid was carried out during daylight on the 21 September when six Canberras from IAF No. 16 Squadron flying from Agra managed to sneak in and deliver their payload of rockets and bombs on the Badin radar station, putting it out of service for a considerable duration.

The PAF B-57 crew in comparison preferred to pull up to 8,000ft over targets, and then deliver their payload in multiple dives at 4,000ft. This put them at greater risk of being hit by airfield AAA, but accuracy over safety concerns seems to have been preferred. At later stages of the war, when orders came in from top brass to deliver the attacks from 8,000ft to minimise exposure to AAA, it was strongly protested by the pilots, deeming it to be ineffective area bombing.[87] The B-57 crews were also quick to adapt to the threat by masking their attacks using innovative techniques such as cutting engines during dives to increase accuracy, yet at the same time throw off the enemy AAA crews about the direction of their attacks. Well planned approach routes and skip bombing techniques were employed to stay out of the engagement envelope of rumored SA-2 SAM sites while attacking Ambala airfield.

No. 31 Wing ended its war by flying 195 sorties out of which 167 sorties were deemed successful, delivering close to 600 tons of bombs. One pilot and navigator ended up as POW, and two other pilots and navigators gave their lives in the line of duty. The true extent of damage caused by the B-57 raids was only known decades later when the official Indian history of the war was made available online, which admitted to losing 35 aircraft on the ground in total.[88] Out of these, 13 were credited to the raids by the B-57s.

Cloak-and-Dagger

The role played by No. 24 ELINT Squadron based at Peshawar had always been shrouded in secrecy due to the very nature of their work. The fact of U2 flights being staged via Peshawar by the CIA is well known largely due to the U2 piloted by Francis Gary Powers being shot down on 1 May 1960, resulting in a diplomatic crisis between USA and Soviet Union. What is less known are the ELINT and telemetry missions flown by the US Navy, also from Peshawar, against Soviet missile tests sites such as Kapustin Yar among others, which were deemed so valuable to the National Security Agency, that after the US Navy team was evicted in the early 1960s for repeated violations of restricted Pakistani and Indian airspace, a compromise was reached which allowed US-owned special mission aircraft, but flown by PAF aircrew, to conduct the same missions.[89]

No. 24 Squadron was unique in the sense that it was raised as part of that compromise, manned by both US and Pakistani aircrew and had aircraft on strength that which were Pakistani- and US-owned. The squadron was raised on 5 December 1962, with Squadron Leader Mohammad Iqbal as its first OC and with a skeleton staff of pilots, navigators and maintenance crew.[90] The squadron was equipped with two specially modified RB-57Bs (S/N 52-1536 and 52-1573) between December 1962 and February 1963. These modifications were done at General Dynamics under the Big Safari program, which was a USAF-run program to modify aircraft for special purposes. These two special mission RB-57Bs, US-owned but sporting PAF insignia and marking were housed at one of the two large hangars available at Peshawar air station. While the USAF team maintained the telemetry suite, the maintenance and missions were conducted by the PAF. These aircraft were withdrawn from Peshawar in March 1964 and replaced with two RB-57F, S/N 63-13286 and 63-13287. The extensively modified RB-57Fs were entrusted with missions of telemetry collections against launches at Soviet missile ranges and like earlier examples, while US owned, were fully maintained and manned by PAF aircrews.[91] Approximately 40 PAF officers and enlisted personnel had been trained earlier in the USA for maintaining these sensitive aircraft along with flight training for pilots and navigators.

Two additional modified RB-57Bs (S/N 53-3934 and 53-3961), based on two B-57Bs taken from PAF No. 31 Wing, were also modified and these being PAF-owned were fitted with an ELINT suite and 40" focal length cameras, allowing them to be used against targets that interested Pakistan. While the US-owned RB-57F aircraft were used to fly telemetry intercepts against the USSR usually at 65,000ft by PAF aircrew wearing full pressure suits, the PAF-owned RB-57Bs were used to map ELINT signatures and photograph the entire length of the border with India.[92] This data was shared with various Pakistani intelligence services and also with Survey of Pakistan, allowing them to produce updated large-scale maps of the border regions.

Once the war broke out on 6 September, all telemetry missions for the US were stopped as the focus shifted towards supporting their own forces. Members of No. 24 Squadron were also listening in, when OC No. 19 Squadron, Squadron Leader Sajad Haider, was briefing his pilots for the first strike on Pathankot in the borrowed air-conditioned crew room of No. 24 Squadron. As part of a secret inhouse project, engineers from No. 215 R&D Squadron, which was also deployed at Peshawar, had developed a prototype airborne R/T (radio transmission) jammer. To support the initial strikes by jamming the communications, and spreading chaos, the jammer fitted RB-57F (S/N 63-13286), piloted by Flying Officer Jaweed Ahsan with Flight Lieutenant Tassawar Elahi in the backseat took off at 1530hrs. Setting up station south of Sargodha at 45,000ft, the RB-57F crew went to work as a strike formation of No. 19 Squadron headed towards Pathankot. After detecting the VHF transmission frequency of the Russian-made P-35 radar, the aircrew turned on the jammer, only to find it ineffective and describing it as a *'cat mewing in front of a lion'*.[93] Apparently to maintain secrecy, the jammer had not been tested thoroughly enough before the war. Hearing the Amritsar GCI vector airborne fighters from Halwara and Adampur towards the incoming Pathankot raid, the quick-thinking Ahsan and Elahi decided to improvise and started to interfere by mimicking the GCI's voice and vectoring the fighters in the opposite direction. In the chaos that ensued, the leader of the IAF formation, after exchanging some harsh words with the GCI, decided to abandon the intercept. No. 19 Squadron in the end was able to deliver the attack unopposed and the RB-57F recovered at Peshawar after its 4½ hour sortie. The squadron continued to fly similar sorties throughout the war to lesser effect, as the Indians became wiser after 6 September and had started changing frequencies regularly, along with using coded language and call signs.

The squadron lost its OC, Squadron Leader M. Iqbal, and his navigator, Flight Lieutenant Lodhi, in a tragic case of fratricide on 11 September, while they were practicing homing technique against an old Marconi radar deployed at Rahwali. The newly deployed Army air defence unit, entrusted with guarding the radar was not notified of the practice raid. Iqbal was considered something of a genius when it came to electronic warfare and was considered by the USAF to be absolutely essential for the successful standup of the operation.[94] As the USAF-PAF operation wound up after the war, and remained shrouded in secrecy for decades to come, one of the few senior USAF personnel who eventually spoke about it, recalled Iqbal as '…one of the finest officers with whom he had ever worked.'[95]

Towards Impasse

As the war progressed and the threat to airfields subsided, PAF turned its attention to providing maximum support to the various Army units and conducting fighter sweeps. Prior to the war, during the months of June, July and August, the PAF allocated one to two sorties every fortnight to various Army formations to enable them to practice the close air support procedures.[96] The Army units took this opportunity to train additional Forward Air Controllers (FAC), e.g. 6th Armoured Division, which only had four qualified FAC's in the entire division before June, managed to train enough soldiers to have two per major unit and one per minor unit by the end of August. During each training sortie, four to five FAC would participate and in the process would also be entertained by some low-level Sabre aerobatics.

Some of the aerial engagements took place when fighters from opposing forces ran into each other during CAS missions. Flight Lieutenant Saiful Azam, who had been seconded to No. 32 Wing[97] from No. 2 Squadron where he had been serving as instructor prior to the war, narrated one such mission to the authors:

> Around midday 19th September I was sitting in the alert tent listing to accomplishments of pilots who had flown missions the previous day against Indian Convoys of trucks, tanks and equipment on trailers, moving towards the Pakistan border in the Sialkot Sector.
>
> I had also flown one such mission on the 17th and wondered at their wisdom of sending such convoys without adequate air cover. The whole convoy was stretched along the road bumper

Sabres being prepared for another mission at Peshawar. (Authors' collection)

to bumper. The spacing between vehicles was so small that one could destroy or damage up to 5–6 soft skin vehicles in a single pass! We flew several missions that day destroying or damaging many. Anti-aircraft fire was generally small-arms fire, one could actually ignore it.

At about midafternoon a flight of four x F-86s was scrambled from Sargodha to an urgent army call for ground support in the Chawinda sector of Sialkot. I was #4 of this element led by Squadron Leader Azim Daudpota with Flight Lieutenant Mujtaba Quereshi #2 and my flight commander Flight Lieutenant S.M. Ahmed #3. On identifying the target we carried out, if I recall correctly, a total of six attacks including two rocket attacks. As we were preparing to exit four Gnats jumped us. I was still recovering from the dive of my last gun attack when I could make out calls from the leader to the formation members. The transmission was garbled, and I could not make out what he said. A section of two Gnats had got behind #3 piloted by SM Ahmad. Just then I saw two Gnats coming from my left trying to position behind me. I gave a call "Leader from Four, I am breaking off to engage Gnats" There was no response from anyone! I made a hard chandelle type left turn to engage the Gnats. The height was around 1,000 to 1,500 feet. As I gained height and crossed over the Gnats, instead of reversing I instinctively converted my chandelle to a barrel roll, inverted I could keep them in sight, when I recovered from the barrel roll I was comfortably placed behind the #2 of the pair.

I reduced power and used intermittent airbrakes to remain inside the turn of the Gnat. I quickly adjusted the gun sight settings to the wingspan of a Gnat, (I had mistaken them for Hunters) laid the "pipper" on the aircraft and fired a very short burst, perhaps ¾ of a second and immediately observed hits on the aft section of the aircraft. I recall flashes and pieces flying off and saw the pilot gently pull up and mercifully eject.

As I pulled up, the combat had occurred around 500 feet, I unexpectedly found the first of the pair of Gnats bang in front of me, slightly to my left and closing alarmingly. The Gnat probably responding to calls from his wingman appears to have slowed down and was in a 20 degree bank. I was less than 500 feet and closing fast, the pilot had his head turned looking back and I "felt" our eyes meet. I recall he did not have his smoked visors down. All I had to do is to make slight adjustment of the controls and fire. At that point, I still can't figure out, even after 40 years, what came over me! I banked away without opening fire. Could it be "looking" into the eyes of a fellow human being who appeared so helpless at that point, afraid of being hit by debris of an exploding aircraft or being fearfully low on fuel. Today I am a very happy man, completely satisfied with my action on that day, although many friends chided me for this decision.

I headed towards Sargodha at 500 feet. I could hear my leader asking other members of the flight if they had seen me eject. He repeated the call and said "I hope Azam has ejected and is safe". I was very moved by his concern for me and was desperate to inform him that, not only was I safe but had also shot down an enemy aircraft.

I heard #3 SM Ahmed's call telling the leader that he was hit and had lost his pressure instruments but as the aircraft was controllable he was heading for Sargodha. I also heard #2 Mujtaba give an all well call. Low on fuel I decided to slowly gain height. While climbing I took off my mask to check on the microphone connection, the plug had come off! As I reconnected the plug I had my transmitter functioning again. I joyfully informed my leader that I was fine and had shot down a Gnat. He was much relieved and directed us to land individually. At this point SM Ahmed requested me to give a chase up to the landing point, I declined politely, my fuel gauge was showing zero. I, however, had SM Ahmed on visual on his straight final. Suddenly I saw his left wing dip and the Sabre hit the ground short of the runway and explode in a ball of fire. I landed through the pall of thick black smoke, parked the aircraft in the pen and declared to the ground crew that SM Ahmed was no more. Bad ending to an otherwise successful mission.

SM Ahmed had skillfully nursed a disabled aircraft only to crash a few hundred feet from the runway. I went to my tent without talking to anyone. In the evening I decided to go to the mess to and try to forget the SM Ahmed tragedy. As I approached the bar, I could not believe my eyes! The man, I thought had been killed in the crash, was sitting on the bar stool nursing a broken wrist and a drink! It transpired that the ejection seat had somehow miraculously fired on impact and SM was thrown clear of the exploding aircraft![98]

The Gnat shot down by Saiful Azam was piloted by Flight Lieutenant Vijay Mayadev who managed to eject safely and was captured by the Pakistani troops. The IAF pilot on whom Saiful Azam took mercy is not known.[99]

Other than chance encounters during the CAS missions, PAF pilots also conducted CAPs, sometimes well inside Indian territory in the hopes of drawing out IAF fighters for combat. One such mission, flown by the very popular Squadron Leader Munir, is narrated by Flight Lieutenant Imtiaz Bhatti:

It was the 10th of September, 1965. Pilots assembled in the vicinity of Operations Room were discussing in a confident manner, their plans of shooting down Indian Jet fighters. Our Operations Officer, Sqn. Ldr. Munir, who was the central figure of this group said to me that since the 1st of September he had been waiting to shoot down an Indian aircraft, but was not afforded a chance as the Wing Commander M. Anwar Shamim had stopped him from participating in any mission likely to involve air combat. This was done because Sqn. Ldr. Munir stammered quite a bit, especially when he was excited. I had known Munir since I first joined a fighter Squadron where he was posted as a Flight Commander. Besides being a dashing pilot, he was an extremely good shot. He found his true metier only in the air. He was a man of endearing personality, always full of wit and humour. He was a popular figure throughout the Air Force.

Sqn. Ldr. Munir told me that if I agreed to fly as his wingman, he would be permitted to undertake a mission where he would be able to shoot down an Indian aircraft. I offered to fly as his wingman. Munir being the boss of operations, placed our names on top of the list of pilots detailed for air defence duties.

Pilots who lost their turn due to us, though equally eager, did not mind this sacrifice for Munir. We did not have to wait for long before we were placed on 'COCKPIT STANDBY'. We were scrambled soon after. After getting airborne, Munir contacted the radar controller. On radio, a cool, calm and collected voice said, 'Steer 120° (i.e. towards Khem Karan), climb to 20,000 feet'. When we reached Khem Karan we were told to patrol North to South a few miles inside Indian territory. With the passage of time, Munir was progressively becoming impatient with the radar controller for not being able to direct him on to an enemy aircraft. Controllers could not be blamed because apparently there were no Indian aircraft yet airborne to accept our challenge of patrolling inside their territory. 'Pu-Pu-Put me on them' was Munir's reply when radar controller told him that two bogies (un-identified enemy aircraft) were airborne from Halwara and were heading toward Khem Karan. The same cool, calm but now joyous voice said, "Steer 110°, when steady bogies will be 11 o'clock 15 miles". We whipped the aircraft towards the given direction. A minute later we were told that the bogies were very fast and high and were turning in for attack from left 9 o'clock. Both of us had not been able to spot them as yet. Munir called "... punch tanks". I saw his tanks leave the aircraft and tumble earthwards. We spotted two Gnats attacking us from the left. Munir called "B..... reak left". Before we could whip our aircraft into a sharp turn towards left, I saw smoke puffs being emitted from the nose of the Gnat formation leader's aircraft. He had opened fire. I continued turning hard towards the attacker. Gnat Leader stayed behind me firing. His No. 2 climbed up towards our right, perhaps to attack us again. I then saw Munir manoeuvring his aircraft hard to shoot the Gnat off my tail. I decided to continue the turn. Within no time Munir closed in range and I saw his .50 machine guns emit flames. Next moment Gnat behind me started trailing smoke and then spinning towards the ground. Before I could take a sigh of relief, I saw the other Gnat corning in to attack Munir. I called out, "Leader bogie 6 o'clock, break right". But Munir had his radio transmitter button pressed and was not listening.

This upset me a lot, because I did not like him getting shot without knowing and putting up a good fight. I continued transmitting the warning and tried to position myself behind that Gnat before it could open fire. The Gnat pilot had not yet positioned himself to fire when Munir left the transmitter button, heard my warning, whipped his aircraft into a right turn and threw the Gnat off his tail. In the meantime, I had just about closed into the firing range and opened fire. The Gnat dived away with a few bullet holes. After the war I was talking to some Army officers, one of them describing this fight told me that the Gnat which dived, hit the ground and exploded like a bomb. Munir had landed earlier and was waiting for me. As we shook hands he said "Bh – – – - atti Thank y ... ou very much. Th ...... rough out the fight l was t ... t ... rying to tell you that there is an aaa ... a ... aircraft firing at you.[100]

Squadron Leader Munir was to perish the next day on his ninth mission of the war when his Sabre took a direct AAA hit while attacking Amritsar radar.

Squadron Leader Sajad Haider, OC No. 19 Squadron and Flight Lieutenant M. Akbar stand beside an F-86 partially parked on perforated steel planking and alongside a sandbagged revetment. (PAF Museum)

The well camouflaged and heavily guarded IAF P-35 mobile radar deployed close to Amritsar city received considerable PAF attention throughout the war. Days earlier another Sabre, this time flown by Flight Lieutenant Sadruddin Hossain had been lost, but this time to friendly AAA. Sadruddin narrated that mission to the authors:

On 9 September 1965, I was one of the eight F-86Fs on a low-level strike mission: target Amritsar radar complex. Wing Commander M.A. Shamim, OC 33 Wing (later Air Marshal and C-in-C, PAF) was to be the leader with my squadron commander Squadron Leader M. Arshad (OC No. 15 Squadron) as the deputy leader of the formation. For reasons still unexplained, the formation leader made a navigational error and turned towards the target two minutes earlier than planned which actually brought us over Lahore rather than Amritsar. Everyone in the formation seemed to realise the mistake except for the leader who pressed on despite repeated warning from the deputy leader and others in the formation. Realising the mistake, Squadron Leader Arshad, who was the leader of the four aircraft in which I was No.4, decided to circle and hold in one place while calling the leader to correct the mistake. As a result, the two formations were soon separated considering the fact that we were flying at a speed of some 420 knots (approx. seven miles a minute) at tree-top level. The place was very close to the border and we were still in our territory when the Pak Army ack-ack units from the ground opened up on us taking us to be enemy aircraft. My aircraft picked up one of the shells under the left wing and began to spill fuel which soon turned into fire. I was asked to turn back towards the base and begin climbing. By the time I was around 1,200–1,500 feet above the ground, I realised it was time for me to go as by then the fire had engulfed part of the left wing. ... I was able to perform a perfect ejection and within a few minutes I was on the ground safe and sound.

I was picked up by the Army unit which had shot me down and, needless to say, they were totally surprised to see me. A lack of communication between the Army and the Air Force resulted in this unfortunate incident. Some Indian writers claiming that I was shot down by Indian ground fire are wrong. It was a classic case of same side which are not uncommon in such conflicts.[101]

On 13 September, while conducting CAP close to the Khem Karan Sector, around 30 nautical miles inside Indian territory a pair of two Sabres led by Flight Lieutenant Yousuf was vectored towards two Gnats that had taken off from Halwara. The wingman Flight Lieutenant Imtiaz Bhatti narrates the ensuing encounter:

Flt. Lt. Yousaf gave a call "Punch tanks". My tanks left the aircraft immediately, but I saw only one of his tanks tumble earth wards. I was about to inform him on the radio when I heard his brave and confident voice "My one tank has not gone, but we shall fight regardless". Soon after we saw two Gnats climbing towards us almost head on. We picked one each and within no time I saw the Gnat ahead of Flt. Lt. Yousaf smoking and spinning downwards. In the meantime, I had closed into the firing range. As I opened fire, a funny idea came to my mind. I decided to close in further and film the complete sequence of aircraft getting shot from point blank range. I stopped firing and tightened my turn to cut in and get closer. The Gnat surprised me by barrel rolling downwards and running away; something which a Gnat could do with F-86 so easily. I again opened fire and kept on firing till he was out of range. I came back with a heavy heart and at times laughing at

Pilots pose in front of their Sabres at Sargodha. Second from left is Flight Lieutenant Imtiaz Bhatti. (Authors' collection)

Squadron Leaders M.M. Alam and Jamal A. Khan engrossed in conversation. (Authors' collection)

myself. A few hours later we heard All India Radio announce the name of a brave pilot who had got injured in action and brought the damaged Gnat aircraft home and died in the cockpit after landing.[102]

Yousuf's victim was Flight Lieutenant Arvind N. Kale from IAF No. 2 Squadron, who managed to eject safely. Bhatti's quarry was Squadron Leader N.K. Malik who died of his injuries at the hospital after landing his damaged Gnat back at base. A few of the other aerial engagements were not so one sided. One of those took place on 16 September, when a pair of Sabres led by Squadron Leader M.M. Alam along with his young wingman Flying Officer Shaukat-ul-Islam while on CAP ran into another pair of Hunters from IAF No. 7 Squadron close to the Amritsar area. While Alam easily shot down the No. 2 Hunter flown by Flying Officer F.D. Bunsha using guns, his own wingman fell to the Hunter lead piloted by Flying Officer P.S. Pingale. As Shaukat-ul-Islam was descending by parachute after his successful ejection, he recalls seeing the No. 2 Hunter of the formation fly close to his parachute at approximately 10,000ft and then going into an uncontrolled dive, from which he never recovered, with his head resting on the left side of the canopy. Approaching close to the ground, Shaukat-ul-Islam noticed two persons, with one in uniform, aiming their weapons at him quickly followed by a few shots, one of which hit him. After being rescued from the baying crowd by the police, he was to become the third and final PAF POW of the war.

Flight Lieutenant Sharbat Ali Changezi bagged a Hunter over Lahore on 20 September, this possibly being a gun-camera film frame of the event. (Authors' collection)

Another aerial engagement took place close to Lahore on the afternoon of 20 September. Four Sabres that had taken off from Sargodha for CAP and led by Squadron Leader Sharbat Ali Changezi were soon to mingle with a mixed sweep of Hunters and Gnats. Changezi had Flight Lieutenant A. Malik as his wingman and the second pair was led by No. 3 in formation Flight Lieutenant Nazir Jilani with Flight Lieutenant Amanullah as his wingman. As Amanullah called contact with a pair of Hunters flying at 15,000ft, the rest of the Sabre formation after calling contact, armed the switches and dropped their tanks. Changezi and Malik dived after one, while Jilani and Amanullah went after the other.

The GCI had warned the formation about four bogies and in the heat of the battle, and perhaps due to the hazy conditions that are prevalent in the subcontinent during September, the formation had failed to pick up the two small Gnats lurking below. As Changezi was busy shooting down his Hunter, piloted by Squadron Leader L.D.P. Chatterjee from IAF No. 7 Squadron, Malik – busy in keeping his leader's tail clear – was surprised by a volley of 30mm cannon shells from a Gnat flown by Flight Lieutenant A.K. Mazumdar. Malik tried to nurse his damaged aircraft back to the base but ejected successfully enroute after aircraft became unflyable. Changezi's quarry, Chatterjee, went down with his aircraft. Jilani also managed to score hits on his target, a Hunter flown by Flight Lieutenant S.K. Sharma, who managed to eject safely just after crossing the border. This was the last aerial engagement of the Sabres that drew blood. The ceasefire came into effect on 23 September, bringing down the curtains on this short 17-day war.

The Tally and the Lessons

During the war PAF flew a total of 2,364 sorties and lost 20 aircraft to all causes. Out of these 20 losses, seven were lost in air combat, an equal number to combat and non-combat related accidents, two to fratricide, three to enemy AAA, and just one on the ground. Three aircrew ended up as POW and 13 were killed in action. After the war PAF gave generous access to many of the international aviation reporters, allowing the pilots to be freely interviewed. Since all the PAF fleet was made up of US-supplied aircraft, the US Military Assistance Advisory Group deployed in Pakistan, and which had intimate knowledge of the inventory, also confirmed the PAF losses.

IAF flew a total of 3,937 sorties and for its part had admitted the loss of 71 aircraft in total.[103] Fifty-nine aircraft are accepted as being lost in combat, and out of these, 35 are accepted to be lost on the ground, 18 during air combat and six lost to other causes. The remaining 12 aircraft including three Gnats, four Hunters, three Mysteres, one Canberra and one Austere are accepted as being lost in accidents or to other causes.[104] India also accepted the loss of 19 aircrew as killed and five who managed to eject safely within its own territory. Seven IAF aircrew ended up as being POWs.

Table 7: Breakdown of Armament Expended during the 1965 war[108]	
Type	Consumption
GAR-8	33
Bombs, HE	1,711
Bombs, Fire	73
20mm (B-57)	22,324
20mm (F-104)	942
.50 Cal (F-86 & T-33)	349,642
.303 (T-6G)	15,711
Rockets, 2.75"	8,024
Rockets, 5"	724
Rockets, 3" (T-6G)	198

If one takes into consideration all types of serviceable fighter, bomber, recconnaissance, training or transport aircraft (five C-130) types that were used in combat roles,[105] the attrition rate for PAF based on 20 aircraft lost to all causes turns out to be 10.41 percent. If only serviceable fighter and bomber types are taken as the benchmark,[106] the attrition rate works out to be 14.7 percent. The attrition rate drops to 5.72 percent and 8.08 percent respectively with the same aircraft strength, if taking into consideration only the 11 aircraft lost to enemy action and excluding the nine combat and non-combat related accidents or fratricide. The IAF for its part accepts an attrition of 12.8 percent which is counted based on available fleet strength of 460 aircraft and loss of 59 aircraft, while excluding aircraft lost to accidents.[107] The complete list of all PAF kills and losses is provided in the appendix.

Ground crew work on the Sabres at Dacca flight line. (Authors' collection)

Originally intended principally as an interceptor, the PAF came to employ the F-86 as a multi-role combat jet. It did yoeman duty delivering bombs during two Indo-Pakistan wars. (Authors' collection)

considered strictly "non-transferable". As things stood at about midday on 6 September, an increasing number of F-86s had been diverted for army air support (and some even kept on quick-reaction alert in the rocket-bomb ground-attack configuration) to provide emergency air support to Pakistan Army on the Lahore and Shakargarh fronts. As at other fighter bases, Sargodha too was required to hold a minimum number of F-86s committed to the air defence role, and all of them held a minimal number in reserve. However the decision to divert some of the Sargodha air defence planes would have posed a severe dilemma for the Theatre Headquarters. It was the first day of the fully-fledged war. There was a very high probability that the IAF would continue with its airfield attacks as it had since the early morning. The Air Defence AOC at Sakesar would have justifiably opposed any reduction, even temporary, in the protection that the AOC was mandated to guarantee to the PAF's critical launch bases. The Chief of Operations (Air Commodore Rahim Khan, who was later to command the air force) would have agreed with the AOC, even though the C-in-C could overrule the AOC. However, the C-in-C would not even consider such a weakening of the PAF's air defence guard at a most critical time. In 1940, the RAF was in a similar dilemma during the Dunkirk retreat and the Battle of Britain. There is a record of angry exchanges between the RAF's tactical and air defence air marshals on even temporary transfers of air defence planes to meet the Allies' urgent tactical-strategic air demands. At one point, Prime Minister Churchill had to intervene personally in favour of the air defence staff.

During the war, PAF pilots fired a total of 33 Sidewinders, resulting in three confirmed kills: a poor ratio that needs to be understood in the context of unreliability of early generation heatseeking missiles, and their deployment at low level where much of the air combat took place.

Even though PAF had managed to perform well against a numerically superior foe, it too learned a few lessons of its own. The few hours delay in giving clearance for the launch of the initial strikes, had a ripple effect. With not enough time to reconfigure the aircraft or make additional aircraft serviceable, could there have been another option? Could the developing crisis have been resolved by temporarily taking away eight F-86s out of those assigned strictly for the air defence role at Sargodha? The air defence F-86s for the entire north were assigned to and controlled by a separate AOC, who ordered and watched over their use from his Sakesar radar air base. In principle, the F-86s committed for air defence were, however,

Another lesson learned was the overreliance on just one major airbase in the north. It was PAF's good fortune that repeated Canberra night attacks had failed to deposit any bombs on the runway, which would have severely hampered air support efforts for the hard-pressed ground troops. A few deficiencies in terms of operational tactics were also noted, one of these being the F-104 pilots' night interception training against only high-level ingress profiles of Canberras, resulting in limited success for the F-104 during the war.

3
THE INTERLUDE

During 1965–71, the Pakistan Air Force had to absorb, at the cost of significant combat capacity, five years of the US arms embargo which was imposed on Pakistan at the start of 1965 Indo-Pak war. During this period PAF had continued structurally to suffer a growing offence-defence imbalance with a dwindling number of B-57s and F-86s that had to be replaced by the lighter and shorter-range Chinese F-6s and a worsening obsolescence in its combat force. The older F-86s and B-57s were being supported with difficulty by clandestine and piecemeal purchases of spares and by some indigenous manufacture.

A foursome of B-57s are captured in a series of an aerial images of their formation. (Authors' collection)

Nevertheless, these years were also the most interesting, due to some highly innovative solutions adopted by PAF. These included inducting Chinese MiG-19s (called F-6 in PAF service), ex-Luftwaffe CAC Sabre F.Mk 6s through Iran (called F-86Es by PAF) and a more conventional solution of inducting French Mirage IIIs.

After the 1965 war, the most significant improvements occurred in the field of infrastructure. Between the wars, a number of new airfields were built or upgraded. Compared with the 1965 war, the PAF had twice the number of air bases for the 1971 war. All these bases had hardened aircraft shelters, protected command centres and enlarged fuel storage.

The PAF's peacetime communication network and war command communications were upgraded and modernised during 1966–1971. Owing to limited budgetary allocations in foreign currency, the PAF could not acquire a low-level radar network that it badly needed to cover the approaches to the likely land battle areas, the seaward threats to Karachi and some of the country's other vulnerable areas.

Adapting to the US Arms Embargo

The US arms embargo was damaging to the PAF in many ways. The adverse effects relating to spares support were, to some extent, made up by clandestine purchases from the world's black markets and also by indigenously producing some spare parts. Flying hours per pilot were more stringently rationed but the quality of training was not allowed to suffer. The PAF's leadership and its personnel seem to have applied exceptional inventiveness to offset a few of the many harmful consequences of the US arms embargo, and to maintain training standards and in keeping their tactics up to date.

The PAF introduced several measures to offset the adverse effects of the reduced hours that each combat pilot could fly during the five years of the arms embargo. A few of these measures that are known were the PAF temporarily set up new flying training areas that were closer to the air bases, thereby reducing, by about 30 percent, the flying time spent in travelling to and from the permanent training areas. The closer proximity entailed some risks in air traffic management, but the change enabled the squadron pilots to begin training manoeuvres very soon after take-off, and thus to consume more economically the available flying hours on each aircraft before it became due for its next scheduled inspection.[1] By this and other such means, the PAF pilots got attuned to flying shorter-duration sorties but with more training time packed in each.

The value of training sorties was enhanced by requiring more comprehensive ground briefings and whenever feasible the squadrons' veterans of the 1965 war briefed and led the training missions. For this purpose, pilots with war experience were kept in flying appointments longer.

Solo flights were discontinued as a rule, owing to their lower utility in combat training. Whenever a technical malfunction forced either a pair leader or wingman to abort his mission after starting engine(s), the other pilot was required also to shut down and not proceed, as was previously done, with a solo flight. The munition loads on each aircraft were reduced for all armament delivery sorties, to induce each pilot to deliver each attack with greater skill while he endeavoured to get a good armament score and grading.

EAGLES OF DESTINY VOLUME 2: GROWTH AND WARS OF THE PAKISTAN AIR FORCE 1956–1971

Originally aiming to establish four units of 24 operational aircraft and six reserves each, but then downsizing the complement in order to have a bigger number of units, through the late 1950s, the PAF received a total of 120 North American F-86F Sabres. The number grew to 150 as a result of attrition replacements. Pakistani Sabres were largely left in their bare metal overall livery decorated with coloured markings for each unit. The main artwork shows aircraft 53-1075 (c/n 202-5) from No. 17 Squadron (further recognisable by a small unit insignia in the form of a ram on a green circle with a green star), the colours of which were red and yellow. Inset is shown an example from No. 11 Squadron, which marked its Sabres in blue and red. (Artwork by Tom Cooper)

As standard for the entire PAF Sabre fleet early on, No. 15 Squadron applied its unit colours as red and white chequerboards on its F-86Fs. Notable is that the main serial – 55-5005 – (using an entirely different font to that used in the previous examples) was applied on the rear fuselage, and that the 'last two' were then repeated on the forward fuselage. Another minor difference in comparison to jets from other units was the size of the unit crest (a cobra in black and yellow on a white disc). (Artwork by Tom Cooper)

Another unit worked up on F-86Fs was No. 14 Squadron, which converted to this type in late 1956 at Mauripur AB. As shown on this reconstruction of the F-86F serial number 55-3856 (c/n 227-41), squadron colours were black and white, and thus its aircraft were decorated correspondingly. Unit insignia (hand with a sword on a white disc) was applied in the usual position, but the serial on the rear fuselage was in a much thicker font than usual. No aircraft of this squadron are known to have worn the 'last two' of their serial on the forward fuselage. On 2 February 1958, a joint formation of 16 Sabres from Nos. 11, 14, 15, 16, 17, 18, and 19 Squadrons made history by performing a loop in diamond formation over Mauripur. (Artwork by Tom Cooper)

This is a reconstruction of perhaps the most famous F-86F to serve with the PAF: serial 52-25026 (c/n 227-211). While it remains unknown if it was a 'personal' bird of Squadron Leader M. M. Alam, after the Indo-Pakistani War of 1965 it was decorated with a total of nine 'confirmed' and two 'possible/probable' kill markings in commemoration of his achievements, especially air combats fought on 7 September 1965 on the approaches to Sargodha air base. Later research by historians credit Alam with five confirmed kills during the war. The jet is shown with a slightly worn-out anti-glare panel on the top forward fuselage and equipped with the 200-gallon 'Misawa' drop tank. (Artwork by Tom Cooper)

Little known abroad, in Pakistan Squadron Leader S.A. Rafiqui was at least as famous as M. M. Alam for his achievements from the Indo-Pakistani War of 1965. He scored three confirmed kills, including two against de Havilland Vampires of the Indian Air Force, on 1 September 1965, and one against a Hunter on 6 September 1965. This is a reconstruction of the F-86F most likely flown by Rafiqui during the first engagement: serial number 53-1182. The jet is known to have served in more or less the same livery into the early 1980s. While Rafiqui used his six Browning 12.7mm machine guns for all three victories, this Sabre is shown as armed with an AIM-9B Sidewinder infrared-homing air-to-air missile: still a relatively unusual appearance within the PAF Sabre fleet of the time. (Artwork by Tom Cooper)

In 1966, Imperial Iran purchased a total of 90 Canadair-built Sabre F.Mk 6s from West Germany. On arrival, these were forwarded to Pakistan, ostensibly 'for overhauls'. Actually, Pakistan retained and pressed them into service with four squadrons under the designation 'F-86E'. These Orenda 14-powered jets were more powerful than older F-86Fs. The majority of Sabre F.Mk 6s arrived in Pakistan painted as shown here, in RAL 7012 *Basaltgrau* (basalt grey) and RAL 6014 *Gelboliv* (yellow-olive) on upper surfaces and sides, and RAL 7001 *Silvergrau* (silver grey) on undersurfaces. 120-gallon drop tanks were usually painted in *Basaltgrau* and *Silvergrau*, but many of the 200-gallon drop tanks delivered from Germany were painted in matt black overall. The jet is shown with a SNEB pod for 68mm unguided rockets under the centre underwing hardpoint, and an AIM-9B Sidewinder under the inboard pylon. (Artwork by Tom Cooper)

A handful of ex-German Sabre F.Mk 6s underwent overhauls prior to delivery and thus arrived in Pakistan painted in non-standard colours, including RAL 7015 *Schiefgrau* and RAL 6015 *Schwarzoliv* on upper surfaces, and BS381C/636 PRU Blue on undersurfaces. One of these was the example wearing the serial number 1592, shown here as 'fully packed' for a close air support sortie during the Indo-Pakistani War of 1971. This included (from outer towards inboard underwing hardpoints) a 200-gallon drop tank, a SNEB launcher for unguided rockets (or an AN-M65A1 1 000lb/500kg bomb), and an AIM-9B Sidewinder. (Artwork by Tom Cooper)

The first US-made jet-powered aircraft to be operated by Pakistan was the Lockheed T-33A Shooting Star, a two-seat jet trainer. In 1955–1956, Initially Pakistan was given 10 T-33 aircraft and a further 33 were delivered in later years. Initially, all were operated by No. 2 Squadron from Mauripur AB, and served for jet fighter conversion. When it became obvious that a new war with India was inevitable, in 1971 No. 2 Squadron had its T-33As modified through the addition of underwing hardpoints for US-made AN-M64A1 500lb (250kg) bombs: painted in dark green overall, jets of this unit flew a total of 39 combat sorties during the Indo-Pakistan War of 1971. Pakistani T-33As continued serving into the 1980s, when replaced by more modern types. (Artwork by Tom Cooper)

In addition to T-33As, Pakistan received six RT-33A reconnaissance jets. This variant received quite a sophisticated outfit including three Kodak K18 and one K22 camera in the nose, additional equipment for which was installed inside the rear cockpit. The type was initially operated by the 1st Tactical Reconnaissance Squadron. This example was one of two that served with No. 14 Squadron in East Pakistan as of the late 1960s and early 1970s, by when it received a camouflage pattern consisting of light blue and dark green on top surfaces and sides, and light grey on undersides. Unlike T-33As, RT-33As were never armed. (Artwork by Tom Cooper)

After the shootdown over the USSR of the U-2 piloted by Gary Powers, the USA concluded that there was a Soviet threat to Pakistan, and thus decided to supply 10 Lockheed F-104A Starfighter interceptors. The first arrived by ship in Kharachi in August 1961. Pakistani Starfighters were left in their original, highly polished 'bare metal overall' livery, and had their wings painted in white for the first few years of service. Initially, they could carry AIM-9B Sidewinder missiles on their wingtips only: underwing pylons were reserved for drop tanks. This example was modified through the installation of the Short-range Low Altitude Radar Detection system in the left side of its radome: it was shot down by anti-aircraft defences protecting the IAF radar in Amritsar on 5 December 1971. Flight Lieutenant Amjad Hussein ejected safely and was captured. (Artwork by Tom Cooper)

By the early 1970s, the era of air combat at high altitudes was over. The original weapons configuration of the F-104A caused much aerodynamic drag at low altitudes and thus technicians of No. 9 Squadron rewired the underwing hardpoints of surviving Starfighters to enable the installation of AIM-9Bs there. Henceforth, drop tanks were usually installed on wingtips. This jet was one of only eight still operational as of 1971: on 4 December that year, it was flown by Squadron Leader Rashid Bhatti into an air combat in which it shot down a Sukhoi Su-7BMK of the Indian Air Force. 56-879 survived that war and presently serves as a gate guard at the PAF Academy in Risalpur. (Artwork by Tom Cooper)

As well as serving as conversion trainers, the PAF deployed its two two-seat F-104Bs into operational service during the wars with India in 1965 and in 1971, when the fleet – although depleted to just eight operational airframes – flew 104 combat sorties. During the latter conflict, the backseater usually operated a reconnaissance camera. Both two-seaters survived more than 10 years of operational service with No. 9 Squadron and were preserved: 57-1309 as a gate guard in Risalpur and 57-1312 can be seen at the PAF Museum in Risalpur. (Artwork by Tom Cooper)

Between November 1959 and March 1960, the PAF received 24 Martin B-57B and two B-57C bombers from USAF stocks, thus becoming the sole export customer for the US-variant of the English Electric Canberra. The aircraft in question were former mounts of the 345th Bomber Group taken from storage, and thus retained their glossy black overall colours, red serials applied on the fin, and the usual set of maintenance- and warning stencils. They entered service with Nos. 7 and 8 Bomber Squadrons, organised into the 31st Bomb Wing, the crews of which were trained in Pakistan by a Mobile Training Detachment of the US Air Force. (Artwork by Tom Cooper)

As of 1959, the PAF considered the B-57 to be obsolete and would have preferred the Douglas B-66 Destroyer. US President Eisenhower was against the delivery of the latter: instead, he accepted the Pakistani demand for B-57s to be delivered with equipment to the same standard as that of the US Air Force. Because the B-57Bs arrived without the RB-1A George Peach bombing systems, these were drawn from stocks held at the Warner-Robins Logistic Centre, transferred to Masroor AB and in 1961–1962 retrofitted to all the aircraft by PAF technicians (the original noses were returned to the USA). Pakistani B-57B/Cs thus soldiered for most of their service in the configuration depicted here. This B-57C wore the three-star insignia and title of the C-in-C PAF, Air Marshal Asghar Khan, who preferred to pilot it instead of travelling on a lumbering transport whenever visiting Dacca in East Pakistan. (Artwork by Tom Cooper)

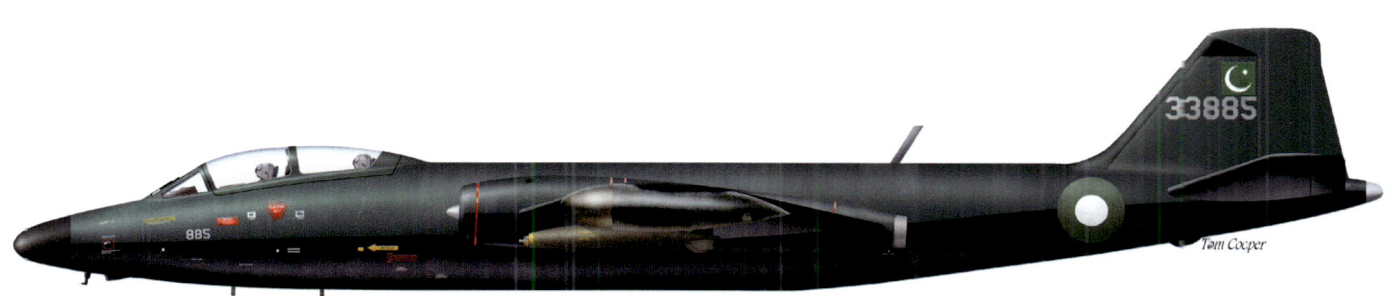

The PAF applied several additional modifications to its B-57 fleet: one included expansion of the fuel system to enable the carriage of underwing drop tanks, while another resulted in two jets being converted to RB-57B high-altitude strategic reconnaissance aircraft. Pakistani B-57s are known to have flown 167 combat sorties during the Indo-Pakistani War of 1965. By 1970, the surviving 17 B-57B/Cs and the sole RB-57B were suffering from shortages of spares, and the fleet was consolidated within No. 7 Squadron. By this time, all had their top surfaces painted in dark green, and serials reapplied in light grey, as shown here. Like all US-made examples, they could carry up to two US-made Mk.83 (1,000lbs/500kg) bombs on underwing pylons, in addition to nine Mk.82 (500lbs/250kg) bombs in the internal bomb bay. (Artwork by Tom Cooper)

This Mirage IIIEP is shown configured for quick-reaction alert and intercept operations. Its armament consisted of a pair of AIM-9B Sidewinders installed on outboard underwing pylons, and a single Matra R.530 air-to-air missile under the centreline, while two 500-litre 'supersonic' drop tanks were usually installed on inboard underwing pylons. R.530s proved too limited due to their short and narrow engagement envelope – especially at low altitude – and their operational deployment was discontinued after only a few days of the Indo-Pakistani War of 1971. All PAF Mirage IIIs wore a standardised camouflage pattern in *gris bleu tres fonce* (dark grey) and *vert fonce* (dark green) on top surfaces and sides, and *gris bleu clair* (light blue) on undersides. (Artwork by Tom Cooper)

Although the Mirage IIIEP could carry heavier warloads, during the Indo-Pakistani War of 1971 the range and speed were at premium, and thus No. 5 Squadron usually configured its aircraft as shown here: a pair of US-made M117 (750lbs/375kg) bombs was installed tandem under the centreline; inboard underwing hardpoints were occupied by 1,300-litre drop tanks, while a pair of AIM-9Bs was carried for self-defence purposes – in addition to the two internally-installed DEFA 552 autocannons (with 125 rounds per cannon). Eventually, the fleet undertook 38 offensive counter-air operations during that conflict, without suffering any losses. (Artwork by Tom Cooper)

In addition to 18 Mirage IIIEP interceptors and fighter-bombers, PAF acquired a total of three Mirage IIIDP two-seat conversion trainers (shown in the main artwork) and three Mirage IIIRP reconnaissance fighters. Both retained their combat capability but only the reconnaissance jets of No. 5 Squadron – which had five Omera Type 31 cameras installed in their nose, in place of the Cyrano II radar – undertook operational sorties in 1971. Twenty-two of the 36 sorties were concluded as successful in collecting precious intelligence about developments on the frontline. While both the IIIDP and the IIIRP are shown as equipped with 1,300-litre drop tanks under their inboard pylons, the lower inset shows a 1,700-litre ferry drop tank used for long-range combat air patrols, or for ferry sorties during peacetime. (Artwork by Tom Cooper)

Pakistan received the first four Lockheed C-130B Hercules within the MDAP program in 1963–1964. The first batch included serials 58-073 (coded X), 61-2646 (coded B, later M), 61-2648, and 62-3494 (coded R). Two additional Lockheed L-100s (civilian variant of the C-130B were acquired via Pakistan International Airlines and wore the serials 64144 (coded T) and 64145 (coded U). As of 1965, five served with No. 6 Squadron and originally wore the bare metal overall livery, shown here on the C-130E 62-4140/B, acquired with the second batch, to replace several losses in mishaps. Other aircraft from the same batch included 62-4141/F (later A), 62-4142, and 62-4143/O. (Artwork by Tom Cooper)

By 1964, the PAF Hercules fleet had been reinforced through the acquisition of six C-130B/Es from Iran. These included aircraft with Iranian serial numbers 5-101 (redesignated as 62-3488/P in Pakistan), 5-106/5-102 (10687/D re-coded H), 5-108/5-103 (10689/S), 5-109/5-104 (64310/J), 5-111/5-106 (64312/L), and 5-114/5-108 (14727/S). Like other C-130Bs, C-130Es, and L-100s acquired around the same time, all were initially kept in their bare metal overall livery. This is a reconstruction of one of the ex-Iranian C-130Es: the former 5-109/5-104, which received the serial number 64310 in PAF service, and wore the large crest of the Pakistan Air Force applied behind the cockpit. (Artwork by Tom Cooper)

Nominally a 'lumbering transport' not supposed to venture anywhere near the combat zone, the Pakistani C-130 fleet saw intensive action during the war of 1965. CO No. 6 Squadron, Wing Commander Eric Gordan Hall, began deploying his aircraft as bombers loaded with 45 Mk.82 (500lb/250kg) bombs which were rolled out on pallets from the rear ramp. In addition, three Hercules were deployed for dropping parachute commandos into Indian territory by night; for this purpose, the ex-Iranian C-130B (former 5-104, redesignated as 23491/W), received a makeshift camouflage pattern in a colour similar to light stone (BS381C/361) on upper surfaces and sides, with big splotches in olive green on top wing surfaces and the fin only. (Artwork by Tom Cooper)

The C-130s of No. 6 Squadron saw yet more action during the Indo-Pakistan War of 1971, when its crews flew five nocturnal air strikes on IAF air bases, five close support- and one interdiction sorties as 'bombers'. By this time, this C-130E (62-4143/O) was painted in the same light blue and dark green as used on B-57s and T-33s, applied to a standardised camouflage pattern on top surfaces and sides. In addition to the undersides, the lower half of the fuselage was oversprayed in BS381C/636 PRU Blue to better conceal the aircraft during nocturnal operations over enemy territory. (Artwork by Tom Cooper)

The PAF's sizeable fleet of Bristol B170 Freighter C.Mk 31s was phased out by 1966. By then, many aircraft – including S4417 shown here – had received makeshift camouflage patterns in olive green and dark green, often applied crudely atop of their original livery in white on the top fuselage, and bare metal elsewhere. Codes – in the case of this Freighter C.Mk 31M: 'J' – were still worn on the front cargo doors. (Artwork by Tom Cooper)

About 20 North American T-6B/C Harvards acquired in 1948, reinforced by additional examples purchased from the USA and Canada during the 1950s, served as basic and advanced trainers at the PAF Academy in Risalpur through the 1960s and into 1970s. All were painted in yellow overall, with a black anti-glare panel along the forward fuselage, some additionally marked with red on the spinner and around the front engine cowling. Classic, large black codes were positioned near the centre of the fuselage and completed by serials to the rear. Reportedly, by 1971, the overall yellow was replaced by overall dark green but sadly, there are no visual references. (Artwork by Tom Cooper)

In 1966–1967, the People's Republic of China supplied 12 bombers as a reinforcement for the PAF. While designated 'B-56' in Pakistani service, it remains unclear if these were Soviet-manufactured Ilyushin Il-28s, or their Chinese copy, the Harbin H-5, which is known to have entered production around the same time (this had a slightly different form for the power-driven barbette with two 23mm cannon in the rear, as depicted here). All were painted in semi-glossy black overall and received at least a minimal set of maintenance and warning insignia. As with the B-57s, they wore serials applied in red. After proving tough to fly and operate at low altitude by night, all the B-56s were withdrawn from service before the war of 1971. (Artwork by Tom Cooper)

Another Chinese-made type proved much more successful in service with the PAF: the Shenyang F-6. Pakistan originally received 90 aircraft from early production batches: these replaced old F-86Fs of No. 11 Squadron in 1966, and subsequently enabled the establishment of two new units, Nos. 23 and 25 Squadrons. The PAF was quick to start applying numerous modifications to them, and thus by December 1971 the majority of its F-6s appeared as depicted in this example from No. 11 Squadron, including launch rails for AIM-9B Sidewinder missiles on outboard pylons and ORO-57 pods for unguided 57mm rockets on inboard underwing pylons. (Artwork by Tom Cooper)

During the Indo-Pakistan War of 1971, the threat of IAF raids on its bases forced the PAF to start applying camouflage colours to its fighters. In the case of F-6s, the colours used depended on availability and timing: some aircraft received dark grey (or grey-green) on upper surfaces and sides, and light blue on undersides, applied atop a layer of varnish, which gave them a relatively clean appearance, as illustrated here. A few other jets received much more elaborate patterns including sand, dark brown, and dark green colours, but applied without varnish: this resulted in colours suffering wear and tear and starting to chip off. (Artwork by Tom Cooper)

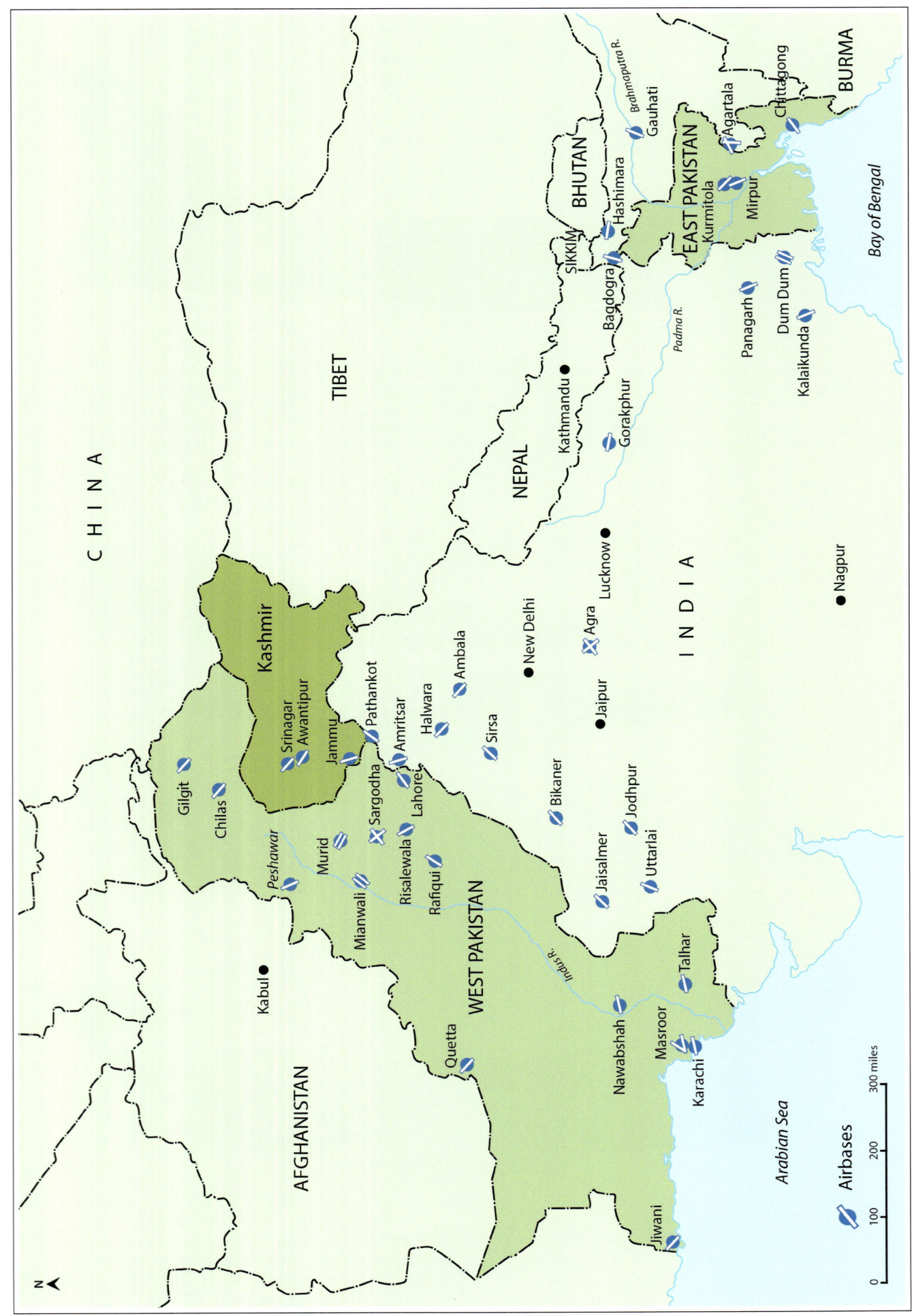
The opposing air force bases for the 1971 Indo-Pakistan War. (Map by George Anderson)

Table 8: PAF Rocketing Standards in Terms of USAF Standards[2]			
USAF standards	Percentage of PAF Pilots achieved standards in terms of USAF standards		
	1964	1967	1968
Exceptional 0'– 30'	10.9%	21.2%	59.9%
Above Average 31'– 45'	21.8%	46.2%	28.5%
Average 46'–60'	21.8%	26.3%	8.5%
Below Average 61'– and above	45.5%	6.3%	3.1%

element of combat expertise and leadership in each squadron.[3]

The PAF introduced one other training aid, better to prepare the pilots who were gearing up for the 1971 war. After collecting all the air combat and air-to-ground gun-camera films of the 1965 war, these were spliced together and compiled by mission types. Several sets of copies of each type were prepared for the combat units. These hundreds of short movie clips included many examples of both skillful and incompetent shooting by pilots in the heat of battle. For each combat wing, a set of this wartime footage was provided for frequent screening and discussion in the crew rooms, to draw both lessons and inspiration.

RAF and PAF officers mingle after a training exercise at Peshawar, early 1971. (Rod Dean)

Following the USAF, the PAF was one of the first air forces to introduce Dissimilar Air Combat Training (DACT) during the period. Unlike the past, now the Pakistani pilots began to train in simulated air combat by confronting PAF aircraft types that were unlike their own and behaved more like their enemies. For example, (starting from both defensive and offensive positions) pairs of F-86s would be pitched against two or four Mirages or F-6s that would use power and manoeuvre boundaries similar to those of the MiG-21 or Su-7s. The object was to train the F-86 pilots in the various ways in which to exploit the F-86 characteristics and strengths to defeat the MiG-21s and Su-7s, whose profiles would be acted out by the Mirages and F-6s. The PAF used the DACT training program to train Mirage, F-6 and F-104 pilots as well, in different settings. The programme is

Throughout the embargo years, the PAF maintained professional contacts (some of them discreet) with the leading combat training institutions of the USAF, the RAF and the French Air Force. This helped the PAF to reassure itself that its knowledge base was not eroding and that it was able to keep itself updated. The PAF quickly evaluated for their relevance any new tactics or techniques and adopted them where necessary. Those veterans of the 1965 war who had been promoted to the rank of Squadron Leader or Wing Commander and had been transferred to training, staff or other non-flying duties were returned to the squadrons to be employed as regular combat pilots for the 1971 war. This injected a heavier

Squadron Leader Sharbat Ali Changezi (in the middle) flanked by two Turkish Air Force exchange pilots during a training exercise at a PAF base. (Authors' collection)

An F-6 caught in the crosshairs of a visiting RAF Hunter, tries to dive and get away – early 1971. (Rod Dean)

believed to have significantly enhanced the confidence of younger pilots who fought in the 1971 war.

The PAF also benefited significantly from its investments in India-based intelligence resources. These agents provided the PAF invaluable data on the IAF's state of training, tactics, morale, aircraft serviceability rates and many other pieces of information, during both the pre-war months and the actual war. It bears mentioning here that throughout the 1971 crisis, the PAF pilots (as most Pakistanis) were furious at the Indo-Soviet collusion that was clearly aimed at exploiting Pakistan's internal turmoil and at the egotistical and mutually destructive policies of its political leaders in the two wings. While they were acutely conscious of their crucial role in the imposed war, their anger was focused on India and they remained aggressively motivated throughout.

The PAF also adopted a wide range of operational-logistic measures to minimise the effects of the US arms embargo and the very tight budgetary allocations during the five years between the two wars. Some of the logistic measures included periodic aircraft inspections being compressed to reduce the number of days that the aircraft would remain on the ground. The PAF authorised its senior engineering officers to exercise their best judgements in deciding not to change certain component and structural part on the mandated calendar-basis, provided they were satisfied that the subject part was in good physical condition.

So long as an aircraft was fit to fly and deliver armament effectively, the PAF also authorised its experienced engineers to waive the requirement of removing minor technical faults that would ordinarily call for new spare parts. This was always done in consultation with the squadron commanders and the procedure made it possible for the PAF to maintain a larger number of aircraft on a combat-ready status.

The recommended grade of fuel that was different for F-6 fighters from that used on the other PAF jets was standardised to one type. At a slightly increased safety risk, this enforced fuel commonality removed the necessity of maintaining two types of jet fuel and their costly separate storage at most air bases.

Several spare parts were manufactured indigenously at the PAF's own engineering depots. The civil industries in Karachi, Lahore, Sialkot, Gujrat and some other cities were also enlisted to produce a number of simpler spare parts that were not available, or whose delivery was subject to long lead times or exorbitant costs.

The F-104 fleet was hit the hardest due to the US arms embargo. Almost all the No. 9 Squadron pilots were very experienced on the F-104 and did not need more than about 8–10 hours per month to maintain proficiency on it. Invariably, they also had hundreds of hours experience on the F-86 and many had converted effectively on the F-6 as well. Due to the very restricted availability of F-104 spares from the black markets, the PAF decided to augment the F-104 squadron pilots' overall flying per month by allocating to them some of the flying hours being generated by the F-6 fleet. This was not a unique arrangement and had the benefit of some dual-qualification pilots being available for combat duty on the two larger fleets (F-86 and F-6) in the event that the number of F-104s diminished in war. If the need arose in war, a substantial number of the F-104, Mirage and F-6 pilots could, at short notice, switch proficiently to fight on at least one other type of fighter.

These measures increased substantially the PAF's combat effectiveness and helped in creating a less adverse balance between the unequal rival air forces.

Induction of the F-6

After the imposition of American sanctions, forestalling any further chances of receiving new hardware or spares for the existing fleet from American sources, PAF availed the opportunity to acquire a substantial number of F-6 aircraft from China. The initial lot of 60 aircraft was supplied as a goodwill gesture by the Chinese government at no cost. This was to be the second supersonic aircraft to enter PAF service.

In October 1965, a team of 13 pilots selected from various staff and training units, along with a group of technicians and engineers assembled at Drigh Road for their onward journey to China.[4] The team was to be led by Wing Commander Mian Sadruddin who many years earlier had also led the induction of F-104 into the PAF service. It was only at Drigh Road, that the assembled team was told that they would be proceeding to China for two months for conversion on F-6 aircraft. The team flew to Dacca on board a PIA 720B and from there to Beijing on board a Chinese Il-18 and finally to their destination, a training base 200km southeast of Beijing.

The PAF team found the conditions at the base primitive but adequate. The major hurdle was the language barrier along with the more rigid training system patterned on the Russian style with an overemphasis on safety. Interpreters were used in bridging the language barrier during ground school and also during initial conversion sorties, conducted in dual-seat UMiG-15s, where if a PAF pilot had any questions, he would call the tower where an interpreter would translate it for the Chinese instructor pilot seated in the back seat, and relay back the answer in English. During the two months, each pilot flew approximately 10 hours comprising about 20 sorties.[5] The team returned to Pakistan and after two months, on 20 December 1965, 12 pilots left Sargodha in a C-130 for Hotien to ferry the first lot of F-6 aircraft accompanied by PAF C-in-C Air Marshal Nur Khan. During the flight, the C-130 pilots were asked to fly as high as possible to gather wind speed data that could be utilised for the F-6 ferry flights. After reaching Hotien, a basic ceremony was conducted for formal acceptance of the aircraft. The C-in-C Nur Khan – forever eager to lead from the front – wanted to be part of the first ferry flight, which would also have been his first solo on the type but was persuaded against it after much trepidation considering his minimal experience on the type and the overcast conditions. The aircraft also came with a rudimentary attitude gyro that did not install any confidence.

Wing Commander Mian Sadruddin recalls:

> All 12 aircraft took off in succeeding flights of four breaking out of cloud at 30,000ft heading for Gilgit – the first leg. It was covered and they turned on time for Risalpur where the clearing of the undercast allowed a clear run to destination. Sargodha welcomed the arrival with a large gathering of all ranks. Another three ferries were completed before year end, bringing the inventory to 48 F-6.

After the delivery of the initial lot, the more demanding task of creating operational and maintenance procedures from scratch commenced. There was no English documentation available, except for a pamphlet called pilot notes, which noted that in case of spinning, it was caused by a 'pilot blunder', and no recovery procedure was outlined. A team of six Chinese technicians was at hand to assist with technical training but there was no such support for flight training. Flight instruments in metric with Chinese characters, along with other hand brakes and temperamental engines did not make the transition any easier.[6] Eventually through

created from scratch along with checklists following the USAF style of documentation.

In the process of creating aircraft manuals, PAF pilots also modified numerous Chinese operating instructions, one of these being the approach speed which was judged by experienced PAF pilots to be excessive. The approach speed was reduced by 20km to 300kph, this resulted in brakes not fading too rapidly in hot summer conditions and in case of chute failure, the aircraft could avoid barrier engagement in most instances.

While one challenge was the operational conversion of pilots to the F-6, another was the maintenance aspects of a completely new system devoid of documentation and procedures that varied substantially from what existing PAF technicians were accustomed to.

Wing Commander Abdul Latif recalls:

Air Marshal Asghar Khan with visiting dignitaries on the flightline, and inspecting a PAF hangar, with an F-104 under repair, Sargodha. (Authors' collection)

a process of improvisation, and innovation, where PAF pilots even carried out high altitude stall and spin recovery sorties to verify and document the flight characteristics of the aircraft to remove any worries owing to the absence of such information for air combat manoeuvring operational training. The aircraft flight manual was

The small group of technicians and engineers that was sent to China for training, learned about the aircraft systems through interpreters, who in most of the cases happened to be non-technical persons. The information so acquired had inherent draw-back of interpretation and inadequate description. The total technical literature that became available to PAF

Squadron Leader M. M. Alam poses with the visiting Chinese dignitaries. China assisted with several aircraft acquisitions during the period of the American embargo. (Authors' collection)

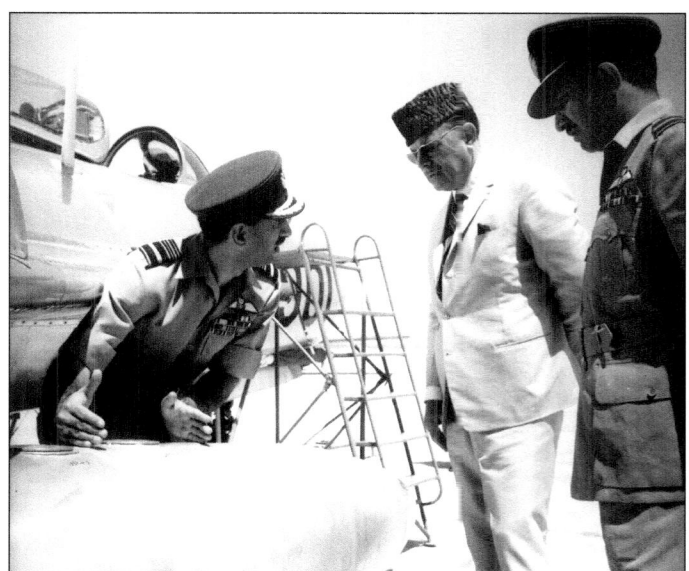

Air Marshal Nur Khan briefs the President after the delivery of F-6 aircraft to Pakistan as Air Commodore Masroor Hussain looks on – Sargodha. (Authors' collection)

consisted of the handwritten notes prepared by these technicians and certain wiring diagrams in the form of blueprints marked in Chinese. The aircraft came with a set of spares, toolboxes and a limited number of support equipment items. These were the circumstances under which flying and maintenance of F-6 aircraft was started at Sargodha. The most immediate requirement at the time was to prepare the inspection cards and maintenance manuals for the aircraft so that proper maintenance could be performed, and safe flying could be conducted. The notes available with various technicians were collected and scrutinised for authenticating their accuracy. Many cases of variations were detected which were clarified by actually checking the systems on the aircraft. A team was set up for preparing, as the first step, the inspection cards and then the aircraft maintenance manuals. This is perhaps the only case in the history of PAF where a Base produced a "Dash Two" (-2) for a newly inducted aircraft. The language barrier kept posing difficulties for a long time but it was never allowed to come in the way of reliable aircraft maintenance. A comprehensive training programme was started and a sizeable strength of trained technical manpower was built up in a few months. The training classes were conducted in the afternoon for allowing the instructors to attend to maintenance work during working hours. Using the parts breakdown manuals, that were in Chinese language, pre-issue and bench stocks were established for use by various work centres. The maintenance procedures were studied and modified to suit PAF requirements. Aircraft markings were changed to English, and a number of minor modifications were incorporated to improve aircraft operation or maintenance. A comprehensive programme was undertaken for fabricating the testers for testing pneumatic, hydraulic, electrical, instrument and electronic systems components. Some of the testers were liked so much by the Air Headquarters staff that they tasked the Base to mass produce these for use at other Bases once those Bases received F-6 aircraft.[7]

No. 23 Squadron, which was number-plated on 4 March 1964 after phasing out of Fury aircraft was reactivated and became one of the first two squadrons to be equipped with F-6 on 8 February 1966 at Sargodha. The other squadron to be equipped with F-6 during 1966 was No. 25 Squadron, which was formed at Sargodha on 1 June 1966. Both the squadrons were also entrusted with the additional responsibility of converting pilots on the F-6 aircraft and managed to convert 25 pilots each from other squadrons within the first three months. The third squadron to be equipped with F-6, also during 1966 was No. 11 Squadron, which was earlier equipped with Sabres.

Over the next few years, a large set of modifications were carried out to either increase the effectiveness of the system or to make maintenance easier and more efficient. This included modifications to allow employment of Sidewinder missile in April 1967 and carriage of additional underwing fuel tanks during February 1971. The additional fuel tanks allowed greater range for close air support missions but came at the cost of manoeuvrability and were not recommended for air-to-air engagements.

A two-seater trainer version (later to be called FT-6) for the F-6 was not available in the beginning and going solo after only ground

Flight Lieutenant Aftab Alam poses in front of newly inducted F-6s at Sargodha, which are then seen being manned. (Authors' collection)

instructions, no matter how thorough, was a demanding task on such a difficult aircraft. As the F-6 instruments and controls were quite different from the American aircraft, to which pilots were used too, PAF acquired three dual-seat MiG-15UTI (known as UMiG in PAF) to assist with the pilot transition to F-6.[8] The UMiGs were used for introducing the pilots to Chinese instruments and cockpit controls, along with checkout of pilots who had not flown for more than 30 days. The aircraft was found to be very basic and did not have the flight characteristics of the F-6, it was never used for advanced training.

Induction of the Mirage Aircraft

As the ratio of combat aircraft between the IAF and the PAF grew worse, and USA as a source of new major weapon systems remained shut, PAF evaluated various European options for its needs. In 1968, after two years of search and analyses, the Mirage IIIEP (single seat) was chosen for the PAF out of the very few non-US aircraft that met the PAF's Air Staff Requirements (ASRs) in some measure. The ASRs called for a multi-role strike aircraft that could gradually replace the ageing fleet of F-86s and B-57s but would also have some night/all-weather interception capabilities at low altitudes. The Mirage III did not fully meet the second requirement but was inducted as the best *available* aircraft meeting most of the ASRs. Eighteen Mirage IIIEPs were ordered along with three Mirage IIIDPs (two-seater) trainers and three Mirage IIIRPs with photoreconnaissance capability. The DPs and RPs could be used for strike missions as well. All these 24 Mirages were delivered prior to 1971 war to a single squadron, No. 5 Squadron based at Sargodha.

These aircraft were ordered under project code-name Blue Flash One. PAF at that time envisaged the phased induction of Mirage aircraft with these 24 being the first phase of this programme. A further batch of 28 Mirage 5PAs and two Mirage IIIDP aircraft were ordered in 1970 under Blue Flash Two. Delivery of these aircraft started well after the 1971 war. Two more batches consisting of 10 Mirage IIIRPs under Blue Flash Three and 18 Mirage 5PA2s, 12 Mirage 5PA3s and two Mirage-5DPA2s under Blue Flash Four were ordered in 1975 and 1979 respectively. The mix of the first 24 aircraft was determined to fill the most glaring gaps in the PAF orbat. The three RP variant aircraft would strengthen its tactical reconnaissance capability (till date limited to increasingly obsolescent RT-33s), the three DPs would allow local conversion of PAF pilots to Mirages while the 18 Mirage IIIEPs were equipped with Cyrano II radars and Doppler navigation systems. The latter would allow at least some night and all-weather operation capability. These aircraft were complemented with the purchase of R.530 AAMs while PAF's existing stock of AIM-9B Sidewinders were also made compatible with the Mirages.

The First Six in France

To ferry the initial lot of six aircraft from France and to become the nucleus of the future instructor force for the Mirage fleet, six pilots were handpicked for initial training in France. These were Wing Commander M.M. Alam, Squadron Leaders Hakimullah, Farooq Feroz Khan, Flight Lieutenants Arif Manzoor, Akhtar Rao and Farooq Umar.

Wing Commander Alam, the new OC for the squadron, was the leading scorer of the 1965 air war, Squadron Leaders Hakimullah, Farooq Feroz Khan and Flight Lieutenants Arif Manzoor and Farooq Umar were also '65 war veterans and the first two along with Flight Lieutenant Arif Manzoor were also F-104 pilots. Before proceeding to France for Mirage conversion, all six pilots spent some time flying F-104s with No. 9 squadron to gain more supersonic aircraft experience.

The initial lot of six pilots travelled to Paris at the end of 1967 and from there to conversion school at Mont-de-Marsan close to the Spanish border. They stayed there for approximately a month and a half doing MTD (Mobile Training Detachment) studying various systems of the aircraft. Afterwards these pilots went to Strassbourg to do Link Simulator training and having completed that returned to Mont-de-Marsan and there flew the dual-seat Mirage IIIDP with French instructors. After as little as three to five sorties in the dual seat, the pilots – in spite of European winter weather – were cleared to go solo. Most of the subsequent sorties were flown by the pilots to get acquainted with the tailless delta characteristics of the Mirage aircraft. They were also checked out on radars, though most pilots being experienced F-104 Starfighter jockeys were quite experienced with airborne radars and found the transition easy and comfortable.

The first batch of six aircraft (S/N 67-101 to 67-106) was ferried to Pakistan at the start of March 1968. After taking off from Mont-de-Marsan and a brief stop in Istres the formation flew over the Mediterranean and crossing over Milan, landed at Brindisi. After an overnight stay at Brindisi, the formation took off for Turkey

Air Marshal Nur Khan prepares to fly a sortie in one of the newly inducted Mirages at Sargodha. (Authors' collection)

A Mirage IIIEP photographed in France before delivery flight to Pakistan. (Mercillion Patrick, MBDA)

next morning and landed at Murted Air Base near Ankara. Next stop was Tehran International Airport where after an overnight stay, the formation took off for Mauripur (now called Masroor) Air Base and landed there on 8 March 1968. After a brief refuelling stop at Mauripur the aircraft took off for the last leg of their journey to the squadron home base, Sargodha.

The last Mirage III, a single-seat EP variant was ferried alone at the start of 1970 by Squadron Leader Farooq Umar, the Flight Commander of No. 5 Squadron and Flight Lieutenant Khalid Iqbal as reserve pilot.

Pre-War Training

The PAF Mirage conversion course included a lot of ground schooling, technical and especially avionics familiarisation, the theory and operation of the Doppler navigation system, and AI radar training. The first four course exercises were called C1, C2, C3 and C4 and flown in dual-seat Mirage IIIDPs with a qualified instructor. The exercises would be repeated in case the student was slow on the uptake. Finally, he was sent in the first solo chase mission, chased by an experienced pilot and this was followed by a second and in an odd case, third chase. Afterwards they were given a few solo missions to fly the aircraft near its performance envelop. This was followed by high level GCI missions to familiarise and make trainee pilots proficient in blind interceptions.

PAF has a tradition of rigorous training and unsurprisingly a high tempo training schedule was also maintained on Mirages with pilots clocking about 20 hours per month. Regular dissimilar air combat training exercises were held, and new tactics were developed on the Mirage, with Mirages preferring to keep fights at 400 knots plus, using afterburners and the vertical plane against better low-speed-turning Sabres and F-6s. Mutual support tactics between lead and wingman were practised with the lead engaging bogeys and wingman maintaining a higher energy level; intervening at a point where lead got into a low energy state. Delta winged Mirages would quickly bleed speed in a turn and had higher angle of attack limitations than the approximately 16-degree AoA limitation on Sabres and Hunters. These characteristics were used to develop specific tactics against better angle fighters. As a last-ditch escape maneuver a Mirage would in a descending vertical turn use higher AoA coupled with its full airframe for braking in a bid to force an overshoot by a tail-attacking bogey.

A limited quantity of Matra R.530 missiles were also obtained from France. On some air defence missions, Mirages would be configured with one underbelly R.530 and two AIM-9B Sidewinders (though only one R.530 was fired in the 1971 war). Some pilots using partial pressure suits also trained for high altitude intercepts and within No. 5 Squadron a batch of pilots also trained for photo recconnaissance missions on the three Mirage IIIRPs.

The Dwindling Starfighters

PAF lost two Starfighters during the 17-day conflict with India. Unlike the past these two losses were not replaced by the US given the arms embargo imposed on Pakistan. Therefore No. 9 Squadron was left with only eight F-104s and two F-104Bs after the hostilities.

In addition, PAF faced the problem of dwindling spare parts stocks for the aircraft which were also embargoed and had to be sourced from third party sources and the black market.

One F-104A aircraft (tail number 56-805) was written-off in 1967 in a ground accident. During aircraft start-up the starter unit did not disengage automatically due to an electrical failure and became overheated due to high revolutions per minute and caught fire. This fire spread to the engine and the aircraft was switched off. Despite efforts by fire tenders the aircraft was completely burnt. Yet another

Air Marshal Nur Khan with Squadron Leader Hakimullah in front of newly delivered Mirages. (Authors' collection)

Two Turkish Air Force officers smile as a PAF pilot makes air combat gestures. To date, the Turkish Air Force (Türk Hava Kuvvetleri) and PAF had maintained close contacts and pilot exchange programs. (Authors' collection)

F-104A was lost in 1968 when Flight Lieutenant G. Abbasi had a fatal crash while practicing low-level aerobatics near Mianwali (S/N 56-807). It is believed that during this practice mission he faced multiple technical problems which Board of Inquiry could not exactly pinpoint.

Flight training during this period added more emphasis to low-level night interceptions, which was not routinely practised before the 1965 war. This was made possible by PAF's acquisition of some low-level radars which were deployed to cover important areas and valuable points. To test the effectiveness of this radar system extensive night training was carried out for F-104 pilots and radar operators. In addition, air combat training missions were flown against other PAF aircraft. With the induction of Chinese F-6s in PAF and PAF's increasing experience of flying Soviet-built aircraft in the Middle East,[9] comparison between the types was increasingly common.

In terms of general handling, F-104 flight controls were slightly heavier than those of the F-6, and control response also slightly slower. However, the J79 engine responded much better to throttle inputs than the F-6. The Starfighter within its operating limitations had few vices while the F-6 exhibited adverse yaw at high angles of attack during low speed or high-G maneuvering which could lead to the aircraft entering a spin.

Within PAF it was assessed that F-104 was inferior in all flight regimes to the increasingly numerous MiG-21s with the Indian Air Force but superior to the Su-7s, also inducted by IAF. Especially in a close fight, the Starfighter was considered to be outmatched by the MiG-21 given its superior manoeuvrability and similar speed and acceleration. The PAF F-104 tactics made use of the aircraft's high speed to hit targets quickly, ideally using AIM-9B Sidewinder, and quickly egressing. Turning with more nimble fighters was not considered advisable.

Slowly but surely, the arms embargo on Pakistan started affecting F-104 flying, with the result that the aircraft were practically cocooned starting from December 1969. While some flying was managed on a regular basis, squadron pilots did the bulk of their day flying on F-6 aircraft with other squadrons. The Starfighters were pulled out of storage in July 1971 as hostilities with India built up.

Modifications and Innovations

Given its ageing reconnaissance capability with RT-33 aircraft, PAF attempted to use the F-104's high speed performance for such missions. During 1968–69, at least one of the two F-104Bs was modified to carry Swedish-made TA7M reconnaissance cameras in the rear seat. There were three cameras in one set of equipment, two oblique cameras and one vertical, with the vertical camera installed in the centre and oblique cameras installed on either side of the vertical camera. This setting provided a total photo coverage angle of 170 degrees. This gave the F-104B the capability to look deep inside enemy territory from a safe distance with the coverage area depending on the height at which the aircraft would be flying. This modification flew quite a few trial missions before the war and the results were very encouraging, though during the 1971 war the three available Mirage IIIRPs were considered sufficient, and the modified F-104Bs did not log any reconnaissance mission.

Another important modification was the installation of a radar detection device on a single F-104A aircraft. This device called SLARD (Short-range Low Altitude Radar Detection) and alternately Radar Locator (RALOR) was procured through an American source and initial trials were carried on a twin-engine communication plane. Based on results of such trials it was decided to fit an F-104A aircraft with this equipment.

Aircraft tail number 56-875 was modified with this equipment (near the war perhaps due to maintenance related issues the equipment was removed from 56-875 and installed on 56-804). Initial trial fitting on the aircraft made the cockpit very uncomfortable for the pilot and was also considered a safety hazard in case of an ejection. Such issues were resolved during the testing phase which included extensive missions against various PAF radars. The SLARD had two sensors on the right and left of the nose cone. The device had a pick-up range of about seven–10 miles at low level. The display in the cockpit would indicate the location of radar about 30 degrees either side from the nose of the aircraft. A vertical line/mark would appear after every 2 to 3 seconds to guide the pilot about exact location of the target radar with reference to the aircraft.

The F-104s also had an infrared (IR) sight however its pick-up range was too short to be of any operational use. After the 1965 war, a serious effort was made by PAF engineers to improve its performance. These efforts did succeed in increasing the pick-up range from less than half a mile to seven–eight miles against a single jet engine source by cooling the infrared cell with liquid nitrogen. The modified system did give the pilots good pick-up ranges but because of ice formation, the system would clog and shut down. It required a good 15 minutes for the ice to clear and the system to start functioning again. Unable to find a satisfactory solution to the problem, the effort was finally abandoned.

Yet another major modification was to make the underwing fuel tank station a weapon station capable of carrying Sidewinder missiles. Both the F-104 A and B versions that Pakistan had acquired had four external stores positions, one on each wingtip capable of carrying either an external jettisonable fuel tank or a Sidewinder

Flight Lieutenant Rashid Bhatti prepares to step up into the cockpit of his F-86F. Later Rashid Bhatti would convert to F-104s, and bag himself a Su-7 during the 1971 war. (Authors' ocllection)

missile, and one under each wing capable of carrying a jettisonable fuel tank only. Of these external store stations, the wingtip station was much cleaner and far less drag-producing than the underwing station. For all operational missions, when Sidewinder missiles were carried, the pilots had either to fly with no external fuel tanks at all or carry them on the underwing station.

Operationally the ability to carry both wingtip tanks and Sidewinder missiles was considered very desirable. It was thought that the underwing stations could be modified to carry Sidewinder missiles. After the 1965 war, efforts were made locally for this modification. PAF's technical staff were able to fabricate a set of Sidewinder launcher racks for the underwing station and completed other necessary modifications like wiring, sighting and emergency jettisoning.

After thorough ground and flight testing, several live firing tests were carried out and the modification was declared successful. The entire fleet of F-104s was then modified at PAF's main engineering depot at PAF Base Faisal.

To address the shortfall in spares caused by the embargo, some changes were also made to daily operational routine. One example is the modification carried out on the starting system of B-57s, which used cartridge-powered starting. The cartridge produced gas, which energised the starter. To conserve cartridges, gas with enough force was injected directly to into the starter from gas bottles and the engine started slowly but surely. Gas bottles were placed at three bases; Mauripur, Mianwali and Peshawar and the aircrew were given training to handle the system. Cartridges were carried in the aircraft to cater for bases where the aircraft may have to land in emergency or to operate from, i.e., Sargodha, Risalpur and Shorkot. Another modification made to the B-57s allowed the carriage of eight 500lb bombs in the rotating bomb bay, thus increasing the total bomb load to 13. This was done to allow for area bombing from 500 feet skip runs as dive bombing was ruled out due to enemy's enhanced radar-controlled AAA and improved SAM capability.

Induction of the F-86E

The cloak-and-dagger procurement of 90 surplus ex-Luftwaffe Canadair Sabre F.Mk 6s from West Germany could have made for a gripping Hollywood movie. Even though

Air Marshal Nur Khan prepares and then straps into a Canadair Sabre Mk 6 for a sortie with 'brass' looking on in Mauripur. Note that aircraft is still sporting a Luftwaffe colour scheme and serials. (Authors' collection)

Pakistan was under the American arms embargo, it was able to procure the 90 surplus Canadair Sabre Mk.2s from West Germany via Merex AG, an arms dealing firm, opened and run by a decorated ex-Nazi Gerhard Mertins.[10]

The deal is believed to have been done with the blessing of German government and intelligence services but keeping in mind the sensitives around the imposed arms embargo and selling to an active conflict zone country, was to be done via a third nation. American intelligence was also believed to be in the know but turned a blind eye. Even though the deal was struck with the Iranian government, it was known right from the start that the aircraft were intended for Pakistan.[11]

The deal was worth 10 million dollars and Gerhard Mertins is believed to have negotiated directly with the Pakistan embassy in Bonn during 1966, and in subsequent negotiations PAF officers, wearing Imperial Iranian Air Force uniforms and ID badges also participated.[12]

The first 10 aircraft were ferried to Vahdati Air Force Base located in South Iran by Luftwaffe pilots in April 1966, hopping across various European bases to refuel. The aircraft flew into Vahdati in four-ship formations once a week or every few days, where the Luftwaffe pilots would park the aircraft, switch off and then would be flown to Tehran for their subsequent flight back to Germany.

At Vahdati Air Base, the aircraft were test flown by a group of PAF pilots led by Squadron Leader Ali Kazim. Over the following months, the rest of the aircraft were also ferried, with the last 20 aircraft delivered in December 1966. The ferrying of the first two F-86Es from Iran to Pakistan was done by Wing Commander F.S. Hussain and Waqar Azim. Ali Kazim recalls:

> The first ferry was done by the legendary F. S. Hussain and Wing Commander Waqar Azim (retired as an Air Marshal). The boss told me that he will fly Vahdati–Mauripur direct! Looking at the expression on my face he said 'Ali don't fret, I have worked out everything. Just have them parked just short of the runway, top up to last drop, have two APUs to start up both at the same time and off we will go.' Was done that way. I took a deep sigh of relief the moment I got the message that they had landed at Mauripur. All 90 went to Pakistan in Luftwaffe colours. The other 88 went Vahdati–Shiraz–Mauripur.[13]

The acquisition of these Sabres was a shot in the arm for PAF. These aircraft equipped four squadrons, No. 17, 18 and 19 Squadrons in West Pakistan and No. 14 Squadron, which was still deployed in East Pakistan.

While Gerhard Mertins was negotiating Sabres with Pakistan, he was also negotiating for the supply of 28 surplus Bundesmarine Sea Hawk 100s and 101 fighters to the Indian Navy.[14] These aircraft were delivered via ship to the Indian port of Cochin (now Kochi) on 23 June 1966.[15]

Touch and go with the Il-28

To support the dwindling numbers of B-57s, it was decided to procure additional aircraft of similar category to supplement the bomber force. The Il-28 (a Soviet aircraft to be supplied by China) was selected, primarily because it was readily available from a friendly source and also most likely due to its very affordable cost.

A team of three experienced B-57 aircrews led by Group Captain Rais A Rafi, a B-57 veteran from the 1965 war, along with Flight Lieutenant Khadim ul Bashar,[16] Flight Lieutenant Sikandar Mehmood,[17] and navigators Flight Lieutenant Muhammad Akhtar,[18] Flight Lieutenants Salah ud Din Qazi, and Iftikhar Ghauri proceeded to China for conversion on the Il-28 and their subsequent ferry to Pakistan. The tail gunners were NCOs of the Armament trade. The team also included two engineers and about 15 airmen from different trades.

The aircrew flew to Beijing via Dacca and then onwards to the air base at Xinjin where PAF pilots had already been trained on the F-6 and seemed to have created a very good impression of their abilities.[19] The Chinese hosts were very courteous, friendly and keen on training PAF aircrew and also at the same time wanted to learn from them. Rais A Rafi takes up the story:

> They had selected Muslim Kitchen staff from Sinkiang province who prepared food according to our Muslim requirements. I remember the name of the cook, Abdul Hye. We often called him HYE and would respond by answering HAAYE, which in Chinese or Uighur language meant" YES SIR". It was great but innocent fun. Only the interpreter "friends" knew English. But soon we could talk to each other in sign language. After formal receptions and "Kumbais" of "Maut Aiees", which some of us enjoyed, we settled down to normal life. They operated the Air Force like the Army, based upon the Soviet system. Most of the senior commanders were serving Army. But squadron commander downwards were Air Force. The Base Commander often sat in the mobile. The morning briefing started with reading of Mao's sayings from the Red Book. Everyone had to fly strictly according to the briefed exercise; not a slight diversion was allowed. Our instructors sitting by the side and interpreter, often a woman, sitting in the tail gunner's cockpit had no problem in teaching us. We could have gone solo after one dual [flight] but had to do four sorties as per the syllabus. Result were very good. Their flight safety and maintenance record was outstanding. Throughout our flying, we could not put a single unserviceability on their Form 781. No accidents either. Amazing. At the end of the course their senior officers from Beijing HQ with Group Captain Inam ul Haq, our Air Attache, visited us. I was asked to give my impressions. After consulting Group Captain Inam, I pointed out to our friends that they ought to give more freedom of flying to their pilots. This was appreciated.[20]

The aircrew returned to Pakistan after completing their conversion and after approximately a month proceeded back to Hotien in China in a C-130 and this time lead by Air Commodore

Air Marshal Nur Khan briefs the Pakistan President on a Sabre. (Authors' collection)

This low quality photograph is the only known image of Chinese Il-28 (known as B-56 in PAF service) at Mauripur. Never put to good use, these aircraft withered away and were eventually sold as scrap. (Authors' collection)

Air force aircrew are intereviewed by a media serviceman. (PAF Museum)

F.S. Hussain, along with several F-6 pilots to ferry the aircraft to Pakistan. After the usual Chinese welcome, the F-6s took off under the leadership of Wing Commander Mian Sadruddin. The three Il-28s, to be officially known as B-56 in PAF, took off for Pakistan, led by Wing Commander Rais A Rafi.

The aircraft flew in trail with no radar coverage, and only relying on radio compasses, joined over the clouds and flew over the Himalayas, which they could not see due to extensive cloud cover, hoping to home to Gilgit. The navigators took a sigh of relief when Gilgit beacon responded. The aircraft maintained a strict RT silence, so there was no contact with the F-6 formation and while the F-6s landed in Peshawar due to their short range, the B-56s pressed on to Sargodha. After a quick refuelling stop, the three aircraft took off for Mauripur where they landed just before dusk.

Next day Rais A. Rafi gave a dual check to Air Commodore Masroor Hussain, the Base Commander. After an assessment of the aircraft based on aircrews' feedback, it was decided not to fly this type against heavily defended targets. The Il-28, being a first-generation makeshift light bomber, had hard controls and was found to be very unmaneuverable. It was difficult to fly at night, particularly at low level and was deemed no match to for the B-57. In PAF it was nicknamed by the pilots as TONGA,[21] who had hoped that they would not be required to fly it over AAA-infested IAF airfields as that would be a one-way journey.[22]

However, No. 8 Squadron was converted to B-56 and started operating the type along with B-57s. The squadron carried out some day and night skip bombing attacks at Sonmiani using B-56s and also took part in a PAF level day and night exercise, while deployed at Mianwali Air Base. The aircraft was deemed very reliable from the serviceability point of view but considered a dead duck operationally. It was kept for use in emergency situations and that against only lightly defended targets.

An idea to use these aircraft for maritime roles was conceived and considered but abandoned quickly as the aircraft presumably did not offer much space and flexibility to house the required equipment. Due to their limited operational utilisation the aircraft were retired after just a few years and well before they could be used in the 1971 war. Three aircraft were seen parked at Mauripur for several years, before eventually disappearing, believed to be sold for scrap.[23]

4

THE INDO-PAKISTAN AIR WAR OF 1971

During December 1971, the PAF was once again in the thick of action, this time under trying civil war conditions and against a much better prepared and motivated foe. The failure to find a political solution to the transfer of power to the East Pakistan-based Awami League, which had won a clear majority in elections, lit the flames of a full-fledged civil war in the Eastern Wing of Pakistan during early 1971, fully instigated and supported by India, which saw a great opportunity for a decisive victory.

Since India seemed determined to exploit its strategic opportunity without restraint, Pakistan's apex leaders had only two options: to take bold and risky political initiatives to give East Pakistan the autonomy it demanded, or to prepare for a war to resist the emergence of Bangladesh via the force of India's military power.

General Yahya Khan (President and C-in-C of the Army) had failed to take initiatives or to seize opportunities to bring about a political compromise between March and October 1971 that could have neutralised India's strategic plan. By mid-October, the President's options had been reduced to just two: declare full autonomy of East Pakistan and unilaterally withdraw Pakistani forces from the East or fight a war as best as he could with the adverse military balance that existed in both wings.

A defensive or attritional war would not have secured any military or political gains for Pakistan. Therefore, if war was to become the only option, the top Pakistani leaders – including the armed forces chiefs – determined that the chosen offensive strategy in West Pakistan of a powerful armour- and air-supported thrust by Pakistan Army's strike corps deep into Indian territory was the only course of action that could dissuade India from dismembering Pakistan.

This offensive was to be led by Pakistan Army's General Tikka Khan, and for the 1971 war, the PAF's difficult but crucial mission was dictated by the need to guarantee the success of this offensive into India. In developing its operational concept, PAF drew some lessons from the most recent air wars of the time, in the Middle East and in Vietnam. PAF's war plan incorporated all such lessons that were relevant to the anticipated nature of the impending war. Additionally, PAF was compelled to adopt some unconventional measures to minimise the effects of its unusually adverse operational and logistic shortcomings.

A B-57 touches down at Mauripur after a sortie. (Authors' collection)

A Sabre pilot prepares for another sortie. (Authors' collection)

The PAF leadership considered it important for the commanders of the air bases, wings and squadrons to understand the rationales underlining their assigned tasks. The leadership disseminated both the relevance and the difficulties of their assigned missions, as well as the unusually adverse war environment for which the tactics for the air support and counter-air campaigns had been evolved. Personally, and through his operational staff, C-in-C Air Marshal Rahim Khan had taken the top air force commanders into confidence about the rationale and ultimate aim of PAF's war plan. The senior operational staff officers had visited the air bases regularly during the pre-war months and in discussions with the senior combat commanders, clarified the particular features of the prescribed operational plan. In turn, the base commanders and wing leaders had also held preparatory discussions with the squadron commanders and their combat aircrew on the reasons for the tactics and strategy that had been laid down for PAF.

The consensus among the senior commanders of air bases, wings and squadrons was that if Pakistan could not use diplomacy to avert a war, it should follow an offensive, not defensive (attritional in the case of Pakistan) strategy. Most of them understood the necessity of keeping PAF ready for the intense centrepiece air campaign in support of Pakistan Army's deep retaliatory thrust into India when it was launched. They supported the tactics being adopted in the interim to minimise PAF's combat losses to SAMs and AAA. There was, however, a segment of younger pilots, less aware of the bigger strategic design, which felt that even in the early phase, all the ground-attack missions should be executed without restraints or regard for attrition, and with all the weapons available to the air force. Some of them later understood that had the Army's strike corps achieved even half of its assigned mission and sustainably occupied sensitive Indian territory, PAF's strategy would have stood fully justified.

PAF's Operational Concept During the War

PAF's day and night strikes against Indian airfields and radars which began on 3 December were in accordance with the high command's operational concepts. The overriding priority of PAF was to give maximum support to Pakistan Army's proposed land offensive into India from West Pakistan; every other air force objective was to be subordinated to this requirement. The proposed land offensive itself was in line with Pakistan's grand strategy that in the event of Indian aggression against East Pakistan efforts would be made to capture strategically important Indian territory in the West and force a political settlement. This strategy was in turn driven by Pakistan's limited resources which could not be split between its two wings separated by thousands of miles of hostile India. The Air Chief and Air Headquarters staff considered this commitment to be pivotal because the success or failure of PAF's support would in all likelihood determine the fate of Pakistan's crucial offensive. When the estimated 'cost' of fulfilling this commitment was calculated by the planning staff in July 1971, it worked out at a loss of 100–120 combat aircraft and pilots over the projected 7–10 days period. Air Marshal Rahim Khan was aware that this would amount to losing one third of his force, but he had the full support of his senior commanders when he directed them in August to prepare their units to pay this price for ensuring the success of the Army's offensive.[1]

Until the Army's offensive was launched, the PAF was to maintain offensive pressure on the IAF with sustained strikes against some of its forward and rear bases. The objectives of these strikes were:

1. Inhibit to the extent possible – both physically and psychologically – the enemy's ability to launch operations against either the Pak Army in the field or other targets on Pakistani territory, including PAF's own air bases and other installations.
2. Try to force the IAF to deploy its strike aircraft at rear air bases and thus deny them full flexibility.
3. Provoke the IAF in retaliating against PAF's own airbases where PAF will use advantages that go to a defensive force and inflict attrition on the IAF.

PAF understood that crippling strikes on IAF bases like those carried out in the 1967 Arab-Israel War or similar to its own strikes in the 1965 war (against Pathankot and Kalikunda) were not possible. This was simply because the IAF, having learned its lesson well from the 1965 war, when PAF was able to destroy a considerable number of IAF aircraft on the ground as they lacked proper dispersal facilities, had upgraded its air bases. The IAF air bases were now far better protected in terms of aircraft shelters, dispersal, camouflage and air defences. Other than the upgraded air base infrastructure, PAF also lacked some essential tools, such as runway denial/penetration bombs.

During this same period, PAF was also to provide whatever air support was needed for the Pak Army's 'holding' actions along the entire 3,700-kilometer border from Kashmir to Kutch. These relatively shallow penetrations were meant to tie down as many of the enemy's resources as possible and to try to achieve a favourable tactical posture in the process.

The IAF bases that PAF planned to attack on 3 December, and on subsequent dates, were chosen for their relevance to the combat zones in which Pakistan Army's current operations were taking place or where these were imminent. The intensity of PAF airfield strikes was deliberately varied and controlled to harmonise it closely with Pakistan Army's operations. The targeted IAF bases, the TOTs and the weapon loads were chosen specifically for creating the indirect effect of minimising or eliminating the IAF's interference with Pakistan Army's most important ongoing operations. Both air forces possessed airfield

What appears to be the remains of a downed Indian MiG-21. (Authors' collection)

Table 9: PAF Combat ORBAT during the 1971 War

Base	Units	Aircraft	Remarks
Western Theatre as on 3 December 1971			
Masroor	No. 2	10 x T-33	
	No. 7	7 x B-57, 1 x RB-57B	
	No. 19	10 x F-86E, 12 x F-86F	
Talhar	No. 19	4 x F-86E	
Faisal	-		Maintenance base
Jacobabad	-		Special contingency base
Okara	-		Forward transit base
Risalewala	No. 23	16 x F-6	
Rafiqui	No. 17	16 x F-86E	
Sargodha	No. 5	18 x Mirage IIIE/R/D	
	No. 9	8 x F-104	Moved to Masroor on 6 December
	No. 11	16 x F-6	
	No. 18	16 x F-86E	
	No. 25	8 x F-6	
Chander	-	-	Forward transit base
Peshawar	No. 26	16 x F-86F	
Chaklala	No. 6	8 x C-130	Aircraft which were dispersed at different airfields after each bombing mission
Murid	No. 15	16 x F-86F	
Mianwali	No. 5	5 x Mirage IIIE	Airbase only activated for the war
	No. 7	10 x B-57	
	No. 25	8 x F-6	
Eastern Theatre as on 3 December 1971			
Tejgaon (Dacca)	No. 14	14 x F-86E, 1 x T-33, 1 x RT-33, 2 x Alouette	
Kurmitola	-		Tejgaon's alternate base
Chittagong	-		Forward transit base

repair teams and neither anticipated nor planned to deliver crippling strikes against each other's air bases in the Western Theatre.

As the war progressed, PAF was to be brought to higher readiness for launching its heaviest sustained counter-air campaign that was expected to last several days. The IAF bases which were to be targeted for that campaign were especially relevant to General Tikka Khan's deep thrust into India, the centrepiece of Pakistan's strategic response to Indian aggression in the East.

The Opposing Forces

In East Pakistan, facing the full might of IAF Eastern and Central Air Commands was the lone No. 14 Squadron deployed at Tejgaon (or Tezgon) air base (Dacca), with 16 F-86E Canadair Sabres on strength. The squadron was to lose two of the Sabres in an aerial skirmish on 22 November 1971, leaving it with 14 Sabres when the official war commenced on 3 December. Before the war, PAF had evaluated the deployment of an additional F-6 squadron at Kurmitola but this could not be completed in time. Against No. 14 Squadron, IAF had deployed 11 squadrons in the Eastern Theatre. These comprised three MiG-21 (No. 4, No. 28, No. 30), four Hunter (No. 14, No. 17, No. 37, No. 7) and three Gnat (No. 15, No. 22, No. 24) squadrons. A Canberra bomber squadron (No. 16) was also deployed.[2]

In the Western Theatre, PAF had a total of 11 fighter/bomber squadrons spread across eight different bases with a total active strength of 200 aircraft, which included 60 F-86E, 44 F-86F, 23 Mirage IIIE/R/D, 17 B-57B/C, 48 F-6, and eight F-104s. The average was about 16–18 aircraft per squadron with No. 9 Squadron having eight F-104 Starfighters on strength and receiving a further nine from Jordan on 13 December. The single B-57 squadron had all 17 B-57B/Cs, and No. 5 Squadron equipped with Mirages had 23 aircraft on strength. About 30 F-6s were undergoing overhaul in China and Pakistan during the war and an equal number of Sabres were also going through their periodic inspections or maintenance. In the Western Theatre the changes in deployment occurred

Pakistan Air Force bases in the north, near the Kashmir border were critical in the 1971 fighting. (Map by George Anderson)

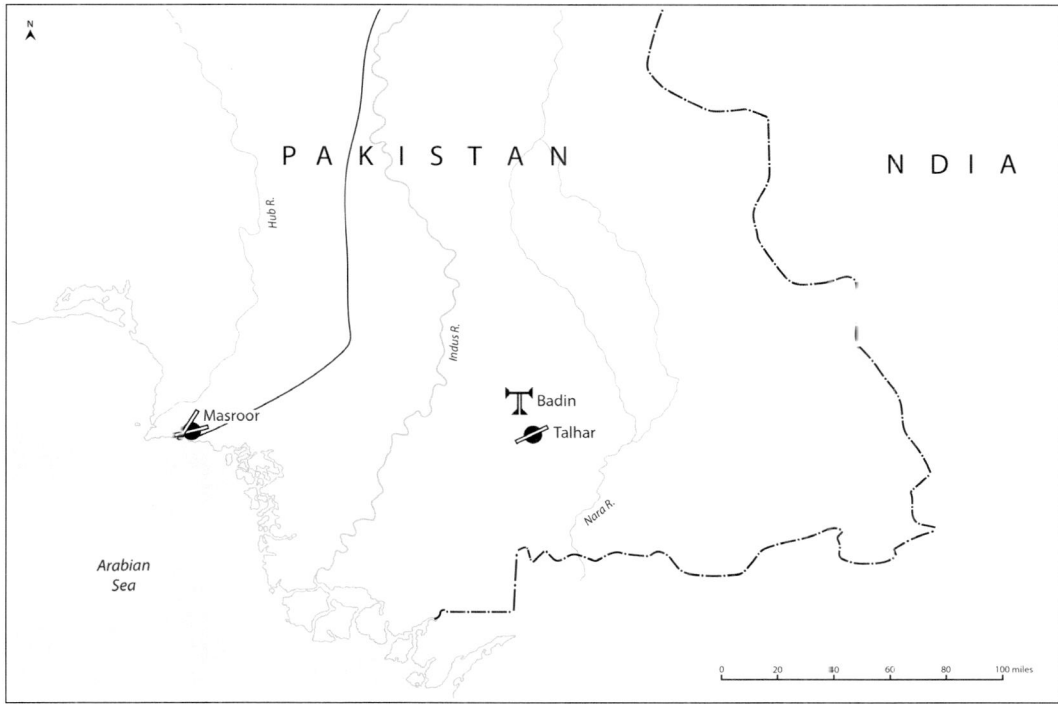

As PAF had shifted its weight north after 1965, the southern fields had remained important. (Map by George Anderson)

regularly during the war and there were no changes in deployment in Easter Theatre.

Opposing PAF was the IAF's Western Air Command with 448 aircraft spread across 28 squadrons. These included five MiG-21, five SU-7, four Hunter, five Gnat, two HF-24, two Mystére and four Canberra squadrons. Two flights of MiG-21s and Su-7s belonging to the IAF TACDE (Tactics and Air Combat Development Establishment) were also deployed to the Western front.[3] The number of aircraft kept in reserve by IAF is not available.

Between the wars, PAF had continued to build its AIM-9B stocks through multiple sources, despite the arms embargo. In addition to the AAM-capable F-104s and Mirages, the PAF had indigenously

Airfields in East Pakistan had proliferated over the years but could serve as little more than targets during the 1971 war. (Map by George Anderson)

Squadron Leader Peter Christy poses in front of the B-57. Peter laid down his life in the line of duty during the 1971 war. The B-57 he was navigating was brought down by Indian AAA during an attack on Jamnagar air force station. (Authors' collection)

parts were replaced when their shelf life expired.

About 8–12 officers, all middle ranking combat pilots and specialists having war experience, constituted the Command Operations Centre staff of the air force. They were connected on secure hotlines to all combat units on a round-the-clock basis for telephone clarifications on operational mission tactics, weapon load and for any related discussions. On a number of occasions, wing and squadron commanders proposed minor changes in tactics or aircraft employment for certain missions. These were quickly assessed and where merited, approved by telephone within minutes. This 24/7 interaction between flying units and the staff of the PAF's Command Operations Centre was maintained throughout the 1971 crisis.

Brothers in Arms

The Base Commander Dacca, Air Commodore Zafar 'Mitty' Masud was strongly opposed to the military crackdown in East Pakistan and had given a forceful fact-based presentation to visiting President General Yahya Khan on 15 March, arguing that military force would not be a solution to what is essentially a political problem. Masud's experienced voice was against the tide of many other officers, who believed that a military operation was the only course of action left.

After the crackdown in East Pakistan on 25 March 1971, the subsequent insurrection was also to impact PAF as about a third of its technicians and about one tenth of its aircrew, totaling close to 5,000 personnel belonged to East Pakistan. Expecting an adverse reaction, the Bengali aircrew were grounded after the crackdown began, with a few exceptions.

made as many of the F-86 and F-6 fighters capable of firing the AIM-9B as it could before the 1971 war began. The high cost and the long lead-time of locally manufacturing the missile modification kits (with electronic parts acquired from the international black markets) made it impossible to equip the entire fighter force with the AAMs before the war began.

All of the 500 AIM-9Bs held by the PAF were fully serviceable. The missiles were stored in environmentally controlled conditions at several locations and regularly tested on simulation test benches to fully maintain their combat worthiness. Rocket motors and other

Shortly after the crackdown had begun, Air Commodore Zafar Masud addressed the entire base and offered leave to those who did not want to participate in the ongoing operations, and at the same time warning against any subversive activities.[4] One reason to offer leave, other than the wellbeing of Bengali aircrew, was perhaps to extend an opportunity of not breaking their oaths – oaths that called for their unquestioning obedience.

At that time in Dacca a group of Bengali officers led by Group Captain A.K. Khandker, OC (Admin Wing) had already planned to defect and join the insurgency. One of the officers in the group, Squadron Leader Sadruddin Hossain, a veteran of the 1965 war, when asked about his role in helping the Indians, told the authors:

> Personally it took me some time before I could start talking. We were flown to New Delhi from Agartala in West Bengal. Our stay was for about 7–10 days, I think. I did not and could not talk for the first 3–4 days. I just kept on avoiding my interrogator on one pretext or the other. The Indians however were very nice to us and they treated us very well. From me, the type of information the IAF was interested in was mainly concerning tactics and operational practices and procedures, locations of various aircraft pens and other facilities of the PAF Base, Sargodha. I do not know if this information helped the IAF or not but I did give them all to the best of my knowledge.[5]

The raging insurgency, pitting what were once brothers in arms against each other, was also to leave personal scars on both sides. One such example is that of Squadron Leader Saiful Azam, a veteran of the 1965 war, during which he had bagged a IAF Gnat, and then went on to add a unique tally of three additional Israeli aircraft (Dassault Mystére IV, Dasault Mirage III and Vatour IIA bomber) while on deputation to the Royal Jordanian Air Force during the 1967 Six-Day Arab-Israeli War, earning him the respect and admiration of his peers. Saiful Azam narrated one personal tale to the authors:

> My sister, a medical student in the Chittagong Medical College, was reported missing and eventually picked up by the Army with her companions. My frame of mind at that time was very disturbed. I was very vocal. Much later I came to know that when they were brought to the Army Camp, she called out to the young Captain in charge saying that she is the sister of Saiful Azam. The captain enquired whether the Saiful Azam in question was from Sargodha School. When she answered in the affirmative, he directed his havildar to take her and her companions to wherever they wanted to go in his Jeep. I never got to know his identity.[6]

Unlike the 1965 war, where IAF had such poor intelligence that it did not know the primary PAF airbases in use, this time it not only had detailed infrastructure knowhow but also the likely tactics of its opponent, and the radar coverage gaps that could be exploited for any interdiction or counter-air mission.

The potentially damaging consequences of about 5,000 absent East Pakistanis were addressed by West Pakistani officers and enlisted personnel by volunteering to work well beyond their normal duty cycles (8 hours) to an extended 12–18 hours daily. Many recently retired officers and technicians were also recalled, filling the gaps. The PAF worked to this extraordinary schedule during the entire June–December 1971 crisis. Despite suffering this handicap, the PAF still managed to keep aircraft combat-ready status to 80–90 percent throughout the war, and a daily generation rate of combat sorties that was twice that achieved during the 1965 war.

East Pakistan – the Last Stand

Between the wars, not much had changed in terms of infrastructure in East Pakistan. A second airbase was still under construction at Kurmitola, well behind schedule. Another squadron equipped with F-6 aircraft that was planned to be deployed to East Pakistan during late 1969 and to be based at Kurmitola never materialised, even though all the planning and groundwork for its transportation was completed. No. 14 Squadron had traded in its nine remaining F-86F Sabres from the 1965 war for 16 F-86E models, only four of which were equipped to fire Sidewinders.

One marked improvement at Dacca air base was the construction of fighter aircraft pens covered with wire mesh and foliage cover on top. The taxi tracks leading to these pens were also camouflaged and two sets of four dummy aircraft were placed at both ends of the runways at Dacca and the still-under-construction Kurmitola.[7] The camouflage was to prove so effective that not a single Sabre aircraft would be lost on the ground to repeated enemy raids.

During the initial months of 1971, early warning was provided by two radars (one P-35, and one low-level AR-1) and a string of MoUs deployed at anticipated ingress routes of enemy aircraft. The P-35 was shipped back to West Pakistan once the insurgency erupted and keeping the MoUs in the field also became unsustainable after units suffered heavy casualties due to Mukti Bahini (Bangladeshi forces) attacks. This left the lone short-range AR-1 radar deployed close to the airbase as the only unit that could provide 2–3 minutes of early warning, not sufficient for routine scrambles. Before the war the 'Killer Control' concept was practised, where a team comprising a fighter pilot and an AAA officer with communication equipment hooked up to the ATC and radar interception frequency and perched somewhere above the tree lines would guide the airborne fighters visually. The idea was that the Killer Control could follow the interceptor profile to the end, thereby controlling the guns effectively.[8]

There was no doubt in the minds of PAF officers that once full-scale hostilities broke out the lone squadron, operating from a single airbase with a single runway would not survive for more than two days. Sajad Haider recalled once such honest appreciation given to Army officers by Base Commander Dacca:

A Sidewinder-armed Sabre rolls down Sargodha's runway. (Authors' collection)

> Air Cdr. Mitty Masud had put together an excellent and graphic information system of maintenance, armaments and logistics of the base. It was from this data and our exercises that he wrote an appreciation of the PAF capabilities during a possible conflict with India. The brief was prepared for presentation to the Army Commander at that time Sahibzada Yaqub

A frame from gun-camera film showing an attack on ground targets. (Authors' collection)

Khan. Briefly, it presented a realistic PAF capability, in the event of a war which we would have to fight without any support from the West after start of hostilities. Essentially, it outlined that PAF Dacca would remain operationally effective for 24 to 36 hours, whereafter the sheer numbers game with 10 Indian squadrons facing a single squadron with one runway and one radar, would be rendered ineffective and the runway untenable.[9]

Even though the 'official' war was to commence on 3 December, No. 14 Squadron had already been in the thick of the action since March 1971 in support of the ground troops. One mission of note that can be described as a textbook case of CAS took place on 15 April 1971, when No. 14 provided continuous air cover to assaulting SSG (Special Service Group) troops that were tasked with capturing the vital Bhairab Bazar Bridge which had fallen to the insurgents and was now believed to be guarded by up to 400 infiltrators and Indian Army troops. The assault by the SSG was proceeded by a strike conducted by four Sabres led by Squadron Leader Abbas Khattak with Flight Lieutenant Khalid Mehmood, Flying Officer Shafqat Mehmood, and Qazi Javed Ahmed as his No. 2, 3, and 4 respectively.[10] For the next five hours additional Sabres launched from Dacca provided continuous cover and support and sometimes fired within a few hundred feet of advancing SSG troops. The rebels routed; the vital railway bridge was captured intact.

It was during another CAS mission on 22 November close to Jessore when three Sabres led by Wing Commander Afzal Chaudhry with Flying Officer Khalid Ahmed as his wingman and Flight Lieutenant Pervez Qureshi as No. 3, were bounced by four Gnats from IAF No. 22 Squadron. The Sabre formation had become easy prey after lingering too long over a contested area and making multiple passes trying to pick off Indian tanks, and with no friendly radar coverage to warn them of incoming bogies. Pervez and Khalil were both shot down with only the leader managing to fight his way out successfully. Both Pervez and Khalid were captured by Mukti Bahini and handed over to the Indian Army and were to remain in captivity for close to two and a half years. This was the third tank busting mission in Jessore sector for the day with ToT of 1530hrs, and the earlier two missions flown at 0700 and 1000hrs had returned safely without meeting any air opposition. By November 1971 the squadron had already flown almost 100 sorties in support of ground troops.[11]

As the PAF struck the IAF bases in the West on 3 December, IAF Canberras attacked the Dacca air base the same night multiple times but without causing any damage.

From the dawn of 4 December 1971, No. 14 Squadron anticipating IAF attacks in strength and at low level, giving little to no warning, had planned to maintain standing CAPs by a pair of Sabres every half hour. The first pair launched at first light and led by Wing Commander Afzal Choudhry made no contact as with the second pair led by Flight Commander Squadron Leader Dilawar Hussain. As the second pair was coming into land, a third pair led by Squadron Leader Javed Afzal with Flight Lieutenant Saeed Afzal as his wingman were getting airborne at 0730hrs.

Soon after taking off, Squadron Leader Javed Afzal and Flight Lieutenant Saeed Afzal made contact with a pair of Hunters believed to be from No. 37 Squadron and as the Sabres jettisoned their drops tanks and were settling behind the Hunters, the Hunters broke off and exited towards home territory. Spotting another Hunter, Javed easily positioned himself behind it and opened fire. Trailing smoke,

A flight line of F-86E Sabres. The E models offered greater power compared to F-86F models. (Authors' collection)

the Hunter flown by Flying Officer Bains of No. 17 Squadron is believed to have made it back with 42 bullet holes. While Javed was busy with his quarry, his wingman Saeed fell to the bullets of another Hunter, flown by Flying Officer Harish Masand of 37 Squadron, who had managed to sneak behind undetected. Saeed managed to eject successfully but is believed to have been killed by Mukti Bahini after landing.

Javed in the meantime had called tally with a MiG-21, which was believed to be part of the escort for a strike formation from No. 28 Squadron. Close to a dozen aircraft in three separate formations had converged over Dacca in short duration and out of these the first two formations of Hunters escorted by MiG-21s had aborted their attacks after running into Sabre CAPs. The third formation was the only one so far to have delivered their attack successfully.

To assist Javed, another pair of Sabres was launched, this time led by Staff Operations Officer Wing Commander S.M. Ahmed, with young Flying Officer Salman Rasheedi as his wingman. Ahmed being fully occupied with staff duties, and a non-regular flier was not expected to participate in any sorties but while at the crew room to cheer up the pilots, and seeing an opportunity, volunteered to lead the next scramble. Soon after getting airborne around 0745hrs, the pair was vectored towards more incoming bogies. In the short and sharp ensuing combat, the Hunter flown by Squadron Commander No. 17 Squadron – Wing Commander N. Chatrath – shot down Ahmed, who ejected successfully but sadly met the same fate as Saeed earlier. Rasheedi, surviving the melee returned to the base unscathed.

The next mission to make contact was led by Flight Lieutenant Iqbal Zaidi with Flight Lieutenant Ata-ur-Rahman as his No. 2 and got airborne at about 0820hrs.[12] As soon as the pair got airborne, they picked up contact with four Hunters lining up to attack the airbase. Taking a pair each, and as Ata managed to settle behind his pair with ease at 2,000 ft, just as he was about to open fire, he was warned of another pair on his tail by the Killer Control. Immediately breaking off, Ata noticed bullets stream past his aircraft. A second later, and he would have borne the full brunt of the Hunters' devasting 30mm ADEN cannons. The Hunters overshot the Sabre, and Ata gave a brief chase but after being outrun at treetop level and being low on fuel, recovered back at base with his wingman.

As Ata and Zaidi were landing, the next pair led by very young Flying Officer Muhammad Shamsul Haq with an even younger wingman Flying Officer Shamshad, was getting airborne around 0845hrs. Shamsul had been waiting patiently since first light for his turn and now finally was to get an opportunity to see action in a target-rich, adrenaline-filled environment. In his own words:

> I was sitting just outside the A.D.A. hut, gazing at the star-flecked sky. I was getting irritated – sitting and waiting; I just wanted to get airborne. I could barely make out my Sabre standing in the darkness – also waiting for someone to give it a ride on the wings of air. I could have taken off in it at a moment's notice but I was chained to my seat, my energies being gradually sapped by the inactivity. I came inside the hut and sat in a chair – waiting. It was already the first light of the day when the telephone rang and I was given the cockpit standby. At last there was some movement, some excitement, some action. Flg. Off. Shamshad was detailed as my wingman. Even in the cockpit, the suspense continued but not for long. Soon, I was told to take off and engage a formation of enemy aircraft approaching Dacca. The big moment for which I had been training and preparing myself had at last come.

> The moment I got airborne I got a call from the controller, "Two bogies (enemy aircraft) 2 miles, 3 O'Clock". My No. 2 was delayed a bit and could not join up although he managed to get airborne in time. As soon as he gained height, I told him to jettison tanks and break into the 'bogies'. I had barely finished talking to him when I saw Su-7s split and come one behind each of us. I broke, dropped my fuel tanks and hit the deck as soon as I broke. There I collected my thoughts for a brief instant and prepared myself for the engagement. I pulled up in order to get behind the Su-7. At that moment, I saw the other Su-7 fire two missiles at my No. 2, Shamshad, but the missiles missed the target completely and went past the F-86. Simultaneously, the 'bogie' which was still somewhere behind me released a missile on me. I sensed the danger immediately and broke in time. The missile missed me and overshot. I heaved a sigh of relief. Immediately I came out of my stupefaction and pulled up for the chase. Spurred as I was by the lucky escape, I manoeuvred myself behind the Su-7 which was zooming past me, selected my guns and started closing in on him. I opened fire at 1,800 feet but to no effect. So I continued the chase and kept firing till I was as close as 400 feet from the target. Realizing that he was in my sights and could not undo the tangled knot, the Su-7 pilot lit the afterburner and tried to out-distance me by sheer speed. His attempt proved futile as by then my burst had landed on his canopy and around. I saw his left wing and exhaust trailing smoke and the aircraft going into a spiral. A few seconds later, it hit the ground.

> The other Su-7 was still behind my No. 2; so I rolled in for it. The pilot of that aircraft lit his burner and disengaged from my No. 2 before I could open fire.

> Next, the Killer Control reported four Hunters behind us. I left the Su-7 to its fate and went for the Hunters. They were in pairs; so each of us took a pair and engaged in an aerial combat. The pair I got behind split and one of them pulled away. I got behind the other Hunter, opened my guns at it from a range of about 600ft. The fire was accurate and hit the aircraft squarely. The Hunter started trailing smoke and after a couple of seconds its pilot bailed out. My No. 2 was still behind the other Hunter. He was firing at him. Meanwhile, I got a call from the controller that another Hunter was in sight. I looked for the Hunter and in a few seconds spotted it. For some inexplicable reason it went into a dive. I used my throttle for extra power and rolled in for the two Hunters still overhead. My bullets had been expended and I had only one missile left. Realizing that I still had a powerful weapon under the belly, I decided to go after the Hunter which was exiting towards the Barrackpur airfield in West Bengal. I continued the chase and went about 9 to 11 miles inside the enemy territory. I was flying at about 400ft., and so was the Hunter. I went further low over tree-tops and got right behind the aircraft. As soon as I heard the missile tone confirming contact I fired the missile. I saw the missile sink initially but then in a flash of a second it went straight into the exhaust of the Hunter. The aircraft immediately turned into a ball of fire like a napalm explosion. I saw the pilot being thrown out at an angle of 45 degrees to the right. Then the parachute opened. I made an orbit over that area and told the controller to try to recover the pilot.

> I was told later that my No. 2 had chased the other Hunter and damaged it. The Hunter was trailing smoke and was exiting towards the home base. Although the enemy activity in the area did not slacken, we had reached the limits of our endurance and so got ready to end our vigil. I told my No. 2 to land. As he approached for landing I saw a Hunter to the left. I got behind it

and chased it for about five minutes. Since I had no ammunition, I asked Dacca to scramble another pair. As soon as another pair got airborne two 'bogies' were reported coming in for a raid. I disengaged myself from the Hunter and came in for the landing. When I was about 200ft from the threshold of the landing strip the control reported two MiGs 8,000ft behind me. I broke away from the landing pattern and exited low level. I saw one MiG-21 about 5,000ft behind me. I broke into it with the result that it overshot and zoomed up to high altitude. I orbited on the area for a couple of minutes when the Killer Control reported one MiG-21 behind the leader of the other pair. The leader broke into it and the MiG-21 overshot and zoomed past. I followed it up to 13,000ft. but I had, by then, exited at high level. Thereafter I came and landed.[13]

The missiles Shamsul had noticed were 57mm unguided rockets that the Su-7 formation had fired after being intercepted by the Sabres. The Hunter shot down by Shamsul over Dacca was being piloted by Squadron Leader K.D. Mehra of No. 14 Squadron based at Dum Dum. Mehra after ejecting successfully managed to escape back to India with the help of Mukti Bahini. No additional information is available from the IAF sources about the second Hunter shot down over Indian territory using the AIM-9B or the third Hunter that was last seen heading towards friendly territory trailing smoke.

The next pair got airborne around 0930hrs, led by Flight Lieutenant Schames-ul-Haq with Flight Lieutenant Mahmud Gul as his wingman. Soon picking visual with a pair of Hunters that were pulling up for an attack on the airbase, the Sabres turned to intercept. While Gul went after the Hunter which had continued its attack run on the base, Schames tangled with the other Hunter that had broken off its run. In the ensuing fast turning, slow speed engagement Schames settled behind the Hunter after a few turns and a short accurate burst of his six 0.5 calibre guns sent the Hunter spiraling down. The pilot, Squadron Leader A.V. Samanta belonging to No. 37 Squadron went down with his aircraft. Gul in the meantime had given up his chase after losing sight of the bogey during the dive and had rejoined, keeping his leader's tail clear.

The hectic morning was followed by a short interlude during which additional CAPs were mounted but without resulting in any contact. The next pair that were to make contact took off at 1600hrs, led by Squadron Leader Dilawar Hussain with Flying Officer Sajjad Noor as his wingman. After being warned by the radar of bogies at their 11 o'clock, Dilawar was quick to discover a Hunter which was well set at about 1,500ft under him.[14] Forcing an overshoot, Dilawar was able to get behind the Hunter and brought it down with a well-aimed burst from the Sabre's six guns. Sajjad had followed a pair of Hunters that had pulled vertical, and in the process had forgotten to clear his tail. Wing Commander R. Sunderesan, the Squadron Commander of No. 14 Squadron, managed to position behind the Sabre, and an accurate burst of his Hunter's 30mm cannons forced Sajjad to eject from his doomed aircraft. A SAR Alouette managed to rescue Sajjad, and in the process also picked up Flight Lieutenant Kenneth Tremenheere, who has been shot down by Dilawar.

To reevaluate its tactics which so far had not put the lone squadron out of action, or perhaps to focus on providing ground support, the IAF did not attack Tejgaon on 5 December with the same vigour. The Canberras made their nightly runs but caused no damage other than one stray bomb which landed on the Officers Mess and killed a pro-Pakistan Bengali officer Squadron Leader Ghulam Rabbani. The No. 14 Squadron also took this brief lull to mount sorties in support of hard-pressed ground troops. It was at 1000hrs on the morning of 6 December, just after a four-ship Sabre formation had retuned from its fighter sweep that a formation of four MiG-21s from No. 28 Squadron and led by Wing Commander B.K. Bishno, deposited eight 500kg bombs along the length of the runaway making it inoperable for the first time. Unable to subdue the Sabres in the air, and what seems to have been an afterthought, the IAF had assessed that putting the single runway out of action offered the best returns. Base Commander Air Commodore Inamul-Haq provided details many years later:

> These craters on the runway were about 20 feet deep and 50 feet wide, with volcano-like upward thrusting lips of runway slabs. Craters were deep due to time-delay fuses on these sleek bombs. Quick repairing of runway needed large amounts of sand, with loading and dumping vehicles, cement slab cutting machines and quick-setting cement. None of the equipment and material was available; nor was repair time available due to frequent strikes by fighter-bombers, now orbiting safely at 10,000 feet beyond the AAA range with no interceptor to chase them. They would dive steeply along the runway for releasing bombs, exposing themselves to AAA for a very short time. Some raids inflicted casualties on the repairing teams which were doing whatever little they could, with all the handicaps. At the end of the third day of bombing, I inspected the big craters. Fully aware that Dacca runway would not be available for fighter operations any more during the war, I decided to fly the fighter pilots to Burma in PIA's surviving Twin Otter. I saw eight or nine remaining pilots at dawn and could sense their sympathetic feelings on leaving me behind. The Twin Otter took off from a taxi track.[15]

With the runway cratered and with no hopes of having it repaired due to paucity of material and resources, the remaining pilots were flown to Burma using one of the remaining PIA Twin Otter aircraft, which managed to get airborne using the undamaged section of the runway. From Burma, the pilots managed to reach Pakistan via China, well after the war was over. The remaining 11 F-86Es, one T-33, and one RT-33 were made inoperable by damaging critical parts or cutting cables on 15 December after Pakistan forces had decided to surrender in East Pakistan. Out of these, five Sabres were later recovered and flown by Bangladesh Air Force for a short duration. The AR-1 radar operated by No. 4071 Squadron was destroyed to stop it from falling into enemy hands. This brought the curtains down on the last stand of No. 14 Squadron in East Pakistan. The Base Commander, Air Commodore Inam-ul-Haq who had decided to stay behind and was to become a POW, rose in ranks after his release and retired as an Air Marshal.

The Battle in the West – Counter-Air Operations

On 3 December at 1630hrs, the President formally declared a state of war. Just 21 minutes later in West Pakistan, PAF's first strike formations were taking off for their targets. Eight F-86Fs led by Wing Commander S.A. Changezi were to strike Srinagar airfield using bombs, some with delay fuses. Another two formations of eight F-86F Sabres were tasked to strike Awantipura and Pathankot airfields also using bombs, led by Wing Commander Abdul Aziz and Wing Commander S.A. Jilani respectively. As part of these first strikes two four-ship Mirage formations led by Wing Commander Hakimullah and Squadron Leader Aftab Alam Khan were also tasked to crater the Amritsar and Pathankot runways and taxiways. This was in accordance with a pre-planned assault against IAF airfields and radar stations, in which Sabres, F-104 Starfighters and Mirage IIIs were to cross the border at the same time and strike their targets between 1709 and 1723hrs. In the words of Wing Commander Hakimullah Khan (OC No. 5 Squadron during the war and later PAF Air Chief):

> I went to a forward radar unit in the afternoon of 2 December 1971. I had gone there to observe the pattern of IAF's airfield mounted dawn and dusk CAPs (combat air patrols) and after discussing them with radar controllers, evolve tactics and procedures of disrupting them. Next day, I was still busy with the controllers when at about 1200hrs my base commander called me and asked me to immediately return to the base. I hurriedly drove back and was with the base commander by about 1500hrs. He handed me the tasking orders for dusk strikes against Amritsar and Pathankot air bases each consisting of four Mirages.
>
> Returning to the squadron, I detailed the two strike missions and asked the boys to update the maps and logs and prepare the aircraft in appropriate configuration (2 x 1,000lbs HE bombs and 2 x 1,300 litre external fuel tanks). I led the mission to Amritsar at dusk on 3 December 1971. The mission was flown as planned except another formation (two F-104s on a mission against a radar unit) which had entered the runway ahead of us occupied it unusually long and thus delayed our take-off by a few minutes. The ingress to the target was as low as 100ft AGL with initial speed of 480 knots. We had planned a dive-bombing attack using north-south axis. The pull-up for the attack was at 540 knots, at 2 miles north of the airfield to about 6,000ft and was uneventful except as we pulled up, we were surprised to see the runway lights were on. Whether someone was landing or taking off, one thing is sure that we caught them by complete surprise. We saw no interceptors and the anti-aircraft guns started intense firing only after we had delivered the attack.
>
> A quick radio check after the attack confirmed that everyone had delivered their weapons as briefed and that we were exiting safely with no interference from the enemy.
>
> The formation returned safely to Sargodha and after a short debrief, where there was nothing unusual to report, the pilots were assigned their new duties and missions and ordered to proceed. Initial damage based on radio monitor showed that the airfield was inoperative for that night and the next day.[16]

While the Sabres and Mirages were tasked to crater the runways at forward IAF operating bases, the Starfighter pilots were tasked to attack IAF radar stations. The aim was to degrade their performance by damaging or destroying the antennas using the Starfighter's Vulcan cannon, affecting IAF capability to interdict PAF raids on the forward airfields. The initial strikes were planned to be carried out on 3 December close to dusk on Amritsar and Faridkot Radar Stations, using guns only. Further strikes were to be carried out on these and other radar installations such as the one operating from Bernala from 4 December onwards.

Wing Commander Arif Iqbal and Squadron Leader Amanullah were to strike the Faridkot and Squadron Leader Amjad along with Squadron Leader Bhatti, the Amritsar radar station.

Arif, along with his wingman Amanullah, got airborne from Sargodha just before dusk on 3 December and set course at low level. During ingress to the target Amanullah maintained tactical formation on the right side of Arif, keeping 20 degrees behind the line abreast position. A few miles from the target Arif pulled up but could not spot the airfield due to limited visibility conditions as it was getting dark. Amanullah instead of pulling up, kept low and went down to 100 feet and spotted the runway. Amanullah recalls:

> I went further down, and on the side of the runway (a small, abandoned airfield of British times) I saw radar vehicles and one temporary camouflaged shelter with a light aircraft. While Arif was orbiting on top still unable to spot anything, I made a 360 turn to line up with side of the runway where all vehicles were parked and made strafing attack with long burst firing 66 rounds per second with the 104's Gatling gun. I managed to hit the target, made another 90–270 degrees turn and made a second pass. After the second pass I exited. Arif had left before I did therefore I was independent and alone. When I was exiting it was dark and I did not see Ravi and continued west 270 and passed south of Sargodha and when I pulled up it was over Indus River close to Mianwali. I realised then and set course back for Sargodha. When

A B-57 banks away exposing its belly for the camera. (Authors' collection)

Pilots sprint for their Starfighters. (Authors' collection)

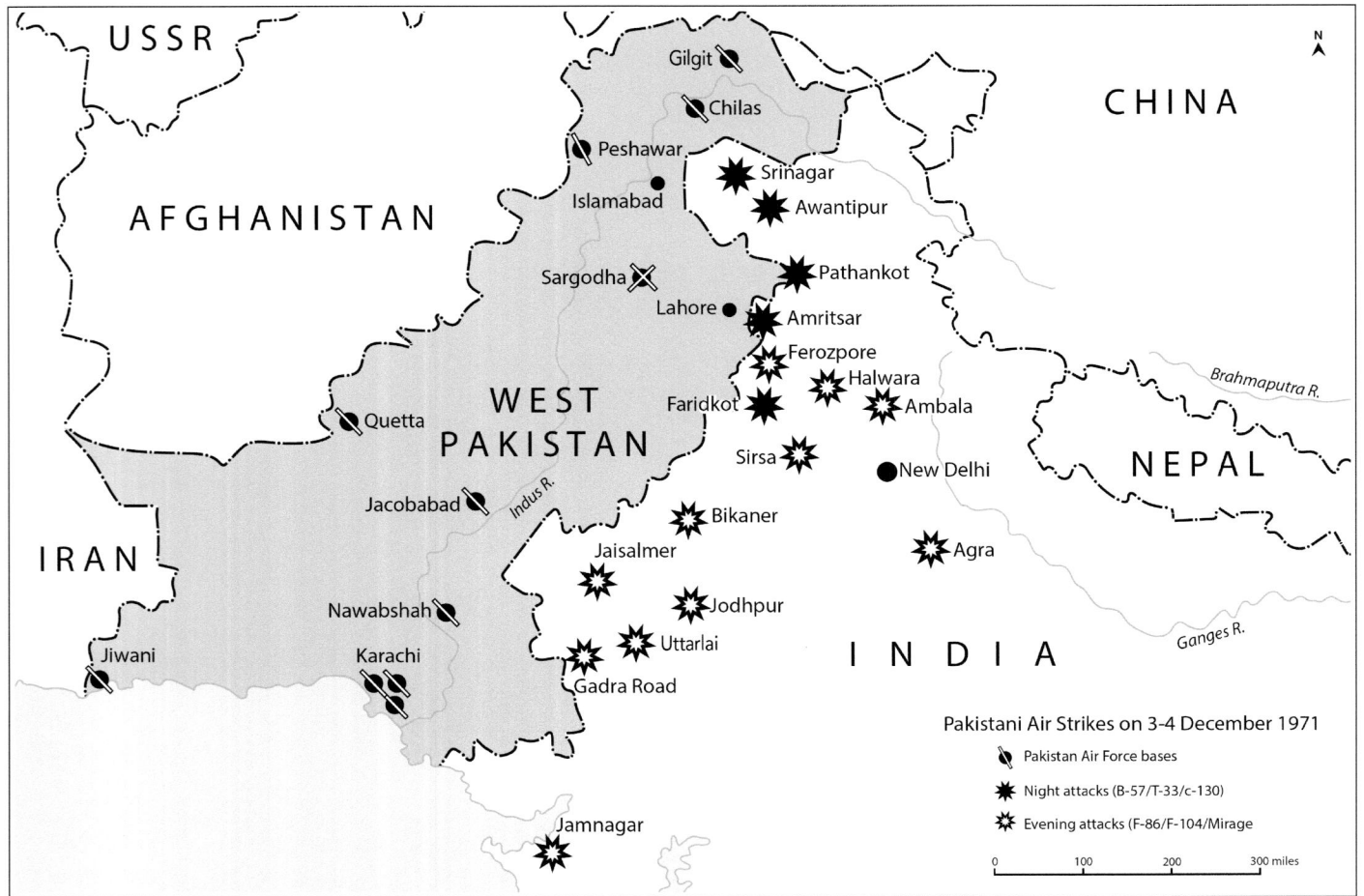

The opening strike on Indian facilities. (Map by George Anderson)

I came to land, as it was the initial moments of war, the Ack-Ack of Sargodha opened on me. I went round shouted at Sargodha ATCO and came back and landed. Base Commander was waiting for me and hugged me since I had come back late. He told me that I have hit an Indian light aircraft at Faridkot (announced by Indian radio). They did not say anything about radar, but the radar was silent after the attack throughout the war. Arif came back without firing while I had expended closed to 400 rounds.[17]

The first raid on Amritsar radar was carried out at 1710hrs by two F-104A aircraft lead by Squadron Leader Amjad Hussain, with Squadron Leader Rashid A. Bhatti as his wingman. Amjad was flying the specially equipped radar locator F-104A (56-804). Both the aircraft took off from Sargodha air base configured with two fuel tanks on pylon stations and two Sidewinder missiles on wing tips. The radar was located and engaged successfully, and it went off the air. All aircraft from the initial strike missions were able to recover safely without any loss.

Next morning, 4 December, pilots were informed that the radar was back on air. Another mission was planned for 0500hrs with Bhatti as lead (in F-104A 56-804) and Amanullah as his wingman. As the formation arrived over the radar, heavy ack-ack opened up. The pilots decided to stay low and make a 180 degree turn to re-attack. While turning and pulling up, Amanullah spotted a Gnat trying to level behind the lead with all guns blazing. Bhatti punched his tanks and engaged afterburners after getting a timely "Gnat behind you, exit" warning from his wingman. While trying to position himself behind the leading F-104A, the Gnat pilot had not noticed the wingman. With Bhatti's F-104A now pulling out of range at supersonic speed, Amanullah positioned himself behind the Gnat and after getting a locked-on tone fired the AIM-9B Sidewinder. While the missile was homing on, the Gnat broke right, and the missile exploded under its belly. Amanullah saw some parts of the Gnat flying off but did not see it crash. After the attack, the wingman also broke-off and headed home.[18]

While flying back, Bhatti looked at his wingtip tanks which were stuck and had not jettisoned. Since he was going supersonic the aileron got stuck due to the tortional effect of the tanks on the aileron. Bhatti popped up his speed breaks and the aircraft came out of turn and he was able to safely exit.

Since the mission was interrupted, another strike was planned on Amritsar radar station around noon on the same day (4 December). This was Bhatti's third mission, and he flew as No. 2 to Squadron Leader Amjad Hussain, who once again was flying the specially equipped F-104 with SLARD. While crossing at the border at low level, Bhatti spotted two Su-7 aircraft crossing above them at approximately 3,000ft which were also visually picked up by Amjad at the same time. Amjad manoeuvred to settle behind the lead Su-7 with the second Su-7 trying to come behind Amjad. Bhatti warned Amjad over R/T of the other Su-7 closing behind him but being focused on trying to track the lead Su-7, he did not respond immediately. All this time Bhatti was also manoeuvring to get behind the second Su-7 to shoot it down before it could shoot down Amjad. With the second Su-7 now even closer to the Amjad, Bhatti gave a tactical call to "break right", and this time Amjad was quick to respond. With Amjad now out of danger, Bhatti closed in on the second Su-7 and after getting a Sidewinder lock-on tone, fired the first missile from a distance of 4,000ft. Bhatti saw the missile hit the Su-7 and the aircraft crashing to the ground. Bhatti then tried to close in on the lead Su-7 and after getting a locked-on tone fired his second Sidewinder and while fumbling with the cockpit switches at the same time, trying to jettison the fuel tanks, Bhatti failed to notice if the second missile found its mark. The fuel tanks failed to jettison and with emergency selection, only the right pylon fuel tank got released. Now with the left pylon fuel tank almost full the aircraft was uncontrollable due to asymmetric conditions at very high speed (550–600 knots). Bhatti however managed to control the aircraft and after crossing the border and getting an all clear from own radar, climbed to a safe altitude and with a reduced speed, recovered the aircraft safely at Sargodha.

Once again, the mission remained unaccomplished. Now the fourth mission was planned for 5 December at 1330hrs with Squadron Leader Amjad as leader and young Flight Lieutenant Samad A. Changezi as his No. 2. Intel had reported the position of this radar at a road going towards Amritsar Airfield. The pilots approached the target from the south and as Amjad spotted the target and made his first strafing pass hitting the antenna, he realised that it was a wooden decoy when he saw it splinter. Right at that moment he saw the actual antenna rotating on the right. As the wingman, Changezi, also called contact, the formation turned around and attacked again, hitting the antenna. This time the radar station was struck successfully, and it went off the air for the second time. During exit, Amjad's aircraft (56-804) was hit by anti-aircraft guns deployed around the radar station. As he turned towards Pakistan hoping to recover, the wingman noticing the spreading fire gave the call to eject. Amjad successfully ejected and was to spend the rest of the war as a POW.

On 6 December, No. 9 Squadron was ordered to move to PAF Base Masroor, Karachi. For the rest of the war the squadron performed day and night air defence and counter-air operations from this base.

The B-57s were once again entrusted with keeping up the pressure on the IAF airfields during the night. On the night of 3/4 December, in 15 separate sorties, the B-57s flying from Mianwali and Masroor attacked Ambala, Agra, Halwara Amritsar, Pathankot, Sirsa, Jaisalmer, Bikaner, Jodhpur, Jamnagar, and Uttarlai Airfields. The B-57 aircrew was to continue attacking the major IAF airfields throughout the war suffering three losses to AAA in the process along with their aircrew being KIA. The first B-57C (S/N 53-3948) flown by the youngest aircrew of the squadron, Flight Lieutenant Javed Iqbal with Flight Lieutenant G M Malik as his navigator, was brought down while attacking Amritsar Airfield on the 5 December. The second B-57B (S/N 53-3943), piloted by Squadron Leader Ishfaq Hamid with Squadron Leader Zulfiqar Ahmed as his navigator, was lost in the south on the same night while attacking Bhuj airfield. The third and final B-57 loss to AAA was on the next night (6 December), when Squadron Leader Khusro and his navigator Squadron Leader Peter Christy were shot down over Jamnagar. After suffering substantial losses to B-57 night attacks during the 1965 war, the IAF had taken necessary precautions this time and did not admit to losing any aircraft on the ground during night raids. The attacks focused on destroying runways and taxiways to disrupt the IAF operations during day time, did cause a varying amount of damage and one of the interesting narrations of the damage caused came from a Sirsa based IAF MiG-21 pilot, Flight Lieutenant Harish Sinhji, who was taken POW on 5 December:

> After one of PAF's night bombing strikes on our airfield, we were all grounded for six hours. The runway had been cratered in many places. The following morning our CO, Wing Commander V B Sawa-dekar, took us all to the runway to show us the Pakistani pilot's bombing accuracy. Pointing to the craters on our runway he said "this is the kind of bombing accuracy the IAF pilots should achieve against Pakistani targets".[19]

Sirsa had been struck on the first night by a lone B-57 flown by Squadron Leader Yousaf Hassan Alvi and Flight Lieutenant S.M. Ali Shah as his navigator, and they consider the IAF pilot's remarks as the best compliment they ever got.[20]

Just before midnight on 4 December, the Indian Navy successfully struck Pakistan Navy (PN) ships and oil storage installations at Karachi harbour using missiles fired from Osa-class missile boats. Ill-prepared to defend against missile attacks, the PN requested air support from the PAF. The PAF was to fly 25 missions using B-57, F-104, F-86, and T-33s in support of PN but since the aircraft lacked the capability to locate and engage ships during the night, the effort had little impact. Another 127 visual reconnaissance sorties were also flown in the support of PN.[21] On the night of 5/6 December a B-57 struck Okha harbour which was believed to be a refuelling stop for the Osa boats, setting fire to fuel storage tanks. Four days later the harbour was attacked again by a pair of F-104s, whose pilots could still see the fires burning.

On the 10 December, Wing Commander Arif Iqbal along with Squadron Leader Manzoor Bokhari took off from Masroor Air Base in two F-104s in search of Indian Navy Osa boats towards Okha

An F-104A Starfighter at Sargodha fitted with wingtip fuel tanks. This Starfighter (56-804) was lost during an attack on an IAF radar during the 1971 war. (Authors' collection)

A Sidewinder-armed F-104s rolls down Sargodha runway for another mission. (Authors' collection)

harbour. The pair spotted an Indian Navy Alize aircraft at a low level. Easily settling behind it in gun range, Arif shot it down with a short gun burst. The Alize with its crew of three crashed into the sea. The formation safely recovered at Masroor.

On the morning of 11 December, Wing Commander Arif Iqbal, this time with Squadron Leader Amanullah as his wingman took off from PAF Masroor for a fighter sweep mission. The aim was to catch any fighters taking off from IAF Base Uttarlai. Navigating at a low level the Starfighter formation pulled over Uttarlai airbase completely undetected and noticed two HF-24 Maruts lined up on the runway for take-off. Quickly aligning, Amanullah aimed for one of the HF-24s and fired 170 rounds in one single burst, destroying the aircraft. As Amanullah pulled up and positioned for another attack, he saw Wing Commander Arif, who was below him, firing at the other aircraft. Amanullah shifted his aim into an aircraft pen and fired another burst. Exiting the area at a low level, the formation safely recovered at Masroor.

It was at Masroor that PAF No. 9 Squadron received nine F-104s (S/Ns 56-774, 56-775, 56-767, 56-777, 56-799, 56-839, 56-843, 56-845, 56-1789) provided by the Kingdom of Jordan in support of Pakistan during the 1971 war. These Starfighters which belonged to RJAF No. 9 Squadron, were ferried by RJAF and PAF pilots to Masroor on 13 December from where they operated for the remaining period of the war. When the Jordanian aircraft were 200 miles out from Karachi, and being unarmed, a PAF F-104 formation led by Amanullah got airborne to escort them to Masroor. Amanullah was in formation with Major Ihsan Shurdom and Awni Bilal to guide them for landing while orbiting over head to give them top cover.[22]

A formation of two F-104s was tasked on 13 December to strike the IAF's airfield at Jamnagar. The experienced Wing Commander Mervin L. Middlecoat was to lead this mission with Squadron Leader Tariq Habib as his No. 2. The formation configured with wingtip tanks and two Sidewinders under the wings, ingressed at a low level. Close to the target the formation pulled up to 2,000–3,000 feet, to line up for their strafing run with the target offset to their right by 2–3 miles. For some reason Middlecoat, who was leading the strike, banked to the left while the target was on the right.[23] As Habib gave the leader a call for correction, the repositioning for the strafing run resulted in formation spending another minute or two near the target area. After repositioning and as the formation was again committing to the run, Habib got a call from Middlecoat that a missile had been fired at him. Habib cleared his six but did not see anything. Moments later while exiting and over the Gulf of Kutch, Habib got a call from Middlecoat saying that he had been hit and was ejecting. Habib inquired if he could make it to overland, but he replied in the negative. Habib saw Middlecoat ejecting and the Starfighter going into the water while inverted. At that moment Habib noticed a MiG-21 to his right. As he pulled up to convert behind the MiG-21 his auto-pitch control malfunctioned, and the aircraft's nose started oscillating. After disengaging the auto-pitch control, Habib safely exited from the area.

Later from various published Indian accounts, it transpired that two IAF MiG-21's had intercepted the Starfighters while they were lining up for the strafing run. The lead MiG-21 had fired an Atoll air-to-air missile at Middlecoat's F-104 which had missed but was able to close-in for a gun kill.[24] Wing Commander M.L. Middlecoat was declared MIA.

During one of the early morning raids on Srinagar airbase on 14 December, the formation of six F-86F Sabres from No. 26 Squadron were challenged by a lone Gnat. Before the Gnat, flown by Flying Officer Nirmal Jit Singh Sekhon could cause real damage, it was brought down by one of the Sabre escorts, piloted by Flight

Note the short, thin F-104 wings which were ill suited for a turning fight. (Authors' collection)

A Sabre performs a roll over the field prior to touching down after a sortie. (Authors' collection)

Lieutenant Salim Baig Mirza. Sekhon who was late in ejecting from his stricken aircraft and perished in the encounter, was awarded the highest award (Param Vir Chakra) by the Indian government.

During the war, the PAF flew a total of 160 day and 130 night counter-air sorties against enemy airfields and radars. The IAF admitted a loss of three aircraft on the ground during these raids.[25]

Air Defence Missions

The IAF response to the opening PAF salvo was swift. The same night (3 December), IAF Canberras conducted 15 raids and struck Rafiqui (2236hrs), Sargodha, Mianwali, Riselewala Murid, Masroor and Chander, only causing minor damage. Most of the bombs had missed the runways, and at Sargodha and Mianwali, loose soil thrown on the main runways was cleared up by quick-reaction parties while Masoor remained unscathed.[26] Only the runway at Chander was cratered and was to receive additional attention over the next three nights, rendering this forward airfield unfit for operations.[27]

As the dawn broke on the morning of 4 December, the PAF was on full alert in anticipation of the coming raids and unlike the 1965 war, this time the IAF struck with force and determination, using around 70 Hunters and Su-7s in streams of twos and fours.[28] Making full use of gaps in the low-level radar coverage, no doubt based on intelligence gleaned from the defecting Benagli officers, the IAF formations targeted 12 air bases and two radar sites. The 'hornets nest' Sargodha was not attacked during the day as perhaps the 20 percent attrition suffered on the opening day of 1965 war still weighed heavily on the minds of IAF planning staff. During these attacks, the PAF lost one F-86F (S/N 53-1187) on the ground at Murid and the radar at Badin received some damage but remained operational.

The raids led to some gut churning air battles, many of which took place at treetop levels. The first blood was drawn by the F-6 pilots of No. 23 Squadron, who intercepted a pair of attacking Su-7s right above Risalewala airfield. In the ensuing interception the F-6 leader Flight Lieutenant Javed Latif was able to bring down one of the Su-7s piloted by Flight Lieutenant Harvinder Singh of Halwara-based No. 222 Squadron with an AIM-9 and damage the second one with his cannons. Latif's wingman, Flight Lieutenant Riffat Munir called off his chase of the damaged Su-7 flown by mission leader Squadron Leader B.S. Raje due to being short on fuel.

At Peshawar, Flight Lieutenant Salim Baig Mirza had returned to his No. 26 Squadron in time from an off-base assignment to witness a pair of Hunters deliver their attack and destroy two dummy aircraft on the tarmac at 0715hrs.[29] Tasked by the Base Commander to man two additional Sabres on ADA, Flight Lieutenant Salim Baig Mirza along with his leader Flight Lieutenant Khalid Razzak made themselves comfortable in their fully refuelled and ready Sabres, parked at the end of the runway in protected pens. The pair finally got their scramble orders around 1030hrs and were retracting landing gear within three minutes. Initially given south easterly vectors towards Cherat Hills, approximately 30 miles from Peshawar, and while flying at 5,000ft, the pair was soon instructed to turn around towards base as the bogies were now closer to the base. As the pair got closer to the base, Killer Control provided warning about a pair of Hunters, which had just exited towards easterly direction. The pair now flying battle formation with 3–4,000ft abreast separation, noticed one of the Hunters at much lower level, in an opposite direction to them. As the pair did a hard turn to settle behind the Hunter, they got another Killer Control call informing them of another Hunter pair pulling up for an attack on the base. Deciding to forego the singleton, Mirza and Razzak turned towards the west and jettisoned their 200 gallon drop tanks to make the aircraft lighter and ready for pursuit. Flight Lieutenant Salim Baig Mirza narrates rest of the story:

> We were now almost overhead the base and I spotted one Hunter turning to the left across the runway well below me. I informed the leader who had also sighted him and saw Flight Lieutenant Khalid Razzak's Sabre diving to position himself behind the enemy aircraft. While looking to the right, I cautioned him about the presence of other enemy aircraft and sure enough there was another Hunter who had seen the lead Sabre diving and was turning left to sneak behind the Sabre. I immediately called leader about this new development and told him that I was going for the second Hunter who was still more than a mile behind.
>
> Diving and throttling back, I got behind the second Hunter who had apparently not seen me. Pretty soon an interesting situation had developed in which four fighter jets were twisting and manoeuvring in high 'g' turns at barely 100 feet above rugged terrain west of Peshawar airfield and were jockeying to shoot each other out of the sky.
>
> People watching the fight from the ground could see the fighters in a tight high 'g' turn at low level with one Hunter in front of lead Sabre firing at him and a second Hunter following and firing at the lead Sabre and I being the last one had this Hunter in my gun sight and was firing with all guns blazing. I was hoping to shoot him before he got dangerously close to the leader. During this melee I was giving a running commentary to the leader about the distance of enemy aircraft behind him. I could clearly see the puffs of dust being raised by impact of bullets of both Sabre and Hunter in front of me. Their bullets were landing well short of the target because of firing out of gun range.
>
> While firing at the enemy aircraft I was getting closer in range but in spite of my bullets hitting the target, there was no sign of smoke or fire. The Hunter was proving to be a tough nut to crack. I was aware that the Hunter's distance from leader's aircraft was becoming less and could be fatal if not warned in time. I, therefore, told leader to 'Break' – a manoeuvre performed by fighter aircraft to avoid extreme danger. At the same time my bullets showed

their effect and the Hunter aircraft started to emanate thick smoke from the right side of its fuselage and wing root and the next instant I saw him hitting the ground. A mushroom of thick black smoke and fire leapt up at the point of impact. The pilot had no chance of ejecting out of the aircraft and was instantly killed.

Since the leader (Flight Lieutenant Khalid Razzak) had broken off from his attack and I was looking down at the fallen aircraft, the first Hunter rolled out in south easterly direction and with full throttle managed to make good his escape. We flew in the general direction of his escape route but could not sight him and he was lucky to have survived. After patrolling the airspace for some time we landed back and were told that the air battle had been anxiously watched by PAF personnel at the base till the time it got so low that they could not see us anymore except hear the guns rattling followed by an explosion and cloud of black smoke.[30]

The Hunter shot down by Mirza belonged to No. 20 Squadron and was being flown by Flying Officer K.P. Muralidharan who had taken off from Pathankot. The other damaged Hunter flown by Squadron Leader Bajpai, also from No. 20 Squadron, landed at the Jammu airfield and ran onto a construction truck at the end of the runway.

Also, at approximately 1030hrs, another Hunter pair was intercepted while egressing from their attack on the Murid airbase by a pair of No. 15 Squadron F-86Fs led by Flight Lieutenant Mujahid Salik with Flying Officer Sarfraz Toor as his wingman. Using guns, Salik managed to bring down one of the Hunters, flown by Flying Officer Sudhir Tyagi from No. 27 Squadron, who went down with his aircraft around 44km east of Murid airbase.

The last daylight raid close to sunset was detected heading towards Mianwali airbase and a pair of scrambled F-6s belonging to No. 25 squadron, piloted by Squadron Leader Ehsan and Flying Officer Qazi Javed stood exposed on the runway, as the Hunters pulled up for the aircraft. As the Hunters made a hasty exit after missing both the exposed F-6s in their strafing run, Javed got airborne to give chase. Quickly catching up with one of the Hunters approximately 25km north-east of Mianwali, which seemed oblivious to the approaching threat in his rear quarters, Javed fired both his AIM-9 Sidewinders in successive shots from a range of 2.5km, both of which failed to connect. Closing in further, Javed let loose the F-6's powerful 30mm cannons and noticed hits on the right wing of the Hunter, followed by the aircraft pitching up and then rolling over to the right.[31] The IAF pilot, Flying Officer Vidyadhar Shankar Chati, from No. 27 Squadron ejected successfully and after capture, still oblivious of what had happened, believed that he was brought down by AAA.

As the night fell on 4 December, the PAF air bases in the south received greater attention from the Canberras, possibly to hinder PAF efforts against ongoing Indian naval operations. On the night of 4/5 December, six air bases were struck again, with Masroor receiving the maximum number of bombs, one of which landed on the main runway and another on the taxiway culvert. Chander runway was also cratered at two places – the damage at both air bases was quickly repaired. The next night, another Canberra raid struck a hangar where the last remaining RB-57 was parked, destroying it completely.

A pilot poses in front of his Sabre. An F-6 can also be seen in the background. (Authors' collection)

Ground crew perform maintenance on an F-6 at Sargodha. Note the rocket pod under the wing. (Authors' collection)

In addition to more conventional strike intercepts, PAF had to prepare for two additional types of intercepts where Mirages were supposed to play a role. The first was interception of high altitude IAF Canberra reconnaissance missions and the second was interception of IAF Canberra night strikes. For the first mission PAF Mirages practised zoom tactics with R.530 missiles. Night interceptions were a bigger problem because of a number of reasons including lack of comprehensive low-level radar coverage, compounded by Pakistan's hilly topography in some regions and 1960s airborne radar technology was inadequate for detecting low-level targets. Also, IAF Canberras would be warned of

A formation of Mirages IIIEPs during a routine training mission. (Authors' collection)

an approaching interceptor by IAF GCI/ELINT assets and its own tail warning radar.

Nevertheless, one success against IAF night intruders was achieved by Mirages and this was in fact the first night kill by a Mirage IIIEP. This came on the night of 4 December when Flight Lieutenant Naeem Atta using an AIM-9B Sidewinder shot down a IAF Canberra B(I) 58 bomber (S/N IF-916) on its ingress route to attack Sargodha air base. The Canberra crew, Flight Lieutenants L M Sasoon and his navigator R M Advani went down with their aircraft.

The Mirages achieved their second kill, awarded as a joint kill to two pilots, on 5 December. At the start of the war a detachment consisting of four Mirage IIIEPs and their pilots had been moved to Mianwali with the aim of protecting the airbase and air defence radar located at Sakesar. During the morning, Sakesar detected an incoming raid, and a pair of Mirages was scrambled to intercept. The pair detected the Hunters as they were diving to attack the radar and Sakesar giving weapons free instruction to friendly AAA. The pair did not follow the Hunters into the dive due to friendly AAA and decided to set up an orbit overhead. Due to bad visibility the Mirages lost the Hunters on pull up. After getting back into the crew room the pilots were teased by Flight Lieutenant Safdar Mehmood for not diving after the Hunters through own AAA. Little did he know that a few hours later, he would be facing the same predicament.

With an incoming raid warning from Sakesar another Mirage pair was ordered to scramble, this time lead by Flight Lieutenant Safdar Mehmood with Flying Officer Suhail Hameed as his wingman. Once again the attacking Hunters were picked up as they were diving in for their attack on the radar site and friendly AAA was firing away. Flight Lieutenant Safdar, instructing his wingman to stay on his tail, dived through the intense AAA after the Hunters. Seeing the Mirages above and behind them the Hunters hit the deck, split and fled in an easterly direction. Instead of splitting and following both fleeing Hunters, Flight Lieutenant Safdar, due to his wingman's inexperience on the type, decided to chase just one Hunter.[32] The fight was a no contest with Mirages closing in fast due to their superior speed. At close range, Flight Lieutenant Safdar fired his guns twice and hit the Hunter on the port wing. At this moment the wingman also acquired a solid lock and fired his Sidewinder which homed onto the Hunter. The pilot Squadron Leader Jal M

Flight Lieutenant Salimuddin stands proudly before a Mirage III, a type he flew into combat and scored a Su-7 kill with two AIM-9Bs. (Salimuddin)

Mistry from No. 20 Squadron was unable to eject, and the wreckage was collected afterwards by a PAF team showing the Hunter tail number as BA1014.

The same day, two additional Hunters that were making their exit after yet another attack on Sakesar just after midday were brought down by a pair of F-6s on CAP, led by OC No 25 Squadron Wing Commander Saad Hatmi and with Flight Lieutenant Shahid Raza as his wingman. While Hatmi hit the trailing Hunter flown by Flying Officer Kishan Lal Malkani and brought it down 25km east of Sakesar, Raza also managed to chase the lead Hunter with ease and shoot it down. The pilot Flight Lieutenant Gurdev Singh Rai perished with his aircraft.

The third kill by a Mirage IIIEP came on 6 December when Flight Lieutenant Salimuddin shot down a Su-7. Flight Lieutenant Salimuddin had joined No. 5 Squadron at Sargodha air base on 4 December, and flew his very first mission, an air defence sortie, on midnight 4/5 Dec. This was followed by an early morning CAP and participation in a strike against Pathankot airbase. In total, Flight Lieutenant Salimuddin flew 17 sorties during the war, including two Air Test flights to certify the airworthiness of the aircraft. It was during one of the Air Defence Alert missions that he shot down an IAF Su-7 over Jammu sector.

In purchasing Mirage IIIEPs, the PAF also acquired R.530 missiles and ensured compatibility with the AIM-9B missile. One of the French missiles was fired in combat during the 1971 war. This example carries the Sidewinders plus rocket pods while an R.530 sits on a trolly ahead of the jet in the display. (Authors' collection)

Pilots from No. 26 Squadron pose in front of their F-86F Sabres circa 1966, Peshawar. (Authors' collection)

Taking off from Sargodha in a Mirage IIIEP (S/N 67-102) at noon on 6 December, along with his wingman Flight Lieutenant Riazuddin Sheikh, they were vectored towards enemy aircraft who were attacking Pakistan Army ground troops south-east of Lahore. While proceeding towards the Lahore sector the pair was informed by friendly radar that the enemy aircraft had turned tail and fled to their bases. They were now asked to set up a CAP inside friendly territory, awaiting new vectors. They did not have to wait long, as the PAF air defence controller started vectoring them towards four new contacts that were attacking Pakistani ground targets in the Shakargarh sector. Flying at combat speed at 5,000ft, they ended on top of four enemy aircraft, identified as Su-7s in no time. Closing in further Flight Lieutenant Salimuddin's wingman being in a better tactical position called in for the attack and Salimuddin followed him after clearing his tail. Noticing the Mirages, the enemy formation broke off their attack, jettisoned their payload and headed eastward, towards friendly territory in two separate formations at low level and maximum speed. Seeing the enemy hit the deck and flee the Mirages started chasing one of the Su-7 formations and soon both the Mirages ended up behind an Su-7.[33]

Flight Lieutenant Salimuddin's aircraft was configured with two supersonic fuel tanks, two Sidewinders and a Matra R.530 on the centre pylon. Wanting to improve the manoeuvrability, Salimuddin fired the Matra R.530 with an intermediate lock, watching the missile dip and hit the ground. Pressing on his attack, Salimuddin soon heard the lock-on tone of the AIM-9B missile and pulled the trigger. For a moment nothing happened and fearing a misfire, Salimuddin immediately fired his second Sidewinder. As soon as he pressed the trigger, he saw both missiles flying away towards the trailing Su-7. Without seeing the result of the missile attack, he broke away for a gun pass on the lead Su-7, which was at slightly right position and ahead of the trailing Su-7. While maneuvering for the gun attack Salimuddin was cheerfully informed by his wingman that his missiles had connected with the trailing enemy Su-7. Flying close to 600 knots, Salimuddin started closing in on the lead Su-7 and fired his guns without noticing any result as the SU-7 still seemed to be well outside the gun range. Deciding to give up the chase after a low fuel call from Sheikh, the pair recovered safely back at Sargodha with dry tanks.

After the first two days of intense attacks on the airfields and radar stations, the IAF perhaps not too content with the high attrition rate, switched tactics by focusing on interdiction of the major lines of communications running parallel to the border. These shallow attacks coupled with the lack of radar coverage in many areas, offered the attacking IAF aircraft greater safety and ample warning via friendly radars of any vectored PAF interceptors. PAF was to suffer its biggest single loss of the war on 8 December, when a fully armed and fuelled F-86F parked outside its protective pen at Murid was hit by the Hunters from No. 20 Squadron. The resulting explosions destroyed four other fully refuelled and armed F-86Fs, parked in their pens close by.

A Starfighter cutting a sleek figure for the camera. (Authors' collection)

A formation of Starfighters over the snow-capped peaks of northern Pakistan. (Murtaza Qasim)

Another loss suffered on 8 December by the PAF was due to a case of fratricide when Flight Lieutenant Afzal J. Siddiqui was shot down by his leader Wing Commander S.M.H. Hashmi, OC No. 23 Squadron while chasing two egressing Su-7s. Hashmi had caught up to one of the Su-7s and brought it down using an AIM-9B Sidewinder. Thinking his wingman to be still behind him, Hashmi let go of his second Sidewinder as soon as he made visual in the winter haze with what he thought to be the second Su-7, realising too late the mistake that cost the life of his wingman.³⁴

In the south, to tackle the nightly Canberra raids on Masroor airbase, two F-104s were routinely positioned at the close-by Faisal (Drigh Road) airbase for air defence missions. On 16 December, Squadron Leader Rashid Bhatti, along with the youngest member of No. 9 Squadron, Flight Lieutenant Samad Changezi were detailed to move to Faisal airbase with two RJAF F-104A aircraft. The Jordanian Starfighters lacked the special modifications carried out by PAF on its Starfighters, enabling them to carry two Sidewinders on underwing weapon pylons in addition to two on the wingtips. Due to lack of this modification, Bhatti and Samad had no choice but to fly these aircraft for night air defence with guns only, and with wingtip tanks for extended range. The main idea being that at night PAF wanted the IAF raiding bombers to know that Starfighters were in the air leaving them in a very uncomfortable position to continue their planned attacks.

On 17 December, the last day of the war, Bhatti and Samad were instructed to mount a CAP around the Mirpur Khas and Chor area and afterwards recover at Masroor. Both pilots started a CAP in the designated area with Samad in F-104A S/N 56-767 and Bhatti flying the aircraft with S/N 56-839. After an hour on-station, as both pilots were planning to head back to home base, they heard a call from Badin Radar Station, informing them of two bandits, flying at 10,000ft and heading in their direction. The radar controller asked if they would like to engage and after getting an affirmative from Bhatti, started passing on the instructions to establish contact with the bandits.

As the Starfighters were approaching the targets in battle formation, Samad who was on Bhatti's port side was quick to pick up and call contact with one of the MiG-21s coming head-on. Samad breaking off from his lead, tried to manoeuvre behind the MiG-21. Meanwhile Bhatti who had also picked up both the MiG-21s, also tried to position behind them. Now the situation was such that Samad was behind one MiG-21 trying to close to within gun-firing range (about 3,500 ft) with the second MiG-21 trying to close in on Samad. At this time Bhatti saw the second MiG-21, which while still diving and turning, seems to have let loose a missile at a very high AoA at Samad, which missed the target. Bhatti gave a call to Samad, warning him of the second MiG-21 and the missile threat, and at the same time instructed him to jettison his fuel tanks and go full afterburner and disengage. Samad perhaps fixated on the target to get within gun-firing range, either ignored or was not very attentive in the heat of the situation. The second MiG-21 fired another missile which was a direct hit and Samad's Starfighter exploded in the air giving no chance for the pilot to eject. Bhatti by now had closed

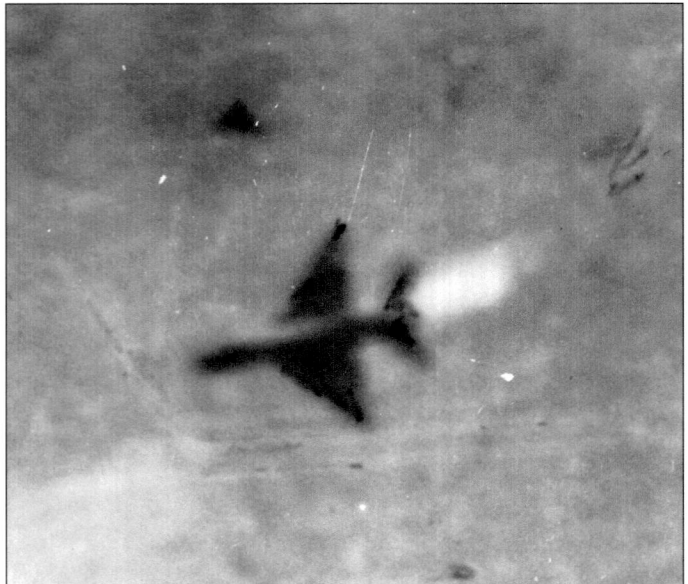

Gun-camera film of an Indian MiG-21 in afterburner turning hard before its PAF adversary. (Authors' collection)

Pakistani villagers pose with what appears to be the wing panel from a downed Indian MiG-21. (Authors' collection)

in behind the second MiG-21, but both the MiG-21s made a hard turn to the right and headed east towards their base. Due to low fuel and lack of any air-to-air missiles, Bhatti also disengaged and recovered at Masroor.[35] This was the third and final Starfighter loss of the 1971 war.

The final air combat of the war on the last day, once again involved IAF MiG-21s but this time they ran into a pair of F-86Es, flown by Flight Lieutenant Maqsood Amir with Flight Lieutenant Taloot Mirza as his wingman. Amir and Mirza belonged to No. 18 Squadron and had taken off from Sargodha for a routine CAP at 5,000ft close to the battle area around Pasrur.[36] To tangle with the patrolling Sabres, a pair of MiG-21s from Amritsar was vectored towards them. Due to lack of low-level radar coverage, the MiG-21s were able to sneak behind the Sabres undetected. It was only through the monitoring of IAF VHF communication and hearing the lead MiG-21 pilot call contact, that the PAF air defence controller sensing something was amiss called for a break. As Amir broke to clear his tail, he saw two MiG-21s in desert camouflage diving down at him from 8 o'clock high.[37] As the MiGs came in hot and high, and judging from their frontal profile that not enough tracking lead was being given for gun attack, Amir settling for an energy conserving turn forced an overshoot. Finding one of the overshooting MiGs within gun range, Amir was quick to place his gunsight just behind the canopy and after a few short bursts, the MiG-21 rolled over and crashed to the ground. The IAF pilot Flight Lieutenant Tejwant Singh beloing to No. 45 Squadron managed to eject in time and was taken POW. Interestingly, Tejwant had flown Sabres during his training at Nellis airbase in the USA, where he also had a few PAF pilots as his course mates, yet he still chose to turn with a Sabre and paid the price.

Reconaissance and Ground Support Missions

Stronger IAF air defence capabilities meant that PAF could not rely on its RT-33s for reconnaissance missions in strongly defended areas. This was a gap which was filled by the three Mirage IIIRPs delivered to the PAF during 1968–1970. These aircraft were equipped with five cameras in the nose cone, one forward-looking long-range F600, a pair of F200s for sideways coverage and pair of F100s for looking up to the horizon, providing a panoramic 180-degree cover, were to prove themselves very useful. Two recconnaissance missions were flown before the war to learn more details of Indian deployment on the western borders. One of these missions, flown about a month before the start of the war, involved a single Mirage IIIRP piloted by Squadron Leader Farooq Umar penetrating Indian airspace near the IAF's Pathankot airbase to gather intelligence on the Indian Army's armour deployment. The pilot flying at a speed of 600 knots and at 3,000ft AGL photographed the area from Katwa (near Pathankot) to Jammu. The photo intelligence gathered from this mission was not conclusive as there were gaps in coverage due to aircraft banking to follow the terrain. A repeat mission was flown over the same area and this time the pilot used left and right rudder so that the aircraft would skid instead of bank and this proved successful. The photo intelligence obtained from this mission allowed Pakistan Army to draw sufficient information about Indian Army deployments.

Later in the war, a major objective for the recconnaissance Mirages was to pinpoint the main Indian armour deployments as this had direct bearing on Pakistan's strategic land offensive in the Western sector. Two missions were flown in the area Kot Kupara–Muktasur on 12 December, covered by the IAF's Halwara and Adampur airbases, the second of these met its assigned objective,

The most numerous photoreconnaissance aircraft in the PAF were six RT-33s delivered in 1957. By 1971 these were too slow to survive in the combat airspace, even when escorted by fighters. (PAF Museum)

Before the war, PAF had managed to make some of its Chinese F-6 compatible with the American AIM-9B Sidewinders. (Authors' collection)

a two-ship CAP towards the intruding Mirages.

Inside Indian territory Squadron Leader Farooq Umar received a call from his own GCI warning him of bogies 40km behind, most probably detecting the trailing No. 2 MiG-21. Hearing this, Squadron Leader Farooq started his photo run at 3,000ft AGL and 400 knots. Shortly afterwards Farooq saw a yellow flash in the rear-view mirror and at the same time GCI called for an immediate break as bogies were closing rapidly. Diving down in a 4g left break, on full instruments in instrument-flight rules conditions, Farooq egressed to Pakistan and while breaking saw a yellow flame passing by and going into the ground. Immediately after, Pakistani ELINT posts overheard calls from an Indian pilot trying to locate his leader and getting no reply. It later transpired that while trying to intercept Squadron Leader Farooq, the No. 2 IAF MiG had shot down his own lead.

During the 14-day war, PAF was to fly a total of 919 sorties in support of various ground formations. Out of these, the largest amount of interdiction, CAS and reconnaissance sorties were flown in support of Pakistan Army's 8th Division, which was hard-pressed in defending the Shakargarh area against a multi-directional Indian attack. In a total of 206 sorties starting from 7 December and lasting until the last day of the war, F-6s and F-86s flown from multiple bases close to the battle area provided extensive CAS and were credited with destroying

disclosing main Indian armour deployments designed to blunt Pakistan Army's offensive south of the Sutlej river.

Another unintended benefit to PAF of these recconnaissance sorties was a blue-on-blue MiG-21 kill by the IAF. On the night of 11 December, Flight Lieutenant Najeeb Akhtar was detailed to fly a recconnaissance mission over the Shakarganj–Jammu area to be followed five minutes later by Squadron Leader Farooq Umar over the area south of Najeeb's route. Most probably alerted by photo flashes from Flight Lieutenant Najeeb's Mirage, the IAF directed

or disabling 56 tanks and 114 vehicles.[38] The F-6s with their three 30mm cannons and eight 57mm rockets were found to be especially effective in the CAS role. Pakistan Army's 23rd Division, which had captured Chhamb by 8 December also received extensive air support in the shape of 117 sorties and the pilots were credited with destroying an ammunition dump and 18 artillery guns.

As would be expected, during many of these interdiction or CAS sorties, the opposing fighters ran into each other. During one such mission over the Shakargarh area on 7 December, four F-6s of No.

Despite a US arms embargo, PAF kept in touch with other air forces to keep its combat knowledge base up to date. Here the resident Sabres and visiting RAF Hunters take a rest as rain stops play – early 1971, Peshawar. (Rod Dean)

11 Squadron ran into four Su-7s belonging to IAF No. 26 Squadron. In the ensuing combat, two Su-7s were claimed shot down. One of the vanquished, Squadron Leader Jiwa Singh went down with his aircraft and the other is believed to have made it back to base. In another engagement over the same area on 14 December, Flight Lieutenant Aamer Sharief flying an F-6, also from No. 11 Squadron, fired a Sidewinder against a fast-receding Su-7. The fate of this Su-7 is not known as no further details have emerged from the Indian side. During one of the interdiction sorties in the Sialkot area on 7 December, Flight Lieutenant Wajid Ali had to eject from his crippled F-6 after receiving an AAA hit and was to spend rest of the war as a POW.

A lack of communication between Army and PAF was to lead to a disastrous campaign for 18th Division. The division commander with a bold plan to capture Ramgarh and Jaisalmer had failed to heed the PAF warnings, delivered well before the war, to notify them of any planned campaign in advance so that the Jacobabad airfield could be made operational for air cover and any ground support requests. The area was otherwise too distant from Masroor or Sargodha for any air support. The IAF on the other hand had three airbases close to the area from where it could provide swift support. Fully exposed in the dessert area, and with no friendly air cover, it only took a flight of Hunters based at Jaisalmer to knock out most of the Pakistani tanks during 4 and 5 December. The PAF rushed in C-130s and B-57s, the only aircraft that could reach the area or strike Jaisalmer, but the damage had already been done. With the advance blunted, the division withdrew its forces back to holding areas, and the sector became largely inactive after 7 December.

Further south, Masroor threw in everything it could muster to blunt an Indian Army advance threatening Hyderabad. The Indian buildup was detected in the Chor-Nagar Parkar sector by an off-course T-33, piloted by Wing Commander Ali Randhawa who was heading towards Uttarlai airfield for his nightly bombing run armed with two 500lb bombs. Just prior to the war, PAF had modified T-33s allowing them to carry two 500lb bombs to supplement the B-57 force in attacking the lightly defended Uttarlai and Bhuj airfields. Noticing a large fully lit area brimming with tanks and vehicles, in an area close to the border with no regular Pakistan Army deployments on the opposite side, Randhawa rang alarm bells as soon as he landed back.[39] The Base Commander, Air Commodore Nazir Latif was quick to react and after verifying Randhawa's initial reports via additional recconnaissance flights, close to 150 sorties comprising of F-86s, B-57s and T-33s were mounted, with top-cover of F-86s and F-104s to wreak havoc and stop the Indian advance.

The Aftermath

As the Pakistan Army surrendered in the Eastern Theatre on 16 December, a ceasefire was also reached in the West and came into force the day after. The much-anticipated Pakistan Army main offensive to be led by General Tikka Khan never materialised, as many of the formations became unbalanced after being committed into piecemeal localised battles, and as the apex military leadership saw little cause to fight when the succession of East Pakistan had already become reality.

During the 14-day war, the PAF flew a total of 3,027 sorties in both theatres.[40] In the Western Theatre the PAF lost a total of 22 aircraft during the 14 days to all causes. Out of these, five were lost in air combat, seven on the ground, seven to enemy ground fire, and three in combat related accidents. In the Eastern Theatre, the remaining 11 F-86Es, one T-33, and one RT-33 were immobilised before the surrender. Before the war, two F-86Es had been lost in air combat, and three additional F-86Es were lost during the war. Despite repeated attacks, not a single F-86E was destroyed on the ground at Tejgaon, and the dummy aircraft placed on the ORP received much of the attention. Out of the two Alouette helicopters at Tejgaon, one of the serviceable aircraft managed to fly to Burma and from where it was shipped to Pakistan after a few months.

The IAF admitted to losing 71 aircraft during the war, out of which it credits 56 to enemy action and the remaining 15 to accidents. Out of the 52 aircraft it accepts losing in the Western Theatre, 16 are attributed to air action, three on the ground, 24 to ground fire, and nine in various flying accidents.[41] In the Eastern Theatre it accepts losing 13 aircraft to Pakistani action, out of which it admits 11 as having been lost in Pakistani territory and two others, that made it back to friendly airspace before crashing.[42] No breakdown in aircraft lost to air action or ground fire is provided. Another independent Indian-researched book admits to losing 18 aircraft in total, out of which it credits 12 as combat and the remaining six as non-combat related.[43] A full list of PAF kills and losses during the war is provided in the appendixes.

Table 10: Fleet-wide Breakdown of Combat Missions in Western Theatre and Type Losses		
Aircraft	Combat missions	Lost to enemy action
F-6	821	3
F-86E	791	2
F-86F	617	7
Mirage IIIRP	390	0
F-104A/B	104	3
B-57B/C	130	3
T-33A	43	0
T-6G	12	0
C-130B/E	11	0
RB-57B	0	1

Out of the total effort generated, most (1,748) sorties were in day/night air defence role, followed by close air support (951) to the ground and naval forces, and 290 were dedicated to counter-air operations. The remaining sorties constituted photoreconnaissance

A formation of Mach 2 capable Starfighters during a routine training sortie. (Authors' collection)

and miscellaneous helicopter operations in SAR, CASEVAC, or transport roles.

There is little doubt that the defecting East Pakistani officers who had intimate knowledge of the deployment sites of PAF's radars and the layout of the air bases provided information to the Indian defence officials. How damaging this intelligence actually proved to be for the PAF cannot be assessed accurately. For example, nearly all the IAF's overland attacks against the PAF bases were detected but that was not conclusive proof that the IAF pilots had failed to use their knowledge of the gaps in the Pakistani radar cover. Similarly, the reason why the IAF could not destroy many PAF aircraft, fuel storage or other air base vulnerabilities was not necessarily a reflection of the IAF's failure to use the valuable intelligence. The more likely reason was its lack of precision weapons or that it became too sensitive to its losses near the well-defended air bases of the PAF. In East Pakistan, the PAF was at a greater disadvantage but there too, little conclusive evidence pointed to the leaked intelligence being the sole or even the principal contributor to the damage inflicted on Dacca air base. The IAF did benefit from the knowledge that from about April onward, the Mukti Bahini's control of the outlying areas around Dacca and other airfields had made it impossible for the PAF to deploy any air defence observer units or radars. Consequently, the IAF fighters enjoyed unchallenged omni-directional routes to Dacca and their only threat came from the intrepid F-86 pilots circling overhead to effect interceptions after visual contact. No. 14 Squadron would certainly have scored more kills had it been served by an effective radar- and observer-based detection system, but that had become an impossibility. One must bear in mind that even that unattainable advantage would have delayed the IAF by just a few more days from gaining total control of the air, owing to the prevailing 10:1 ratio of forces.

PAF had generated almost twice the daily sortie rate compared to the 1965 war, but with greater effort spent on air defence as it had been trying to conserve its strength for the main land offensive, which was not to materialise. Compared to the 1965 war, where it had forced the IAF onto the backfoot at the onset of hostilities, this time PAF had been much more conservative in risk taking. While the IAF was quick to adapt, e.g., deciding to target less protected lines of communication and strategic industrial targets after suffering heavy losses on the opening two days of offensive counter-air operations, the PAF did not recalibrate their response. In hindsight, a case can be made that greater PAF offensive counter-air sorties at the onset, even with higher attrition risk, would have forced the IAF to redirect greater effort towards air defence, and reducing resource availability for offensive missions. Nonetheless, PAF's capability to generate such a high sortie rate, even when hampered by the loss of

The war attracted worldwide attention and Pakistan, normally more restrictive than most, permitted some media access, especially in covering the air war. (PAF Museum)

one third of its technicians and about one tenth of its aircrew which belonged to East Pakistan, reflects well on its resilience and fighting spirit. The PAF was the only service that, despite having lost some aircraft, remained operationally balanced throughout the conflict in the West, and remained fully prepared to perform its assigned task.

The RJAF F-104s that became available in the last part of the war were flown back to Jordan, supported by a PAF C-130, about 20 days after the war had ended. The PAF offered RJAF one of its's own Starfighter in lieu of the single Jordanian aircraft lost, an offer which was politely declined by Jordan.

Three Libyan Air Force F-5As, flown by PAF pilots who had earlier experience on this fighter, landed at Peshawar airbase on 27 December 1971. Although the F-5As had begun their journey to Pakistan on 20 December, a week's delay occurred in getting diplomatic overflight clearances and the need to change their markings enroute. The F-5As flew regularly within a PAF fighter squadron for the next seven months before being ferried back to Libya on 20 July 1972. The three F-5s were only the first batch of fighters, which would have been followed by others, had the war not ended abruptly.

EPILOGUE

PAF had an eventful journey from its very birth.

Developing countries have typically struggled with building state capacity in terms of different agencies of the state being able to successfully deliver on a sustainable basis as per their purpose. In the case of Pakistan its air force has been a noticeable exception, the question then arises as to what contributed to this success. This book has tried to detail the development of PAF from inception until the time it had matured into an effective air force

A group of men highly committed to their profession clearly stands out as one reason, without the motivation and patriotism of the pioneers, the attitude that PAF needed to make the most of whatever limited resources were on offer would not have become part of its culture. Even in the period when the US MDAP made generous support possible, the men at the helm did not stop at what was made available and instead endeavoured to build up institutional capacities as much as possible. PAF was fortunate at the time the US MDAP came about that a core group of officers had built up sufficient experience to realise the value of what was on offer and had the ability to bring about the change that was needed. Even more fortunate was that at that time person like Air Marshal Asghar Khan, who had the reputation of being a highly competent professional, was a dedicated officer and a hard task master, took over the helm of the force. He built up around him a team of officers who were equally committed and this core group of officers provided the leadership that embarked on a transformative journey. The widespread training opportunities that were available to PAF at the time was put to good use and a large number of officers were exposed to new methods and systems and institutional momentum

Inducted into the force in 1959, the B-57s worked hard during the two Indo-Pakistan wars, particularly in night bombing missions, but needed to be replaced by 1971. Choices were limited for various reasons. (Authors' collection)

The F-104 was another unhappy acquisition given the choices offered by the Americans, and then subsequently difficult to support in the embargo period. They were far from being a multi-role combat aircraft. (Authors' collection)

towards this change was created. With this institutional momentum it was possible to break down any resistance to change and new enhanced goals were enumerated for the force to aspire to.

International collaboration was another very important facet, PAF was able to benchmark itself against various practices being followed by other air forces and the body of knowledge this created provided the standards PAF could follow. Even before, this collaboration allowed PAF to train its manpower in technical trades, start meeting its manpower requirements for flying duties and train officers for higher defence planning. This way institutional knowledge was built up on what air power could do and the tools needed to exercise such a capability in practice.

PAF as a service was never lavished with large resources, if it had been resourced better then options more viable than acquiring

PAF had also placed an order for Mirage 5s during 1970 but these were delivered well after the 1971 war. (Authors' collection)

Through all the years of growth and combat the greatest strength of the Pakistan Air Force was its personnel, especially those outside the cockpits as suggested by this support team photo. (PAF Museum)

Equally important was the autonomy PAF was provided with. In developing countries, often, the organisations or institutions that make up a state's functioning capacity see their authority encroached upon. Most often this encroachment is on the part of political actors who intend to use the organisation to further their own interests. As PAF was not seen as an organisation which could be useful for another political actor for its own purposes it was left to its own purposes. PAF leadership was therefore free to concentrate entirely on its own mission. The 1965 war made PAF a darling of the country and this only reinforced its autonomy and provided it the means to secure the support it needed for its own mission. The autonomy thus afforded, along with the strength PAF built as an organisation, worked in tandem to create this success story.

We would see that by end of 1971 blooded in two wars, PAF had performed extremely well against a much bigger and better resourced adversary. It had come a long way from being a marginal force at the time of Pakistan's birth and could look back at its short history with pride. Post the 1971 war, PAF would begin another phase of its journey which would see the air force growing into an even more capable force despite the usual difficulties of periodic sanctions and resource constraints. The story of PAF from the end of 1971 onwards would see a different set of actors, difficulties and triumphs and is a story which deserves its own dedicated account.

second-hand Sabre F.Mk 6s from Germany or Chinese F-6 aircraft would have been exercised. Nevertheless, it got sufficient resources which kept a lifeline open. This is where the aforementioned professionalism and the knowledge base came together, PAF's leadership understood what was important from an operational perspective within the context of modern air power and utilised its limited resources wisely. Without this adequate, if not lavish, allocation of resources it would have been impossible for PAF to continue to build up its capabilities.

APPENDICES

I

1965 INDO-PAKISTAN AIR WAR KILLS AND LOSSES

Table 11: PAF air-to-air combat losses							
Date	Location	Aircraft Type	S/N	PAF Pilot	Pilot Fate	IAF Aircraft	Remarks
4 Sept	Chamb	F-86F	52-4716	F/O N.M. Butt	Ejected	Gnat	Shot down by F/L V.S. Pathani
6 Sept	Halwara	F-86F	52-5248	S/L Sarfaraz Rafique	KIA	Hunter	Shot down by F/L D.N. Rathore
6 Sept	Halwara	F-86F	53-1173	F/O Yunus Hussain	KIA	Hunter	Shot down by F/O V.K. Neb
7 Sept	Kalaikunda	F-86F	55-4027	F/O Afzal Khan	KIA	Hunter	Shot down by F/L Alfred T Cook
16 Sept	Khem Karan	F-86F	52-5232	F/O Shaukat-ul-Islam	POW	Hunter	Shot down by F/O P.S. Pingali
19 Sept	Sargodha	F-86F	53-1199	F/L S.M. Ahmed	Survived	Gnat	Shot down by F/O Vinay Kapilla. Survived the crash landing
20 Sept	Lahore	F-86F	53-1174	F/L A.H. Malik	Ejected	Gnat	Shot down by F/O A.K. Mazumdar

Table 12: PAF aircraft lost to enemy AAA or small-arms fire					
Date	Location	Aircraft Type	S/N	Pilot Name	Pilot Fate
6 Sept	Jamnagar	B-57B	53-3941	S/L S.A. Siddique (P) & S/L A Qureshi (N)	KIA
11 Sept	Amritsar	F-86F	53-1180	S/L Munir Ahmed	KIA
14 Sept	Adampur	B-57B	53-3891	F/L Sheikh (P) & F/L B.A. Choudary (N)	POW

Table 13: PAF losses due to combat and non-combat related accidents						
Date	Location	Aircraft Type	S/N	Pilot Name	Pilot Fate	Remarks
4 Sept	Sylhet	F-86F	55-3832	F/L Hasan Akhtar	Ejected	Bird strike
7 Sept	Kurmitola	F-86F	55-4028	F/L A.T.M. Aziz	KIA	Flew into ground during bad weather while vectored towards enemy aircraft
7 Sept	Mauripur	F-86F	52-4849	F/O Sikander Azam	Fatal	Engine flame out on take-off
7 Sept	Sargodha	F-104A	56-877	F/L Amjad Hussain	Ejected	Flew throw the debris of Mystére flown by S/L A B Devayya
13 Sept	Gurdaspur	F-86F	52-5160	S/L Alauddin Ahmad	KIA	Debris of exploding train or bomb ricochet
17 Sept	Sargodha	F-104A	56-868	F/L G.O. Abbasi	Survived	Thrown clear after landing short in a dust storm
17 Sept	Risalpur	B-57B	53-3942	F/L M.A. Butt (P) & F/L Khalid-uz-Zaman (N)	Fatal	Crashed during night landing possibly due to disorientation

Table 14: PAF losses to own AAA						
Date	Location	Aircraft Type	S/N	Pilot Name	Pilot Fate	Remarks
8 Sept	Kasur	F-86F	51-13427	F/L Sadruddin Hossain	Ejected	Landed among own troops
11 Sept	Rahwali	RB-57B	53-3961	S/L Muhammad Iqbal (P) & F/L Saifullah Lodhi (N)	KIA	Shot down by own AAA while practicing ELINT mission

Table 15: PAF aircraft lost on ground to IAF attacks

Date	Location	Aircraft Type	S/N	Remarks
7 Sept	Sargodha	F-86F	55-3843	Destroyed on ground

Table 16: Indian air-to-air combat losses

Date	Location	Aircraft Type	IAF Pilot	Pilot Fate	PAF Pilot	PAF Aircraft	Remarks
1 Sept	Chamb	Vampire	F/L A.K. Bhagwagar	KIA	S/L Sarfaraz Rafiqui	F-86F	
1 Sept	Chamb	Vampire	S/L V.M. Joshi	KIA	S/L Sarfaraz Rafiqui	F-86F	
1 Sept	Chamb	Vampire	F/L S. Bharadwaj	EOT	F/L Imtiaz Bhatti	F-86F	
6 Sept	Halwara	Hunter	F/L P.S. Pingali	EOT	S/L Sarfaraz Rafiqui	F-86F	
6 Sept	Halwara	Hunter	F/O A.R. Ghandhi	EOT	F/L Yunus Hussain	F-86F	Possibly shot down by F/L Cecil Choudhry
6 Sept	Adampur	Hunter	S/L A.K. Rawlley	Killed	S/L M.M. Alam	F-86F	
7 Sept	Sargodha	Mystère IV	F/L Babul Guha	Killed	F/L A H Malik	F-86F	AIM-9B kill
7 Sept	Sargodha	Mystère IV	S/L A.B. Devayya	Killed	F/L Amjad Hussain	F-104	
7 Sept	Sargodha	Hunter	S/L O.N. Kakar	POW	S/L M.M. Alam	F-86F	AIM-9B kill
7 Sept	Sargodha	Hunter	F/L J.S. Brar	Killed	S/L M.M. Alam	F-86F	
7 Sept	Sargodha	Hunter	S/L S.B. Bhagwat	Killed	S/L M.M. Alam	F-86F	
13 Sept	Sialkot	Gnat	F/L A.N. Kale	EOT	F/L Yousuf Ali Khan	F-86F	
16 Sept	Khem Karan	Hunter	F/L F.D. Bunsha	Killed	S/L M.M. Alam	F-86F	
19 Sept	Chawinda	Gnat	F/L V.M. Mayadev	POW	FL Saiful Azam	F-86F	
19 Sept	Bhuj	Beechcraft	N/A	KIA	F/O Qais M. Hussain	F-86F	Civilian aircraft with CM Gujrat Balwant Rai Mehta, wife and staff on-board
20 Sept	Lahore	Hunter	S/L D.P. Chatarje	KIA	F/L Sharbat Ali Changezi	F-86F	
20 Sept	Lahore	Hunter	F/L S.K. Sharma	EOT	F/L S.N.A. Jilani	F-86F	
22 Sept	Sadiqganj	Canberra	F/O M.M. Lowe (P) and F/O K.K. Kapur (N)	Kapur-KIA Lowe-POW	S/L Jamal A. Khan	F-104	Night kill with AIM-9B

Table 17: IAF losses to Pakistan AAA or small-arms fire

Date	Pilot Name	Unit	Aircraft Type	Pilot Fate	Area
1 Sept	F/O S V Pathak	45 Sqn	Vampire	Bailed Out	Possibly shot down by own troops
7 Sept	S/L Jasbeer Singh	3 Sqn	Mystère IV	KIA	
8 Sept	F/O M V Singh	27 Sqn	Hunter	POW	
9 Sept	F/L I F Hussain	8 Sqn	Mystère IV	EOT	
10 Sept	F/O D P Chinoy	1 Sqn	Mystère IV	Escaped	
11 Sept	S/L R K Uppal	1 Sqn	Mystère IV	KIA	
13 Sept	F/L T S Sethi	31 Sqn	Mystère IV	KIA	
13 Sept	F/L Sadarngani Lal	8 Sqn	Mystère IV	POW	
22 Sept	F/L K C Carriapa	20 Sqn	Hunter	POW	
22 Sept	F/O P R Ramchandani	3 Sqn	Mystère IV	KIA	

Table 18: Indian aircraft lost on ground to PAF attacks

Date	Aircraft Type	Quantity	Airbase	Remarks
6 Sept	Gnat	1	Pathankot	No. 19 Sqn raid
6 Sept	MiG-21F	2	Pathankot	No. 19 Sqn raid
6 Sept	Mystére IV	6	Pathankot	No. 19 Sqn raid
6 Sept	C-119	1	Pathankot	No. 19 Sqn raid
6 Sept	MiG-21F	1	Adampur	B-57 night raid
7 Sept	Canberra	2	Kalaikunda	East Pakistan – No. 14 Sqn 1st raid
7 Sept	Vampire	4	Kalaikunda	East Pakistan – No. 14 Sqn 1st raid
7 Sept	Canberra	2	Kalaikunda	East Pakistan – No. 14 Sqn 2nd raid
7 Sept	Dakota	2	Srinagar	No. 19 Sqn raid. One Dakota belonged to Indian Airlines
7 Sept	Caribou	1	Srinagar	No. 19 Sqn raid. Aircraft belonged to UN Mission
10 Sept	Vampire	1	Bagdogra	East Pakistan – No. 14 Sqn raid
11 Sept	C-119	1	Pathankot	B-57 night raid
12 Sept	Mystére IV	1	Pathankot	B-57 night raid
13 Sept	Mystére IV	2	Adampur	B-57 day raid
13 Sept	Dakota	1	Jammu	B-57 night raid
14 Sept	C-119	1	Barrackpore	East Pakistan – No. 14 Sqn raid
14 Sept	Dakota	1	Barrackpore	East Pakistan – No. 14 Sqn raid
14 Sept	Hunter	2	Halwara	B-57 night raid
14 Sept	Dakota	1	Jamnagar	B-57 night raid
14 Sept	Hunter	1	Jamnagar	B-57 night raid
14 Sept	Vampire	2	Jamnagar	B-57 night raid
14 Sept	Dakota	1	Pathankot	B-57 night raid
15 Sept	Hunter	2	Halwara	B-57 night raid
20 Sept	Gnat	1	Halwara	B-57 night raid

Table 19: IAF losses due to combat and non-combat related accidents

Date	Aircraft Type	Pilot Name	Pilot Fate	Area	Remarks
3 Sept	Gnat	S/L B.P.S. Sikand	POW	Pasrur	Landed in panic after seeing a F-104
9 Sept	Hunter	F/L G.S. Ahuja	Fatal	Halwara	Mid-air collision with another Hunter
15 Sept	Hunter	F/L T.K. Choudhry	Fatal	Halwara	Bird strike

Table 20: Summary of PAF and known Indian losses

	PAF	IAF
Aircraft lost in air-to-air combat	7	17
Aircraft lost to AAA or small-arms fire	3	10
Aircraft lost on ground to enemy attacks	1	38
Aircraft lost in combat or non-combat related accidents	9	3
Total	20	68
The above summary includes only IAF losses and excludes the 3 civilian, 2 Indian Army and 1 Indian Navy losses		

II
1971 INDO-PAKISTAN AIR WAR KILLS AND LOSSES

Table 21: PAF air-to-air combat losses							
Date	Location	Aircraft Type	S/N	Pilot	Fate	IAF Aircraft	Remarks
22 Nov	Chuagacha – East Pakistan	F-86E	-	F/L Pervez M Qureshi	POW	Gnat	Shot down by F/L Donald Lazarus
22 Nov	Chuagacha – East Pakistan	F-86E	-	F/O Khalil Ahmed	POW	Gnat	Shot down by F/L M A Ganapathy
4 Dec	Tejgaon – East Pakistan	F-86E	-	W/C S.M. Ahmed	KIA	Hunter	Shot down by W/C N Chatrath
4 Dec	Kurmitola – East Pakistan	F-86E	-	F/L Saeed Afzal	KIA	Hunter	Shot down by F/O H Masand
4 Dec	Tejgaon – East Pakistan	F-86E	-	F/O Sajjad Noor	EOT	Hunter	Shot down by W/C R Sundaresan
10 Dec	Chamb	F-86F	55-3856	S/L Aslam Choudhry	KIA	Hunter	Shot down by S/L R N Bharadwaj
12 Dec	Jamnagar	F-104A	56-773	W/C M.L. Middlecoat	KIA	MiG-21	Shot down by F/L Bharat B Soni
12 Dec	Risalewala	F-6	1703	F/L Ejazuddin	EOT	Su-7	Shot down by F/L S S Malhotra
13 Dec	Talhar	F-86E	1718	F/O N.N.A. Baig	KIA	Hunter	Shot down by F/L Farokh J Mehta
17 Dec	Naya Chor	F-104A	56-767	F/L Samad Changezi	KIA	MiG-21	Shot down by F/L Aruna K Datta; ex-RJAF F-104

Table 22: PAF aircraft lost to enemy AAA or small-arms fire					
Date	Aircraft	S/N	Pilot	Status	Remarks
5 Dec	F-104A	56-804	S/L Amjad Hussain	POW	Amritsar area
6 Dec	B-57C	53-3948	F/L Javed Iqbal (P), F/L G.M. Malik (N)	KIA	Amritsar area
6 Dec	B-57B	53-3943	S/L I Hameed (P), S/L Z Ahmed (N)	KIA	Bhuj area
6 Dec	B-57B	53-3939	S/L Khusro (P), S/L Peter Christy (N)	KIA	Jamnagar area
7 Dec	F-6	4110	F/L Wajid Ali Khan	POW	Marala area
8 Dec	F-86F	55-4019	F/L Fazal Elahi	KIA	Zafarwal area
17 Dec	F-6	4108	F/L Shahid Raza	KIA	Shakargarh area

Table 23: PAF aircraft lost on ground to IAF attacks					
Date	Aircraft	Quantity	S/N	Location	Remarks
4 Dec	F-86F	1	53-1187	Murid	Destroyed in raid by No. 20 Squadron (Hunters)
6 Dec	RB-57	1	53-3934	Masroor	Destroyed in night raid by Canberras
8 Dec	F-86F	5	53-1095, 55-3839, 55-3848, 55-3851, 55-4018	Murid	Destroyed in raid by No. 20 Squadron (Hunters)

Table 24: PAF losses due to combat and non-combat related accidents

Date	Aircraft	S/N	Pilot	Status	Remarks
4 Dec	F-86E	1689	F/L Nayyar Iqbal	Fatal	Flamed-out after take-off from Rafiqui
7 Dec	F-86F	55-4030	F/O Hamid A. Khawaja	EOT	Flamed-out while chasing Hunter in Khushalgarh area
7 Dec	F-86E	1657	S/L Cecil Choudhry	EOT	SD by own AAA in Zafarwal area
8 Dec	B-57B	53-3945	-	-	Caught fire during servicing at Mianwali
8 Dec	F-6	1508	F/L Afzal J. Siddiqui	KIA	Shot down by own AAA or possible fratricide by leader
16 Dec	11 x F-86E	-	-	-	Immobilised before surrender in East Pakistan
16 Dec	1 x RT-33	-	-	-	Immobilised before surrender in East Pakistan
16 Dec	1 x T-33	-	-	-	Immobilised before surrender in East Pakistan

Table 25: Indian air-to-air combat losses

Date	Aircraft Type	IAF Pilot	Pilot Fate	PAF Plane	Area	Remarks
4 Dec	Hunter	S/L A.V. Samanta	KIA	F-86E	Tezgaon – East Pakistan	Shot down by F/L Schames-ul-haq
4 Dec	Hunter	S/L K.D. Mehra	EOT	F-86E	Tezgaon – East Pakistan	Shot down by F/O Shams-ul-haq. Managed to escape.
4 Dec	Hunter	F/L K. Tremenheere	POW	F-86E	Tezgaon – East Pakistan	S/L Dilawar Hussain
4 Dec	Hunter	F/O Sudhir Tyagi	KIA	F-86F	Duman	Shot down by F/L Mujahid Salik
4 Dec	Hunter	F/O K.P. Muralidharan	KIA	F-86F	Peshawar	Shot down by F/L Salim Baig Mirza
4 Dec	Su-7	F/L Harvinder Singh	KIA	F-6	Rurala	Shot down by F/L Javed Latif
4 Dec	Su-7	F/O V.S. Chati	POW	F-6	Sakesar	Shot down by F/O Qazi Javed
4 Dec	Canberra	F/L L.M. Sasoon (P), F/L R.M. Advani (N)	KIA	Mirage III	Jabbi	Shot down by F/L Naeem Atta – night kill
4 Dec	Su-7	F/L D.R. Natu	EOT	F-104A	Amritsar	Shot down by Squadron Leader Rashid Bhatti. AIM-9B kill.
5 Dec	Hunter	S/L Jal M. Mistry	KIA	Mirage III	Sakesar	Shot down by F/L Safdar Mahmood
5 Dec	Hunter	F/L G.S. Rai	KIA	F-6	Sodhi	Shot down by W/C Saad Hatmi
5 Dec	Hunter	F/O K.L. Malkani	KIA	F-6	Katha Saghral	Shot down by F/L Shahid Raza
6 Dec	Su-7	F/L V.K. Wahi	KIA	Mirage III	Samba	Shot down by F/L Salimuddin
7 Dec	Su-7	S/L Jiwa Singh	KIA	F-6	Samba	Shot down by F/L Atiq Sufi
8 Dec	Su-7	F/L R.G. Kadam	KIA	F-6	Jaranwala	Shot down by W/C S.M.H. Hashmi
10 Dec	Alize	Lt Cdr Ashok Roy, Lt H.S. Sirohi, Ac Vijayan	KIA	F-104A	Arabian Sea	Show down by W/C Arif Iqbal. Indian Navy aircraft
11 Dec	Su-7	F/L K.K. Mohan	KIA	F-86E	Nainakot	Shot down by W/C A.I. Bukhari
14 Dec	Gnat	F/O N.J.S. Sekhon	KIA	F-86F	Srinagar	Shot down by F/L Salim Baig Mirza
14 Dec	Krishak	Capt P.K. Gaur, Capt G.S. Punia	KIA	F-86F	Shakargarh	Shot down by S/L Saleem Gohar
17 Dec	MiG-21	F/L Tejwant Singh	POW	F-86E	Pasrur	Shot down by F/L Maqsood Amir

Table 26: IAF losses to Pakistan AAA or small-arms fire						
Date	Pilot Name	Unit	Aircraft Type	Pilot Fate	Area	Remarks
4 Dec	F/L Gurdip Singh	101 Sqn	Su-7	EOT	Chamb	
4 Dec	F/L P.V. Apte	220 Sqn	HF-24	KIA	Naya Chor	
4 Dec	F/L M.S. Grewal	32 Sqn	Su-7	POW*	Rafiqui	
4 Dec	F/L P.N. Saksena	222 Sqn	Su-7	Escaped	Suleimanki	
4 Dec	F/L V.V. Tambay	32 Sqn	Su-7	KIA	Rafiqui	
4 Dec	F/L A.R. Da Costa	7 Sqn	Hunter	KIA	Lalmunirhat – East Pakistan	
4 Dec	S/L S.K. Gupta	7 Sqn	Hunter	EOT	Lalmunirhat – East Pakistan	
4 Dec	F/O S.G. Khonde	37 Sqn	Hunter	KIA	Tezgaon – East Pakistan	
4 Dec	S/L S.V. Bhutani	221 Sqn	Su-7	POW	Tezgaon – East Pakistan	
4 Dec	W/C K.N. Bajpai	27 Sqn	Hunter	Survived	?	Pilot is believed to have crashed on landing
5 Dec	F/L A.V. Pethia	3 Sqn	Mystère IV	POW	Chishtian	
5 Dec	S/L D.S. Jafa	26 Sqn	Su-7	POW	Lahore	
5 Dec	F/L J.L. Bhargava	220 Sqn	HF-24	POW	Naya Chor	
5 Dec	F/L Harish Sinhji	29 Sqn	MiG-21FL	POW	Suleimanki	
5 Dec	F/L S.C. Sandal (P), F/L K.S. Nanda (N)	35 Sqn	Canberra	KIA	Arabian Sea	
5 Dec	F/L S.K. Goswami (P), F/L S.C. Mahajan (N)	5 Sqn	Canberra	KIA	Bhalwal	
6 Dec	F/L J. Bhattacharya	101 Sqn	Su-7	Escaped	Chamb	
6 Dec	F/O K.C. Kuruvilla	222 Sqn	Su-7	POW	Jassar – East Pakistan	
6 Dec	S/L D.P. Rao	4 Sqn	MiG-21FL	EOT	Gauhati – Eastern Theatre	
7 Dec	F/L S. Dasgupta	14 Sqn	Hunter	EOT	Dum Dum – Eastern Theatre	
8 Dec	S/L Denzil Keelor	45 Sqn	MiG-21FL	EOT	Chamb	Managed to escape
8 Dec	W/C B.A. Coelho	7 Sqn	Hunter	POW	Suleimanki	
8 Dec	S/L Anukul	31 Sqn	Mystère IV	EOT	Haveli – Fazilka	
9 Dec	F/L N. Shankar	32 Sqn	Su-7	KIA	Amritsar	
9 Dec	S/L A.V. Kamat	10 Sqn	HF-24	POW	Hyderabad	
10 Dec	S/L M.K. Jain	27 Sqn	Hunter	KIA	Chamb	
10 Dec	F/L S.K. Chibber	108 Sqn	Su-7	KIA	Sadiqganj	
10 Dec	F/L Dilip Parulkar	26 Sqn	Su-7	POW*	Zafarwal	
10 Dec	F/L L.H. Dixon	17 Sqn	Hunter	EOT	Lalmunirhat – East Pakistan	Managed to escape
10 Dec	S/L R.C. Sachdeva	14 Sqn	Hunter	KIA	Narayanganj – East Pakistan	
13 Dec	W/C H.S. Gill	47 Sqn	MiG-21FL	KIA	Badin	
13 Dec	S/L J.D. Kumar	3 Sqn	Mystère IV	KIA	Suleimanki	
13 Dec	S/L P.S. Gill	28 Sqn	MiG-21FL	EOT	Tezgaon – East Pakistan	Managed to escape
13 Dec	S/L Jatinder Das Kumar	3 Sqn	Mystère IV	KIA	Haveli – Fazilka	
15 Dec	F/O B.R.E. Wilson (P), F/L R.B. Mehta (N)	16 Sqn	Canberra	KIA	Tezgaon – East Pakistan	
16 Dec	F/L T.S. Danadass	26 Sqn	Su-7	KIA	Narowal	

Table 27: Indian aircraft lost on ground to PAF attacks					
Date	Aircraft	Quantity	S/N	Location	Remarks
5 Dec	Alouette III	1	-	Srinagar	26 Sqn raid
6 Dec	Vampire	1	-	Pathankot	7 Sqn raid
11 Dec	HF-24	1	-	Uttarlai	Destroyed by S/L Amanullah – No. 9 Sqn

Table 28: IAF losses due to combat and non-combat related accidents					
Date	Aircraft Type	Pilot Name	Pilot Fate	Area	Remarks
4 Dec	Su-7	F/L Jayant Rishi	Fatal	Adampur	Crashed after tyre burst on take-off
7 Dec	Gnat	F/O M.M. Singh	KIA	Amritsar	Reacting to fake intercept by PAF GCI, hit ground
11 Dec	Alouette III	S/L K.L. Bajaj	Fatal	Kargil	
11 Dec	Canberra	F/L R.D. Naithani (P), F/L G. Theophilus (N)	KIA	Bikaner	Spatial disorientation and may also have been hit by AAA
11 Dec	MiG-21FL	F/L A.A. Dhavle	KIA	Gurdaspur	Shot down by another MiG-21 during night interception of Mirage IIIRP
12 Dec	MiG-21FL	F/O P.K. Sahu	Fatal	Palam	Undershot on landing

Table 29: Summary of PAF and Known Indian Losses		
	PAF	IAF (IN+IA)
Aircraft lost in air-to-air combat	10	18 (1 + 1)
Aircraft lost to AAA or small-arms fire	7	36
Aircraft lost on ground to enemy attacks	7	3
Aircraft lost in combat or non-combat related accidents	18	6
Total	42	63

III
AIRCRAFT TAIL NUMBERS SUPPLEMENT TO VOLUME 1

Since the publication of Volume 1 Of *Eagles of Destiny* the authors have identified several further aircraft tail numbers as detailed in the table below.

Table 30: Tail Numbers of Aircraft that served with the Royal Pakistan Air Force and Pakistan Air Force (Supplement to Volume 1)

Kaman HH-43B Huskie	62-4552, 62-4553, 62-4554, 62-4555, 62-4556, 62-4557	
Sikorsky H-19D Chickasaw	56-4252, 56-4253, 57-5977, 57-5978	
North American F-86F	51-13119, 51-13226, 51-13228, 51-13315, 51-13333, 51-13367, 51-13380, 51-13386, 51-13407, 51-13427, 51-13447, 52-4507, 52-4716, 52-4724, 52-4725, 52-4726, 52-4849, 52-5026, 52-5031, 52-5105, 52-5160, 52-5232, 52-5248, 52-5305, 52-5316, 52-5333, 52-5377, 52-5384, 52-5412, 52-5394, 53-1075, 53-1076, 53-1080, 53-1084, 53-1087, 53-1095, 53-1102, 53-1105, 53-1106, 53-1107, 53-1109, 53-1125, 53-1127, 53-1132, 53-1140, 53-1147, 53-1161, 53-1163, 53-1173, 53-1174, 53-1176, 53-1180, 53-1182, 53-1186, 53-1187, 53-1189, 53-1192, 53-1198, 53-1199, 53-1201, 53-1202, 53-1212, 53-1214, 53-1216, 53-1217, 55-3826, 55-3832, 55-3839, 55-3843, 55-3844, 55-3848, 55-3850, 55-3851, 55-3853, 55-3854, 55-3855, 55-3856, 55-3857, 55-3860, 55-3861, 55-3866, 55-3870, 55-4010, 55-4013, 55-4018, 55-4019, 55-4020, 55-4021, 55-4022, 55-4023, 55-4024, 55-4025, 55-4026, 55-4027, 55-4028, 55-4029, 55-4030, 55-4983, 55-4984, 55-4985, 55-4986, 55-4987, 55-4988, 55-4989, 55-4991, 55-4992, 55-4993, 55-4995, 55-4996, 55-4998, 55-5000, 55-5001, 55-5002, 55-5003, 55-5005, 55-5011, 55-5018, 55-5022, 55-5028, 55-5029, 55-5030, 55-5031, 55-5033, 55-5037, 55-5038, 55-5039, 55-5040, 55-5041, 55-5042, 55-5043, 55-5044, 55-5045, 55-5046	Since the publication of Volume 1, the authors have been able to identity additional serial numbers. In total, 133 serial numbers are now known, leaving only 17 unknown serials. F-68Fs were in natural metal schemes and early pictures show at least some aircraft with squadron markings on the nose and chequer patterns on the nose and tail. These were later removed. Known chequer colours were, No 14 Squadron black and white, No 17 red and yellow, No 15 red and white (see colour section).
Lockheed RT-33	53-5090, 53-5491, 53-5517, 53-5533, 53-5335	Six were delivered in total. The serial number of one aircraft that was abandoned in Dacca during 1971 war is not known.

BIBLIOGRAPHY

Ahmed, K., *Legend of the Tail Choppers, 50 Years of Excellence 1948-1998* (PAF Book Club, 2007)
Ahmed, L. G., *History of Indo-Pak War – 1965* (NUST University Press, 2006)
Anon, *The Story of the Pakistan Air Force: A Saga of Courage and Honour* (Shaheen Foundation, 1988)
Bhatti, I., 3 Encounters of '65 Indo-Pakistan War, *Shaheen Journal of Pakistan Air Force, Volume 30, Issue 1.*
Bowman, M., *Lockheed F-104 Starfighter* (Barnsley: Pen & Sword Books Limited, 2019)
Chakravorty, B. C., *Official History of the 1965 Indo-Pakistan War* (Government of India, 1992)
Chhina, R. T., *The Eagle Strikes: The Royal Indian Air Force 1932-1950* (New Delhi: Ambi Knowledge Resources, 2006)
Fricker, J., *Battle for Pakistan* (London: Ian Allan, 1979)
Grimes, B., *The History of Big Safari* (Archway Publishing, 2014)
Gulati, Y.B, and Palit, Major General (Retd.) D.K., *History of the Regiment of Artillery, Indian Army* (Leo Cooper Limited, London, 1972)
Husain, A., *Men of Steel: 6th Armoured Division in the 1965 War* (OUP Pakistan, 2006)
Hussain, Syed S., *History of the PAF 1947-1982* (Karachi: PAF Press, 1982)
Khan, A. R. *Tactical Operations by the PAF during September, 1965* (Unpublished, 1966)
Khan, J. A. The Emergence of Air Doctrine under Asghar Khan. *Shaheen Journal of the PAF*, 2016
Piracha, T. E., *History of No 24 Squadron 1962 – 1967* (unpublished, no date)
Rab, S. M., Mauripur to Masroor. *Shaheen Journal of the PAF* (no date)
Rafi, R. A., *PAF Bomber Operations 1965 & 1971 Wars* (PAF Book Club, 2001)
Robert P. Grathwol, *BRICKS, SAND AND MARBLE: U.S. Army Corps of Engineers Construction in the Mediterranean and Middle East, 1947-1991* (U.S. Army Center of Military History, 2007)
Sattar, A., *Pakistan's Foreign Policy 1947–2005: A Concise History* (Oxford University Press, 2007)
Shah, A. C., *The Gold Bird – Pakistan and its Air Force, Observations of a pilot* (Karachi: Oxford University Press, 2002)
Sheikh, M. S., Some Sweet Reminiscences of Drigh Road, Shaheen (Vol. 35). *Shaheen: Journal of the Pakistan Air Force* (no date)
Singh, L. C., *1965 War – Role of Tanks in India-Pakistan War* (BC Publishers, India, 1982)
Singh, P., *Himalayan Eagles: History of the Indian Air Force* (New Delhi: Society for Aerospace Studies, 2007)

Archives Used
Bristol Aerospace Museum
Royal Air Force Museum
The British Library, London, United Kingdom
The National Archives, Kew, United Kingdom
The US National Archives

Veterans Interviewed
Air Marshal Nur Khan
Air Chief Marshal Jamal A. Khan
Air Chief Marshal Hakimullah Khan Durrani
Air Marshal Zafar Chaudhry
Air Vice Marshal Mian Sadruddin
Air Vice Marshal Abbas Mirza
Air Vice Marshal Sadruddin Hossain (Former Chief of the Air Staff, Bangladesh Air Force)
Air Vice Marshal Farooq Umar
Air Vice Marshal Viqar Azim
Air Vice Marshal Amjad Hussain
Air Vice Marshal Salimuddin
Air Vice Marshal Hamid Khawaja
Air Commodore Mansoor A. Shah
Air Commodore Sajad Haider
Air Commodore Rais A. Rafi
Air Commodore Muhammad Sultan
Air Commodore Rashid Bhatti
Air Commodore Imtiaz Bhatti
Air Commodore Amanullah
Air Commodore Momin Arif
Air Commodore Viqar Ahmad Abidi
Group Captain Saiful Azam
Group Captain M. Shaukat-ul Islam
Group Captain Cecil Chaudry
Wing Commander Tariq Habib
Wing Commader Salim Baig Mirza
Squadron Leader Nisar ul Haq
Flight Lieutenant Fred Isaacs

Audio Recordings
Air Marshal Asghar Khan, dated 5 April 1986
Air Marshal Zafar Chaudhry, dated 23 April 1986
Air Marshal McDonald, dated 11 August 1986
Air Marshal I.A. Khan, dated 11 April 1986
Air Vice Marshal Haider Raza, dated 29 July 1986
Air Vice Marshal Khyber Khan, dated 7 October 1986
Air Vice Marshal A. Elahi Shaikh, dated 24 November 1986
Air Vice Marshal A. Qadir dated, 7 May 1986
Air Commodore T.S. Jan dated 13 May 1986
Air Commodore B.K. Dass, dated 21 June 1986
Air Commodore P.D. Callaghan, dated 19 June 1986
Air Commodore M.M. Piracha, dated 22 April 1986
Air Commodore Maqbool Rab, dated 17 August 1986
Air Commodore M. Dogar, dated 21 April 1986
Air Commodore M. Ayub, dated 11 April 1986
Air Commodore Mansoor Shah (exact date unknown)

NOTES

Chapter 1

1. Abdul Sattar, *Pakistan's Foreign Policy 1947–2005: A Concise History* (Oxford, UK: Oxford University Press, 2007), p. 35.
2. Sattar, *Pakistan's Foreign Policy*, p. 35.
3. United States National Archives (USNA): General Records of the Department of State, Records relating to Pakistan 1953–57.
4. United States National Archives (USNA): General Records of the Department of State, Records relating to Pakistan 1953–57.
5. Anon., *The Story of the Pakistan Air Force: A Saga of Courage and Honour* (Islamabad, Pakistan: Shaheen Foundation, 1988).
6. Jamal A Khan, 'The Emergence of Air Doctrine under Asghar Khan', *Shaheen Journal of the PAF*, Special Issue 2016, pp. 1–5.
7. Khan, 'The Emergence of Air Doctrine', p. 2.
8. Air Chief Marshal (Retd.) Jamal A. Khan, personal communication, 2006–2022.
9. United States National Archives (USNA): General Records of the Department of State, Records relating to Pakistan 1953–57.
10. The United States federal government's fiscal year is the 12-month period beginning 1 October and ending 30 September the following year. The identification of a fiscal year is the calendar year in which it ends.
11. Department of State, Foreign Relations of the United States: Diplomatic Papers.
12. Air Commodore (Retd.) Sultan Mohammad, personal communication, October 2021.
13. Martin Bowman, '*Lockheed F-104 Starfighter*' (Pen & Sword Books Limited, 2019).
14. Air Vice Marshal (Retd.) Mian Sadruddin, personal communication, 2006–2021.
15. Air Vice Marshal (Retd.) Mian Sadruddin, Air Vice Marshal (Retd.) Amjad Hussain and Air Chief Marshal (Retd.) Hakimullah, personal communication, 2006–2021.
16. Eyewitness accounts of both crashes were obtained in interviews with Air Vice Marshal Farooq Umar and Abbas Mirza.
17. Air Vice Marshal (Retd.) Sadruddin Hossain, personal communication, June 2006.
18. Air Marshal Zafar Chaudhry, Audio Recording, dated 23 April 1986.
19. Air Vice Marshal (Retd) S Moinur Rab, *Mauripur to Masroor* (Shaheen Journal of PAF).
20. Robert P. Grathwol, and Donita M. Moorhus, '*Bricks, Sand and Marble: U.S. Army Corps of Engineers Construction in the Mediterranean and Middle East, 1947-1991*' (Center of Military History, U.S. Army Corps of Engineers, April 2010).
21. Air Vice Marshal Haider Raza, Audio recording, dated 29 July 1986.
22. Air Marshal (Retd) Saeed M Sheikh, '*Some Sweet Reminiscences of Drigh Road*', Shaheen: Journal of the Pakistan Air Force, Volume 35.
23. Sheikh, '*Some Sweet Reminiscences*'.
24. CENTO was the Central Treaty Organization, also referred to as the Baghdad Pact, and in addition to Pakistan included Iran, Iraq, Turkey, and the United Kingdom.
25. Group Captain (Retd) A Majeed Khan, '*Days to Remember*' (Shaheen: Journal of the Pakistan Air Force, Volume 35).
26. Air Vice Marshal (Retd) Saeedullah Khan, '*Sargodha Yesterday*' (Shaheen: Journal of the Pakistan Air Force, Volume 31, Issue 1) pp. 1–6.
27. Saeedullah Khan, '*Sargodha Yesterday*', p. 6.
28. Air Commodore P.D. Callaghan, Audio Recording, dated 19 June 1986.

Chapter 2

1. Air Commodore A. Rahim Khan, *Tactical Operations by the PAF during September, 1965* (John Fricker's private collection obtained by the authors.)
2. B.C. Chakravarty, '*Indian Armed Forces – Official History of the 1965 Indo-Pakistan War*' (Government of India), p. 362.
3. A. Rahim Khan, '*Tactical Operations by the PAF during September, 1965*'.
4. Chakravarty, *Indian Armed Forces*, p. 362.
5. Eid is a religious holiday which marks the end of the month-long fasting.
6. Anon., *The Story of the Pakistan Air Force*.
7. Anon., *The Story of the Pakistan Air Force*.
8. Anon., *The Story of the Pakistan Air Force*.
9. The Rann of Kutch is a disputed area on the border of Gujarat. Indian and Pakistan forces fought a series of skirmishes in this area and tensions here were one of the causes of the 1965 war.
10. Sabres were from No. 17 Squadron and piloted by Flight Lieutenant Ashraf Sami and Jamshed Akber.
11. D.R. Mankekar, '*Twenty-Two Fateful Days – Pakistan Cut to Size*' (PC Manaktala and Sons Private Limited, India).
12. Lieutenant Colonel (Retired) Bhupinder Singh, '*1965 War – Role of Tanks in India-Pakistan War*' (BC Publishers, India).
13. Lieutenant General (Retd) Mahmud Ahmed, '*History of Indo-Pak War – 1965*' (NUST University Press).
14. Imtiaz Bhatti, '*3 Encounters of '65 Indo-Pakistan War*' (Shaheen: Journal of Pakistan Air Force, Volume 30, Issue 1).
15. P.V.S.J. Mohan, and S. Chopra, *The India-Pakistan Air War of 1965*.
16. All three pilots from the second formation perished, these included Flight Lieutenants Satish Bharadwaj, Aspi Kekobad Bhagwagar and V. M. Joshi. Flying Officer S. V. Pathak from the first formation had managed to bale out successfully.
17. Chakravarty, *Indian Armed Forces*, p. 248.
18. Anon., *The Story of the Pakistan Air Force*.
19. Mohan and Chopra, *The India-Pakistan Air War of 1965*, p. 79.
20. Mohan and Chopra, *The India-Pakistan Air War of 1965*, p .79.
21. Air Vice Marshal (Retd.) Yousuf Ali Khan narrated the episode during a private gathering in February 2012.
22. According to various IAF published sources, there were eight Gnats in two separate formations.
23. Air Vice Marshal Abbas Mirza, personal correspondence, 2006–2021.
24. IAF awarded Squadron Leader Trevor Keelor a Vir Chakra for shooting down Yousuf's Sabre.
25. Official IAF History only acknowledges 'one Gnat, short of fuel, failed to return', and provides no other information.
26. Air Commodore (Retd.) Saad Akhtar Hatmi, *I Flew the Indian Air Force Gnat*' (Shaheen: Journal of the Pakistan Air Force).
27. Anon., *The Story of the Pakistan Air Force*, p. 350.
28. From East Punjab, there are three main approaches to Lahore. The shortest is from Amritsar to Lahore astride the Grand Trunk Road. Other two approaches are along the road Harike-Khalra-Barki and from Ferozepur and Khem Karan via a conjunction at Kasur. The BRBL canal is also known as the Ichogil Canal, it was constructed by Pakistan in 1950s partly as a defensive obstacle to prevent an invasion of Lahore.
29. Mahmud Ahmed, '*History of Indo-Pak War – 1965*' (NUST University Press).
30. Y.B. Gulati and Major General (Retd.) D.K Palit, *History of the Regiment of Artillery, Indian Army* (Leo Cooper Limited, London, 1972), p. 228.
31. S. Haider, *Flight of the Falcon* (Vanguard Books, 2009).
32. Haider, *Flight of the Falcon*
33. Gulati and Palit, *History of the Regiment of Artillery, Indian Army*, pp 230–231.
34. Gulati and Palit, *History of the Regiment of Artillery, Indian Army*, pp 230–231.
35. According to published Indian accounts, the Mystére formation had jettisoned their fuel tanks when intercepted by the Starfighter and managed to recover safely to base.
36. Minutes of Conference held at Air HQ on 5 May 1965 to discuss measures to meet situation created by India.
37. Air Commodore (Retd.) Mansoor A. Shah, personal communication, October 2008.
38. Anon., *The Story of the Pakistan Air Force*, p. 360.
39. Haider, *Flight of the Falcon*, p. 134.
40. Anon., *The Story of the Pakistan Air Force*, p. 364.
41. The official Indian war history released decades later accepted loss of 10 aircraft: one Gnat, six Mysteres, one C-119 and two MiG-21s with three other aircraft damaged.
42. When Squadron Leader Alauddin Ahmed, OC No 18 Squadron and the senior most squadron commander, found that his own F-86s were not ready, he forced himself into Alam's formation.
43. Anon., *The Story of the Pakistan Air Force*, p. 365.
44. The Hunter formation was from the IAF No. 7 Squadron and were on a CAS mission.

45	This Hunter was piloted by Squadron Leader Ajit Kumar Rawlley.	91	Grimes, *The History of Big Safari*, p. 66.
46	India accepted the loss of only one Hunter in this engagement.	92	Piracha, *History of No 24 Squadron 1962 – 1967*, unpublished.
47	Mohan and Chopra, *The India-Pakistan Air War of 1965*, p. 110.	93	Piracha, *History of No 24 Squadron 1962 – 1967*, unpublished.
48	Mohan and Chopra, *The India-Pakistan Air War of 1965*, p. 111.	94	Grimes, *The History of Big Safari*, p. 64.
49	Squadron Leader Iqbal was able to recover the aircraft successfully at Peshawar.	95	Grimes, *The History of Big Safari*, p. 65.
50	Rafi, *PAF Bomber Operations*, p. 19.	96	Abrar Husain, *Men of Steel: 6th Armoured Division in the 1965 War* (OUP Pakistan, 2005).

45 This Hunter was piloted by Squadron Leader Ajit Kumar Rawlley.
46 India accepted the loss of only one Hunter in this engagement.
47 Mohan and Chopra, *The India-Pakistan Air War of 1965*, p. 110.
48 Mohan and Chopra, *The India-Pakistan Air War of 1965*, p. 111.
49 Squadron Leader Iqbal was able to recover the aircraft successfully at Peshawar.
50 Rafi, *PAF Bomber Operations*, p. 19.
51 Rafi, *PAF Bomber Operations*, p. 21.
52 The B-57's S/N was 33-941.
53 Chakravarty, *Indian Armed Forces*, p. 251.
54 Air Commodore (Retd.) Najeeb A Khan, *8-Pass Charlie* (Second to None, PAF Magazine).
55 Mohan and Chopra, *The India-Pakistan Air War of 1965*, p. 115.
56 Mohan and Chopra, *The India-Pakistan Air War of 1965*, p. 114.
57 Some had jetisoned their rocket pods, which were recovered and are on display at PAF Museum Karachi.
58 Air Vice Marshal (Retd.) Amjad Hussain, personal communication, February 2009.
59 The British writer John Fricker in his book *The Battle for Pakistan: The 1965 Air War* assigned this loss to Devayya actually shooting down the F-104. However, no evidence was offered to substantiate this claim and Fricker also failed to explain how Squadron Leader Devayya himself was shot down and killed. Later research showed that the wreckage of both aircraft was nearby, along with eyewitness accounts of villagers who saw the mid-air collision from the ground.
60 Air Vice Marshal (Retd.) Sadruddin Hossain, personal communication, May 2006.
61 The Hunter pilot was Squadron Leader Onkar Nath Kakar, who was captured.
62 Anon., *The Story of the Pakistan Air Force*, p. 382.
63 Conducted by Air Commodore (Retd.) Kaiser Tufail and recorded in his book *The Great Air Battles of the Pakistan Air Force*.
64 Filled by pilots after a sortie to outline any issues discovered during flight for remediation.
65 Mohan and Chopra, *The India-Pakistan Air War of 1965*, p. 140.
66 A flight of four Sabres from No. 14 Squadron and led by Flight Lieutenant M M Alam was deployed to Dacca during March 1962.
67 Air Commodore Khaleel Ahmed, 'Legend of the Tail Choppers, 50 Years of Excellence' (PAF Book Club, 2007).
68 IAF No. 14 Squadron equipped with Hunters, No. 16 Squadron equipped with Canberras, and No. 24 and No. 221 Squadroons, equipped with Vampires.
69 Ahmed, 'Legend of the Tail Choppers'
70 Mohan and Chopra, *The India-Pakistan Air War of 1965*, p. 165.
71 Wreckage of his aircraft was discovered 20 miles north of Dacca and showed no battle damage. The IAF Hunters also did not report any contact.
72 Ahmed, 'Legend of the Tail Choppers'
73 Ahmed, 'Legend of the Tail Choppers'
74 India accepted the loss of two Canberras and four Vampires.
75 Ahmed, 'Legend of the Tail Choppers'
76 Ahmed, 'Legend of the Tail Choppers'
77 The aircraft was out of action for the rest of the war as spares could not be flown in from West Pakistan but was eventually repaired and all nine Sabres participated during Republic Day Flypast held at Dacca on 23 March 1966.
78 The IAF accepted a loss of two Canberras.
79 The Indians accepted the loss of one Vampire and one C-119.
80 Mohan and Chopra, *The India-Pakistan Air War of 1965*, p. 201.
81 This might have been done at the direction of the Indian government to preserve strength for the Western theatre.
82 Ahmed, 'Legend of the Tail Choppers'.
83 Air Vice Marshal (Retd.) Amjad Hussain, personal communication, 2006–2010. The incident is also narrated by John Fricker in his book "The Battle for Pakistan".
84 Anon., *The Story of the Pakistan Air Force*, p. 405.
85 Rafi, *PAF Bomber Operations*, p. 52.
86 Anon., *The Story of the Pakistan Air Force*, p. 411.
87 Rafi, *PAF Bomber Operations*, p. 42.
88 Chakravarty, *Indian Armed Forces*, p. 271.
89 Bill Grimes, *The History of Big Safari* (Archway Publishing, 2014), p. 61.
90 Tassawar Elahi Piracha, *History of No 24 Squadron 1962 – 1967*, unpublished.
91 Grimes, *The History of Big Safari*, p. 66.
92 Piracha, *History of No 24 Squadron 1962 – 1967*, unpublished.
93 Piracha, *History of No 24 Squadron 1962 – 1967*, unpublished.
94 Grimes, *The History of Big Safari*, p. 64.
95 Grimes, *The History of Big Safari*, p. 65.
96 Abrar Husain, *Men of Steel: 6th Armoured Division in the 1965 War* (OUP Pakistan, 2005).
97 No. 32 Wing Commanded by Wing Commander Masood A. Sikander was moved to Sargodha at start of the war and designated as Strike Command for ground interdiction, both defensive and offensive across the border into India. No. 32 Wing was constituted of 16, 17 and 18 Squadrons from Mauripur. They were known as the "Mauripur Sabres" throughout the war.
98 Group Captain (Retd.) Saiful Azam, personal communication, 2006–2008.
99 The four Gnats were from IAF No. 9 Squadron, and led by Squadron Leader Denzil Keelor. Other formation members were Flying Officer Rai, and Flight Lieutenants Viney Kapila and Vijay Mayadev.
100 Bhatti, '3 Encounters of 65' Indo-Pakistan War'
101 Air Vice Marshal (Retd.) Sadruddin Hossain, personal communication, May 2006.
102 Bhatti, '3 Encounters of '65 Indo-Pakistan War'
103 Chakravarty, *Indian Armed Forces*, p. 271.
104 Chakravarty, *Indian Armed Forces*, p. 277.
105 192 aircraft in total, excluding the 25 T-37s as they were only used for mail and communication roles.
106 One hundred F-86F, twenty-four B-57, and twelve F-104/B = 136 aircraft.
107 Chakravarty, *Indian Armed Forces*, p. 271.
108 A. Rahim Khan, *Tactical Operations by the PAF during September 1965*.

Chapter 3

1 During such inspections, the aircraft is grounded for several weeks and many of its costly parts are replaced.
2 Taken from a report to C-in-C after the PAF Armament Competition held in January 1968. (John Fricker's private collection obtained by the authors.)
3 During wars, most air forces normally assign only younger pilots that happen to be performing instructional flying or non-operational duties back to the combat squadrons.
4 Air Vice Marshal (Retd.) Mian Sadruddin, personal communication, dated September 2009.
5 Air Vice Marshal (Retd.) Mian Sadruddin, personal communication, dated September 2009.
6 Air Vice Marshal (Retd.) Mian Sadruddin, personal communication, dated September 2009.
7 Wing Commander Abdul Latif, 'Pioneer in Maintenance', *Shaheen Journal of the Pakistan Air Force*, Vol. XXXI No. 1, March 1984.
8 All three UMiGs survived the service and are preserved in different parts of the country with one example on display at PAF Musuem Karachi.
9 PAF pilots flew with Jordan for example and participated in the June 1967 war flying for Iraq.
10 As a major in the German Army, he was the recipient of the Knight's Cross for bravery and was part of the German SS troops that rescued Italian dictator Benito Mussolini after his overthrow.
11 Der Spiegel, *Mit Billetal und BND*, published 17 November 1974.
12 One of the officers involved was late Air Commodore (Retd.) Akbar Hussain, commissioned during 1948 in first batch of Aeronautical Engineers. He participated in the negotiations as Colonel Hussain of the IIAF.
13 Personal communication with Ali Kazim, dated 13 October 2021.
14 According to one PAF officer involved in the negotiations, Gerhard was switching between hotel rooms, negotiating with PAF (disguised as IIAF) officers and Indian Navy officers at the same time.
15 Saurabh Joshi, *How an ex-Nazi arms dealer sold fighters to India and Pakistan during an arms embargo*, Daily O, September 2016.
16 Later rose to become CAS of Bangladesh Air Force and was killed in flying accident at Dacca Airfield.
17 Also a B-57 veteran from 1965 war and retired as a Wing Commander.
18 He was killed in a B-57 accident in Mauripur circuit due to a bird strike. His pilot, Flight Lieutenant Mehboob ul Haq, ejected safely.
19 Personal communication with Air Commodore (Retd.) Rais A Rafi, dated August 2006.
20 Personal communication with Air Commodore (Retd.) Rais A Rafi, dated August 2006.

21. A Pakistani horse drawn carriage.
22. Personal communication with Air Commodore (Retd.) Rais A. Rafi, dated August 2006.
23. Some sources have speculated that the aircraft were returned to China but we found no evidence to support this. The aircraft were in a derelict state and it would not have been possible to fly them back.

Chapter 4

1. Anon., *The Story of the Pakistan Air Force*, p. 447.
2. S.N. Prasad, 'Official History of 1971 War' (Ministry of Defence, Government of India, 1992, unpublished). Placed on the net by *The Times of India*, p. 597.
3. Prasad, *Official History of 1971 War*, p. 455.
4. Air Vice Marshal (Retd.) Sadruddin Hossain, personal communication, June 2006.
5. Air Vice Marshal (Retd.) Sadruddin Hossain, personal communication, June 2006.
6. Group Captain (Retd.) Saiful Azam, personal communication, 2006–2008.
7. Khan, Inam-ul-Haq, Air Marshal (Retd.), 'Saga of PAF in East Pakistan – 1971' (Defence Journal, May 2009).
8. Air Commodore (Retd.) Sajad Haider, personal communication, August 2006.
9. Air Commodore (Retd.) Sajad Haider, personal communication, August 2006.
10. Ahmed, *Legend of the Tail Choppers*, p. 91.
11. Ahmed, *Legend of the Tail Choppers*, p. 93.
12. Air Commodore (Retd.) Kaiser Tufail, 'The Last Stand – Air War 1971' (website: kaiser-aeronaut.blogspot.com).
13. Muhammad Shamsul Haq, 'An Unmtached Feat in the Air' (Shaheen: Journal of the Pakistan Air Force).
14. Tufail, 'The Last Stand'.
15. Inam-ul-Haq Khan, Air Marshal (Retd.), 'Saga of PAF in East Pakistan – 1971' (Defence Journal, May 2009).
16. Air Chief Marshal (Retd.) Hakimullah, personal communication, 2006–2008.
17. Air Commodore (Retd.) Amanullah, personal communication, 2006–2010.
18. The Gnat was being flown by Wing Commander Johnny Green.
19. Anon., *The Story of the Pakistan Air Force*, p. 451.
20. Rafi, *PAF Bomber Operations*, p. 128.
21. Anon., *The Story of the Pakistan Air Force*, p. 466.
22. Amanullah had flown over 300 hours with RJAF at H-5 air base with Awni and Ihsan Shurdom. Ihsan Shurdom later rose to command the RJAF.
23. Tariq Habib, personal communication, 2006.
24. The Indian pilot claims that the missile was decoyed by flares. PAF Starfighters were never equipped with IRCM flares. The Indian MiG-21 pilot most likely saw the F-104's afterburner being lit up and confused it with flares.
25. Prasad, *Official History of 1971 War*, p. 454.
26. Anon., *The Story of the Pakistan Air Force*, p. 457.
27. M.K. Tufail, *In the Ring and on Its Feet: A Concise Account Based on Official War Records* (Ferozsons (Pvt.) Limited)
28. Anon., *The Story of the Pakistan Air Force*, p. 458.
29. Wing Commandere (Retd.) Salim Baig Mirza, *Air Battles, December 1971 – My Experiences*, Defence Journal and personal communication with the authors.
30. Mirza, *Air Battles, December 1971 – My Experiences*, Defence Journal and personal communication with the authors.
31. Tufail, *In the Ring and on Its Feet*
32. According to various published Indian sources this was a lone Hunter piloted by Squadron Leader Jal M Mistry, as his wingman Squadron Leader Karumbaya aborted on take-off due to technical reasons.
33. This formation was piloted by Squadron Leader Ashok Shinde and Flight Lieutenant Vijay Kumar Wahib, both from 101 Squadron.
34. Tufail, *In the Ring and on Its Feet*
35. As narrated to the authors by Air Commodore (retd.) Rashid A. Bhatti, 2009.
36. Tufail, *In the Ring and on Its Feet*
37. Tufail, *In the Ring and on Its Feet*
38. Anon., *The Story of the Pakistan Air Force*, p. 463.
39. Personal communication with Squadron Leader (Retd.) Ali Randhawa, August 2006.
40. Anon., *The Story of the Pakistan Air Force*, p. 469.
41. Prasad, *Official History of 1971 War*, p. 454.
42. Prasad, *Official History of 1971 War*, p. 454.
43. P.V.S. Jagan and Samir Chopra, '*Eagles Over Bangladesh: The Indian Air Force in the 1971 Liberation War*' (HarperCollins Publishers India).

ABOUT THE AUTHORS

Yawar Mazhar was born in Pakistan and has worked in the corporate sector for all of his professional life. Military aviation and especially the history of the Pakistan Air Force has been a passion for him all through his life. Over the years he has collected information on PAF's history and developments and in the process has met and interviewed dozens of PAF officers, most of whom were key part of important developments of PAF. His other interests include philosophy, history and Urdu poetry.

Usman Shabbir was born in Pakistan in 1978 and after his early schooling at Lawrence College, completed his engineering education from IT University of Denmark. He is an avid aviation enthusiast with his primary focus on Asian air forces. He has contributed to numerous aviation publications over the years. Currently, he resides in Copenhagen, working for Deloitte as a manager.